"Weima has written a very timely and important book on how to analyze the apostle Paul's letters. A growing number of scholars, myself included, have had serious questions about the over-rhetorization of Paul's letters. Weima presents a useful and helpful alternative in returning to a robust form of epistolary analysis. We may have some differences of opinion on whether there are four or five major parts to the Pauline letter, but we are in agreement that analysis of the epistolary form of Paul's letters is central to their interpretation. I strongly endorse the approach of this book and Weima's attempt to exemplify it, and I think that other interpreters of Paul's letters will benefit as well."

—**Stanley E. Porter**, McMaster Divinity College

"*Paul the Ancient Letter Writer* is an overdue book that needed to be written. Readers of this comprehensive study will no longer be able to escape the reality of Paul having written real letters. Weima shows how the essential components of ancient letters appear in each of the thirteen texts in the New Testament's collection of Paul's letters."

—**Raymond F. Collins**, Brown University

Paul *the* Ancient
Letter Writer

PAUL *the* Ancient Letter Writer

An Introduction to Epistolary Analysis

JEFFREY A. D. WEIMA

Baker Academic
a division of Baker Publishing Group
Grand Rapids, Michigan

Published by Baker Academic
a division of Baker Publishing Group
P.O. Box 6287, Grand Rapids, MI 49516-6287
www.bakeracademic.com

Printed in the United States of America

Library of Congress Cataloging-in-Publication Data
Names: Weima, Jeffrey A. D., author.
Title: Paul the ancient letter writer : an introduction to epistolary analysis / Jeffrey A.D. Weima.
Description: Grand Rapids : Baker Academic, 2016. | Includes bibliographical references and index.
Identifiers: LCCN 2016024966 | ISBN 9780801097515 (pbk.)
Subjects: LCSH: Bible. Epistles of Paul—Criticism, interpretation, etc. | Paul, the Apostle, Saint.
Classification: LCC BS2650.52 .W435 2016 | DDC 227/.066—dc23
LC record available at https://lccn.loc.gov/2016024966

In keeping with biblical principles of creation stewardship, Baker Publishing Group advocates the responsible use of our natural resources. As a member of the Green Press Initiative, our company uses recycled paper when possible. The text paper of this book is composed in part of post-consumer waste.

16 17 18 19 20 21 22   7 6 5 4 3 2 1

To my parents,
David & Hinke Weima,
who from infancy made known to me the holy Scriptures (2 Tim. 3:15)

To my parents-in-law,
Jan (John) & Dieuwke (Joanne) Zwier,
who even before our marriage welcomed me into their family as a son

Contents

Preface

The origin of this book began over thirty years ago. It was in the early 1980s, during my days as a student at Calvin Theological Seminary, when my Old Testament professor, John Stek, first showed me the importance of looking carefully at not just the *content* of the biblical text (*what* the author says) but also the *form* of the biblical text (*how* the author says it). My first reaction was skepticism as he employed the method of literary criticism to the book of Ruth. When Professor Stek applied this same method in a subsequent course dealing with Hebrew poetry and the book of Psalms, I became a bit more convinced about the importance of form and how a formal analysis of the biblical text can aid interpretation. Yet I still failed to see the implications of literary criticism for the interpretation of a different genre—letters.

A few years later, as I was working on a PhD degree at the Toronto School of Theology, I took a course with John C. Hurd Jr. dealing with letters in early Christianity. It was then that I began to take seriously the form of Paul's letters and how deviations in the apostle's typical or expected letter structure and his skillful adapting of various epistolary conventions were important for a correct reading of his correspondence. This recognition led me to do a formal analysis of Paul's letter closings for my doctoral dissertation, which was later published as *Neglected Endings: The Significance of the Pauline Letter Closings* (Sheffield: JSOT Press, 1994).

In subsequent years, I published essays on the letter closing of Galatians, the epistolary framework of Romans, and the epistolary conventions in Philemon. The research connected with these publications clearly demonstrated (at least to me) that the method of epistolary analysis—the term commonly used for the literary analysis of letters—provided rich insights into not just the letter closing but the opening, thanksgiving, and body sections of Paul's letters as well. This conviction compelled me to include a section on literary analysis in my commentary on 1 and 2 Thessalonians for the Baker Exegetical Commentary series, in which I examined the epistolary form and function of each passage before commenting on it more specifically. My teaching of New Testament letters over the past twenty-four years has also long included an introductory unit on how to read an ancient letter.

This brief historical overview reveals how I have moved from my early skepticism to being a strong advocate for the importance of literary criticism in general and of epistolary analysis in particular. The purpose of this book is to introduce the reader to both the method and the interpretative value of epistolary analysis. Although others have written on this method, their treatment of the four major sections of Paul's letters (opening, thanksgiving, body, and closing) and the diverse epistolary conventions found within each of these four sections is too brief. A bigger weakness of previous studies, however, is their tendency to highlight only the form and epistolary conventions of Paul's letters without demonstrating how this knowledge can help us better understand the purpose and content of the apostle's writings. By contrast, this book provides numerous examples of the exegetical payoff from detailed epistolary analysis. Merely being able to identify epistolary conventions in Paul's letters is not enough. We must also understand the function of these epistolary conventions and how Paul skillfully uses them to aid his persuasive purposes.

I gratefully acknowledge the help of others in completing this book. Péter Balla, rector and professor of New Testament at Károli Gáspár University in Budapest, and Neil Martin, my former student and current doctoral candidate at the University of Oxford, graciously read the entire manuscript and offered helpful suggestions for its improvement. Wells Turner at Baker did an excellent job of editing the book, saving me from embarrassing errors and enhancing the volume's overall quality. Elisabeth (Betsy) De Vries, my teaching assistant for several years, drafted the various tables found in the book and also compiled the indexes. Calvin Theological Seminary, both its administrators and board of trustees, kindly granted me a sabbatical and a publication leave to focus on the writing of this book. I am most thankful to my wife, Bernice, for her constant support of me and my various ministries outside the classroom; she continues to be my best friend and partner in ministry. Finally, I am pleased to recognize the key role that my parents, David and Hinke Weima, as well as my parents-in-law, John and Joanne Zwier, have played in my life and academic career, and so it is to them that this book is gratefully dedicated.

Abbreviations

General and Bibliographic

BDAG   *A Greek-English Lexicon of the New Testament and Other Early Christian Literature*, by W. Bauer, F. W. Danker, W. F. Arndt, and F. W. Gingrich, 3rd ed. (Chicago: University of Chicago Press, 2000)

BDF   *A Greek Grammar of the New Testament and Other Early Christian Literature*, by F. Blass, A. Debrunner, and R. W. Funk. (Chicago: University of Chicago Press, 1961)

chap.   chapter

e.g.   *exempli gratia*, for example

esp.   especially

i.e.   *id est*, that is

lit.   literally

LXX   Septuagint (the Old Testament in Greek)

NIV   New International Version (2011 revision)

NIV 1984   New International Version (1984)

NLT   New Living Translation (2015 revision)

NRSV   New Revised Standard Version (or its versification)

NT   New Testament

OT   Old Testament

TDNT   *Theological Dictionary of the New Testament*, edited by G. Kittel and G. Friedrich, translated and edited by G. W. Bromiley, 10 vols. (Grand Rapids: Eerdmans, 1964–76)

trans.   translation, translated by

v(v).   verse(s)

Old Testament

Gen.	Genesis	Deut.	Deuteronomy	1–2 Sam.	1–2 Samuel
Exod.	Exodus	Josh.	Joshua	1–2 Kings	1–2 Kings
Lev.	Leviticus	Judg.	Judges	1–2 Chron.	1–2 Chronicles
Num.	Numbers	Ruth	Ruth	Ezra	Ezra

Neh.	Nehemiah	Jer.	Jeremiah	Jon.	Jonah
Esther	Esther	Lam.	Lamentations	Mic.	Micah
Job	Job	Ezek.	Ezekiel	Nah.	Nahum
Ps(s).	Psalm(s)	Dan.	Daniel	Hab.	Habakkuk
Prov.	Proverbs	Hosea	Hosea	Zeph.	Zephaniah
Eccles.	Ecclesiastes	Joel	Joel	Hag.	Haggai
Song	Song of Songs	Amos	Amos	Zech.	Zechariah
Isa.	Isaiah	Obad.	Obadiah	Mal.	Malachi

New Testament

Matt.	Matthew	Eph.	Ephesians	Heb.	Hebrews
Mark	Mark	Phil.	Philippians	James	James
Luke	Luke	Col.	Colossians	1–2 Pet.	1–2 Peter
John	John	1–2 Thess.	1–2 Thessalonians	1–3 John	1–3 John
Acts	Acts			Jude	Jude
Rom.	Romans	1–2 Tim.	1–2 Timothy	Rev.	Revelation
1–2 Cor.	1–2 Corinthians	Titus	Titus		
Gal.	Galatians	Philem.	Philemon		

Other Ancient Sources

Add. Esth.	Additions to Esther	*Pol.*	Aristotle, *Politics*
Att.	Cicero, *Letters to Atticus*	1QH	*Hodayot* or *Thanksgiving*
2 Bar.	*2 Baruch*		*Hymns*
2 Esd.	2 Esdras	1QpHab	*Pesher Habakkuk*
Frat. amor.	Plutarch, *De fraterno amore*	Sir.	Sirach
Hom.	John Chrysostom, *Homilies*	Tob.	Tobit
Jos. Asen.	*Joseph and Aseneth*	*T. Benj.*	*Testament of Benjamin*
Let. Jer.	Letter of Jeremiah	*T. Dan*	*Testament of Dan*
3 Macc.	3 Maccabees	*T. Naph.*	*Testament of Naphtali*
Names	Philo, *On the Change of Names*	*T. Reu.*	*Testament of Reuben*
		T. Sim.	*Testament of Simeon*
Nic. Eth.	Aristotle, *Nicomachean Ethics*		

Papyri Collections

BGU   *Aegyptische Urkunden aus den Königlichen* [later *Staatlichen*] *Museen zu Berlin: Griechische Urkunden* (Berlin, 1895–)

P.Cair.Zen.   *Zenon Papyri: Catalogue général des antiquités égyptiennes du Musée du Caire*, edited by C. C. Edgar (Cairo, 1925–40)

P.Eleph.   *Aegyptische Urkunden aus den Königlichen Museen in Berlin: Griechische Urkunden*, Sonderheft: *Elephantine-Papyri*, edited by O. Rubensohn (Berlin, 1907–)

P.Giss.	*Griechische Papyri im Museum des oberhessischen Geschichtsvereins zu Giessen*, edited by O. Eger, E. Kornemann, and P. M. Meyer (Leipzig and Berlin, 1910–12)
P.Grenf. II	*New Classical Fragments and Other Greek and Latin Papyri*, edited by B. P. Grenfell and A. S. Hunt (Oxford, 1897)
P.Lond.	*Greek Papyri in the British Museum* (London, 1893–)
P.Mert.	*A Descriptive Catalogue of the Greek Papyri in the Collection of Wilfred Merton* (London and Dublin, 1948–67)
P.Mich.	*Michigan Papyri* (1931–99)
P.Oxy.	*The Oxyrhynchus Papyri*, published by the Egypt Exploration Society in Graeco-Roman Memoirs (London, 1898–)
P.Yale	*Yale Papyri in the Beinecke Rare Book and Manuscript Library* (1967–2001)

1

Introduction

An Illustration

Eagerly yet nervously, Jack held in his hand a letter from his girlfriend, Jill. The two of them had been dating all through their junior and senior years of high school. Sadly, however, they had been accepted at different colleges and so now found themselves separated from each other for the first time. Yet they nevertheless kept their love relationship alive through the writing of handwritten letters. Yes, it was a bit old-fashioned to communicate this way instead of through email or texting, which they did in addition to writing letters. But it also seemed to both of them quite romantic and a good way to demonstrate the depth of their love for each other.

After two months of being separated and of writing letters to each other, Jack hopped on a Greyhound bus and made a quick visit to Jill at her college some hours away. The visit, however, did not go so well. There was no obvious problem or fight, just a sense of unease and tension at being unable to recapture the way things had been before they headed off to different schools. Jack was thus understandably eager yet nervous to read this first letter from Jill after that not-so-happy visit.

The letter began: "Dear Jack." That letter opening would not sound very significant to anyone else reading the letter, but to Jack's ears it had an ominous tone. This is because all of Jill's previous letters began differently: instead of using the adjective "*Dear* Jack," she had previously always used the superlative "*Dearest* Jack."

This only increased Jack's nervousness about what might come next. The body of the letter began: "I am so busy here! The professors give us tons of readings and assignments—way more than we ever had in high school. I have hardly any free time to spend with my new friends. But I went out anyway last night with my dorm-mate to a coffee shop just to get away from the whole school scene for a while." Again, these observations by Jill about her recent activities would not sound very significant to anyone else reading the letter, but they were to Jack. This is because all of her previous letters began differently: she would first talk about how much she missed him, saying things like, "It is so sad that we are at separate schools! I hate being so far away from you! I can't wait to see you again!" Only *after* these "lovey-dovey," reconnecting statements would Jill then tell him the more factual things about events happening in her life.

Jack is now really getting nervous about his relationship with Jill, and so his eyes jump down to the end of the letter, which reads: "Love, Jill." Again, that letter closing would not seem very important to anyone else reading the letter, but it was significant, even disturbing, to Jack. This is because Jill always ended her letters to him with "Love, *Jillie.*" No one else but Jack called her "Jillie"—only him. It was his pet name for her, and she always used it to end her letters to him. And so when Jack saw that his girlfriend closed her letter instead with "Love, Jill," his heart sank because he knew that his relationship with her was in trouble.

Epistolary Analysis: A Method for Interpreting Paul's Letters

This illustration shows how variations in habitual or expected ways of writing letters can communicate information in and of themselves, and that such changes are therefore important for a correct understanding of what the letter writer was intending to say. The modifications that Jill made in the form of her letter were subtle—so subtle that the naïve reader not familiar with her writing practices would not even notice these changes and consequently be blind to their potential significance. To a careful reader like Jack, however, these subtle changes were important clues to interpreting her letter properly. He rightly perceived that such deviations in the form of her letter were not accidental and insignificant but instead were deliberate and reflected the changed nature of their relationship.

In a similar fashion, the apostle Paul in his letters typically follows a relatively set pattern. This fixed fourfold structure of opening, thanksgiving, body, and closing, as well as the letter-writing conventions that typically make up each of these sections, can be discovered quite easily by looking at the apostle's letters side by side. When Paul deviates from his fixed pattern or expected structure in mostly subtle but sometimes in not-so-subtle ways, the majority of modern readers fail to even notice these changes and consequently miss the important clues that they contain for a proper interpretation of his letters. In this book I will demonstrate that the apostle is an extremely skilled letter writer who carefully adapts and improvises his expected letter-writing practices in ways that powerfully and persuasively express what he, under the leading of the Holy Spirit, intends to communicate. Paul's changes in the epistolary *form* of what he writes, therefore, are never innocent or accidental but instead are conscious and deliberate and therefore provide an important interpretive key to determine his meaning and purpose.

The method that I recommend we follow in interpreting Paul's letters can be classified both broadly and narrowly. The broad classification of my proposed method is that it involves a type of *literary criticism*. It is broad because literary criticism comprises principles of interpretation that ought to be applied to any text in the Bible, not just narrowly to letters. It is difficult to define precisely what is meant by the term "literary criticism." The problem lies in that there is no single literary-critical method of interpretation; instead, a wide variety of interpretative methods have been proposed. Nevertheless, it is possible to identify a set of convictions that are widely held to distinguish a literary reading of the Bible from the historical and theological readings that have traditionally been employed (see Weima 2001).

First, literary criticism involves an appreciation for the sophisticated artistry and aesthetic quality of the text. It recognizes that the diverse books in the Bible are all the result of conscious composition, careful patterning, and the strategic use of literary conventions prevalent in their day. When this first conviction of literary criticism is applied to the letters of Paul, it assumes that the apostle, despite the hectic and challenging demands of his travels and ministry, did not write his correspondence in a haphazard and unreflective manner. Rather, the writing process for Paul involved a very deliberative and conscious process in which he not only carefully selected but also skillfully adapted the letter-writing conventions of his era.

Therefore the influential, early twentieth-century NT scholar Adolf Deissmann, in his desire to distinguish a "letter" from an "epistle," was only half right. He correctly stressed that Paul wrote genuine, real "letters" that addressed the particular issues of specific churches rather than "epistles"— artificial, literary creations intended for wider dissemination. Deissmann wrongly stressed, however, that Paul "was not a literary man," that he "wrote with complete absolute abandon," and that his thoughts in the letters "were dashed down under the influence of a hundred various impressions, and were never calculated for systematic presentation" (1910: 240–41). On the contrary, Paul's letters provide overwhelming evidence of the foresight, care, and precision with which they were written.

Second, literary criticism exhibits a preoccupation with the form of the text. Literary criticism focuses not only on the content of the text (*what* is said) but also on the form of the text (*how* it is said). As Leland Ryken (1993: 367) notes: "We cannot fully comprehend the 'what' of New Testament writers (their religious content) without first paying attention to the 'how' (the literary modes in which the content is embodied)." This preoccupation with form manifests itself in the attempt of modern literary critics to identify the various literary conventions used by a given biblical author and understand the function that these conventions have in the text. This concern with form also shows itself in the great attention given to the diverse types of writing found in the Bible (the technical term is "genre") and how an awareness of genre impacts interpretation.

When this second principle of literary criticism is applied to the letters of Paul, it involves the identification of not just various formulas or fixed expressions in his correspondence, many of which he borrows from letter-writing practices of the ancient world, but also the function these formulas have. One brief example here will be explained more fully in chapter 4: several times in his letters, Paul makes use of a "confidence formula," an expression of confidence that he himself has in his readers. The apostle, for instance, tells his Galatian readers: "I have confidence in the Lord that you will take no other view than mine" (Gal. 5:10). This formula expressing confidence should not be seen as a naïve or innocent remark about how optimistic Paul is that the Galatians will agree with him and his gospel as he has defended it thus far in the letter. In fact, there is much in this letter that indicates the opposite conclusion: Paul is extremely concerned that the Galatian readers will not agree with him but instead side with his opponents. Paul's use of the confidence formula here, therefore, should instead be recognized as part of his persuasive strategy: such a statement places pressure on the Galatian readers to live up to the confidence that the apostle has in them. People typically want to earn the commendation that others give them, and so Paul skillfully uses the confidence formula to create a sense of obligation among his Galatian readers so that they will justify his affirming statement about them.

Third, literary criticism is committed to treat texts as finished wholes. Before the rise of literary criticism in the mid to late twentieth century, liberal scholars did not deal with various books of the Bible in their present form but instead tried to discover the various sources used by the biblical authors and how they edited and arranged these sources. Conservative scholars, on the basis of their belief in the verbal inspiration of Scripture, concentrated on individual words in the text to discover their rich, Spirit-inspired meaning; they also highlighted individual verses that could serve as prooftexts for certain theological positions. Both procedures ended up dividing the biblical text into fragments, as evident in the verse-by-verse commentary that has become a staple of biblical scholarship and the verse-by-verse exposition of the text that characterizes many sermons. A literary approach, by contrast, accepts the biblical text in its final canonical form and is committed to a holistic reading of a particular passage or book.

But the method of interpreting Paul's letters that I am proposing can be classified not only broadly as a type of literary criticism but also more narrowly as *epistolary analysis*. This terminology is a convenient, shorthand way of referring to the three convictions of literary criticism summarized above, yet with the added idea that these convictions ought to be employed *in the analysis of letters*.[1] Other alternative terms for my proposed method include a "letter-structure approach" and "form criticism of letters." Both alternatives reflect certain aspects of a literary approach noted above, namely, the concern with the structure and form of the biblical text, in this case, letters. But the name "letter-structure approach" is inadequate because there is much more to my proposed method than just observations about the structure of Paul's letters. And the name "form criticism of letters" suffers from potential confusion, because form criticism is already a well-established discipline in analyzing the Synoptic Gospels, and it involves many issues that are not relevant to the study of letters.

The term "epistolary analysis" is known and used but not yet universally employed in academic circles. Nevertheless, many scholars recognize how important this method is for a proper interpretation of Paul's letters. For example, already some years ago Robert Funk (1970: 8) claimed: "The first order of business [in the interpretation of Paul's letters] is to learn to read the letter as a letter. This means above all to learn to read its structure." Richard Longenecker (1990: ci), in his commentary on Galatians, similarly recognizes that the interpretation of any Pauline letter must take as its starting point an analysis of the letter's epistolary structure:

> Since form and content are inseparable in the study of any writing, it is necessary to give attention not only to what is said but also to how it is said—that is, to

---

1. For a historical survey of the rise of epistolary analysis as a discipline in biblical and nonbiblical studies, see Weima 1994a: 12–23; also Harvey 1998: 16–22.

the forms used to convey meaning and to the function served by each particular form. Therefore, prior to considering the specific content of Galatians (i.e., prior to exegesis proper), it is essential that we analyze the epistolary and rhetorical structures of the letter, with those analyses then being taken into account at each stage in the interpretation.

Ann Jervis (1991: 35), without explicitly using the term "epistolary analysis," nevertheless asserts that this method helpfully reveals Paul's purposes in his various letters and, as such, can help solve the perennial debate over the reason for Romans: "It is my conviction that by a comparative investigation of certain formal features of the letters of Paul, the function of any particular Pauline letter can be distinguished."

The quote that best captures the kind of issues involved in the method of epistolary analysis that will be introduced in his book comes from Calvin Roetzel (1975: 30): "Once the letter-writing conventions which Paul used are understood, the alert reader will also find clues to Paul's intent in his creative use of those conventions as well." Several phrases in this concise statement can be unpacked in greater detail in order to explain the method of epistolary analysis more fully:

- "letter-writing conventions": This refers to fixed expressions or stereotyped phrases found in ancient Greco-Roman letters and also in Paul's letters. Letter-writing conventions of our day include the opening phrase, "Dear so-and-so," and the closing phrase, "Sincerely . . ." These are fixed expressions or epistolary formulas that we do not create each time we write a letter but simply take over from the writing practices of our modern time. Similarly, when Paul writes a letter, he is not creating a new genre of writing or new letter-formulas but instead utilizes the epistolary conventions of his day.

- "are understood": The contemporary reader can "understand" the letter-writing conventions that Paul used by comparing his letters with the thousands of other letters that have been discovered from the ancient Greco-Roman world. Yet one needs to "understand" not merely the *presence* of letter-writing conventions in Paul's correspondence but, more important, the *function* that these fixed expressions or stereotyped phrases have. By understanding the function of these letter-writing conventions, we can see how the apostle is using them to achieve his purposes, and we can discern the direction of his argument with greater clarity.

- "the alert reader": The typical reader of Paul's letters today is largely unaware of both the presence and the function of his various letter-writing conventions. They also miss the potential significance that an understanding of these things can have for a proper interpretation of the apostle's correspondence. But the alert reader—the reader equipped with the tools of epistolary analysis—anticipates the exegetical insights that will be gleaned from discovering the skilled way in which Paul shapes and adapts his inherited letter-writing conventions.

- "clues to Paul's intent": The ultimate goal of exegesis is to uncover "intent"—to understand what the biblical authors were trying to say and accomplish with what they wrote. The great potential benefit of the method of epistolary analysis is that it provides "clues to Paul's intent" in any given letter. Many of these clues are quite obvious not only to the apostle's original readers, who were naturally familiar with the epistolary conventions of their day, but also to those modern readers who are trained in the method of epistolary analysis. Some of these clues, however, are so subtle that they may well have been missed by Paul's original audience, who had little or no knowledge of his other letters. Consequently, modern readers who have access to all of Paul's extant letters are, at times, in a better position to discern these calculated changes in form and so better grasp the intention behind the apostle's skillful adaptation of contemporary epistolary conventions. The meaning of any given passage in Paul's letters is determined not solely by how his original hearers would have understood his words but instead by what the apostle, under the leading of the Holy Spirit, was intending to say.[2]
- "creative use of those conventions": Paul is not merely a scribe who simply copies or blindly borrows the letter-writing conventions of his day in their traditional form. Rather, the apostle is a gifted writer who has both the freedom and the creative ability to shape and adapt those conventions so that they more effectively strengthen his persuasive purposes at work in the letter.

Competing Methods: Thematic Approach and Rhetorical Criticism

How does the method of epistolary analysis advocated in this book compare with other methods used to interpret Paul's letters? A helpful way to answer

2. The central focus of this book—an introduction to the method of epistolary analysis—does not allow any extended comment on the important issue that is raised here, namely, whether the center of authority in adjudicating debates over the meaning of any given biblical text ought to lie with the reader, the author, or the text itself. See, however, the answer to the question raised in chap. 3 with regard to the missing thanksgiving in Galatians: "Did the Galatians even notice omission of the thanksgiving?"

this question is to revisit the distinction presented above in defining literary criticism, namely, the distinction between the "what" of the text (the *content* of what the biblical author writes) and the "how" of the text (the *form* in which the author chooses to present that content). A method that focuses only on answering the "what" question can be called a *thematic approach*.[3] This method is concerned solely with the content of Paul's letters and so outlines the apostle's correspondence on the basis of the different topics that he treats or the thematic shifts in his letters. A thematic approach involves an examination of the grammar, historical context, and theological claims of any given text and so is a profitable and important method for determining meaning in Paul's letters. This thematic approach is the method that has been used by virtually all exegetes for centuries in the past and is still followed by some today.

The weakness of the thematic approach, however, is that it fails to answer the "how" question and ignores the interpretive clues found in the form of the text. It is not an exaggeration to say that a paradigm shift has taken place in biblical studies over the past three or four decades: the old perspective, illustrated by the thematic approach, which views Scripture primarily as a historical or theological document, has been replaced by a new conviction that the Bible is literature and as such ought to be interpreted from a literary perspective. A central tenet of a literary perspective is how the form and structure of the text provide an important *additional* aid to understanding the meaning of any given text. In other words, form supplements but does not supplant the meaning provided by the text's content. An awareness of both form and content are required for a proper understanding of any biblical passage.

The method of *rhetorical criticism* and the method of epistolary analysis share this recognition of how important form and structure are for a right reading of the apostle's correspondence. More succinctly put, rhetorical criticism is the application of the ancient Greco-Roman rules for speech to the written text of the NT, including the letters of Paul. The popularity of rhetorical criticism as an interpretative method can be readily seen from the opening pages of many recent commentaries that immediately seek to classify a particular Pauline letter according to the three major types of Greco-Roman rhetorical speech (judicial, deliberative, or epideictic) and to divide the letter into the four rhetorical parts of an ancient discourse (*exordium, narratio, probatio, peroratio*). The renaissance of rhetoric is also evident in

---

3. For the threefold classifications of "thematic," "rhetorical," and "epistolary," see Jewett 1986: 68, and esp. the charts on 216–25.

many recently published books and academic articles whose main title or subtitle includes the phrase "A Rhetorical Analysis of . . ."

If one defines rhetoric very broadly as the "art of persuasion," then it can be readily granted that Paul uses rhetoric in his letters. Since the apostle cannot assume that his letters will be accepted and obeyed by all his readers, he is very much concerned with persuasion when constructing his correspondence. It is also clear that Paul employs a variety of literary, or so-called rhetorical, devices that are universally practiced in everyday speech and writing and thus do not necessarily provide evidence for the training in and conscious use of ancient rhetorical rules. Consider, for example, the rhetorical device of paralipsis—a figure of speech that allows speakers and writers artfully to address a subject that they profess does not need to be addressed. Paul uses paralipsis when he says to the Thessalonians: "You have no need to have anyone write to you about brotherly and sisterly love" (1 Thess. 4:9). The apostle's statement allows him tactfully to raise and remind the Thessalonians of a subject about which he outwardly claims they have no need to be reminded. But though Paul employs this rhetorical device, it would be wrong to conclude from such a statement that he was a rhetorician who constructed his letters according to the rules of ancient speech. After all, if a mother who has never been taught rhetorical devices can nevertheless still diplomatically say to her teenager, "I don't have to remind you that you need to be home tonight before your 11:00 p.m. curfew," one should be cautious in drawing any conclusions about Paul's rhetorical training from his tactful statement to the Thessalonians.

Significant objections can be raised against the widespread practice of taking the ancient Greco-Roman rules for speech and applying them in a direct and wholesale manner to the interpretation of Paul's letters (Weima 1997b; also see Porter 1993; Stamps 1995; Classen 2000: 265–91; Porter and Dyer 2012). This book takes seriously the fact that Paul wrote letters and that, consequently, the most important source for understanding the apostle's letters must naturally be the letter-writing practices of his day rather than the rules for oral discourse. Four chapters will be devoted to examining each of the major sections of Paul's letters (the opening, the thanksgiving, the body, the closing) and the diverse epistolary conventions found within each of these four sections. Each chapter will not simply identify the form and function of the various stereotyped formulas and literary devices that occur but will also demonstrate the exegetical payoff that comes from this knowledge. As the saying goes, "The proof of the pudding is in the eating." Thus each epistolary convention will be examined with respect to not just its form and function but also its interpretative significance, thereby demonstrating in a conclusive manner the exegetical benefit that comes from examining Paul's letters according to the method of epistolary analysis. Since these chapters deal in a somewhat atomized way with different texts selected among Paul's thirteen letters, a final chapter engages in an epistolary analysis of one whole letter—Paul's Letter to Philemon—as a concluding test case.

2

The Opening

The first of the four major sections that make up Paul's letters—the opening—plays a more strategic role in the persuasive purposes of the apostle than most modern readers typically recognize. In secular letters the primary function of the letter opening is to establish or enhance personal contact with the letter recipient.[1] Many biblical commentators downplay the importance that this reconnecting function has in Paul's letter openings and view this first major unit of the letter (along with the letter closing) as being entirely conventional in nature, in contrast to the thanksgiving and body sections of the letter, which are judged to be more important since here the apostle takes up the specific issues that he wishes to address. In colloquial terms, the opening is often viewed merely as an "appetizer" and the closing only as a "light dessert," in contrast to the thanksgiving and letter body, which provide the weightier "main course."

The letter opening (and letter closing) sections, however, do have an important role to play in Paul's argument. As Robert Wall (1993: 193) observes:

> The significance of epistolary greetings goes beyond identifying author and audience; it is more than saying hello. The author's salutation, however conventional and formal, specifies the nature of the relationship between author and audience and even draws lines around the conversation being carried on by the letter in hand. Meanings are more readily and rightly determined in terms of this "rhetorical relationship" formulated by the author's opening word.

1. In his early study of ancient letters, Heikki Koskenniemi (1956) referred to this function with the technical term "philophronesis"—the expression of friendly relationship.

Thus, rather than being insignificant, the letter opening serves an important function in the overall argument of the letter. This chapter will demonstrate how Paul skillfully uses these opening sections either (1) to place himself and his readers in such a relationship to each other that his purposes in the letter are strengthened and enhanced or (2) to foreshadow the key themes to be taken up in the subsequent sections of the letter.

The opening is the most formally consistent section of Paul's letters, consisting of three relatively fixed epistolary conventions: (1) the sender formula, (2) the recipient formula, and (3) the greeting formula.

The Sender Formula

Formal Analysis

Whereas modern letters end with the author's signature, ancient letters begin with it, in the form of the sender formula. The only exception to this practice occurs occasionally in letters of petition, where the sender is appealing for help from a person of a higher rank. Paul's practice of opening his letters with the sender formula, therefore, not only follows the common practice of his day but also reflects that he writes to his churches not from a position of weakness (despite his occasional use of the title "slave/servant" to identify himself) but from a position of authority—a fact confirmed by his most commonly used title "apostle." This formula typically consists of four elements (see table 2.1: The Sender Formula):

Table 2.1: The Sender Formula

Letter	Name	Title	Descriptive Phrase	Cosender(s)
Rom. 1:1–6	Paul	a servant called to be an apostle, set apart for the gospel of God	of Christ Jesus,	
			that which was promised beforehand through his prophets in the Holy Scriptures, the gospel concerning his Son, who was from the seed of David according to the flesh, who was appointed Son of God in power according to the Spirit of holiness, from the resurrection of the dead, our Lord Jesus Christ, through whom we have received grace and apostleship for the obedience of faith among all the gentiles for the sake of his name, among whom you also are, the called of Jesus Christ.	

Letter	Name	Title	Descriptive Phrase	Cosender(s)
1 Cor. 1:1	Paul	called to be an apostle	of Christ Jesus by the will of God	and Sosthenes our brother
2 Cor. 1:1	Paul	an apostle	of Christ Jesus by the will of God	and Timothy our brother
Gal. 1:1–2	Paul	an apostle	not from men nor through a man but through Jesus Christ and from God the Father, who raised him from the dead	and all the brothers and sisters with me
Eph. 1:1	Paul	an apostle	of Christ Jesus by the will of God	
Phil. 1:1	Paul	servants	of Christ Jesus	and Timothy
Col. 1:1	Paul	an apostle	of Christ Jesus by the will of God	and Timothy our brother
1 Thess. 1:1	Paul			Silas and Timothy
2 Thess. 1:1	Paul			Silas and Timothy
1 Tim. 1:1	Paul	an apostle	of Christ Jesus by the command of God our Savior and of Christ Jesus our hope	
2 Tim. 1:1	Paul	an apostle	of Christ Jesus by the will of God in keeping with the promise of life that is in Christ Jesus	
Titus 1:1–3	Paul	a servant an apostle	of God and of Jesus Christ for the sake of the faith of God's elect and their knowledge of the truth, which accords with godliness, in hope of eternal life, which God, who never lies, promised before the ages began and at the proper time manifested in his word through the preaching with which I have been entrusted by the command of God our Savior.	
Philem. 1	Paul	a prisoner	of Christ Jesus	and Timothy our brother
James 1:1	James	a servant	of God and of the Lord Jesus Christ	
1 Pet. 1:1	Peter	an apostle	of Jesus Christ	
2 Pet. 1:1	Simon Peter	a servant and apostle	of Jesus Christ	
2 John 1	The elder			
3 John 1	The elder			
Jude 1	Jude	a servant and brother	of Jesus Christ of James	

1. The name "Paul."
2. A title, most commonly "apostle" (Rom. 1:1; 1 Cor. 1:1; 2 Cor. 1:1; Gal. 1:1; Eph. 1:1; Col. 1:1; 1 Tim. 1:1; 2 Tim. 1:1; Titus 1:1) but sometimes also "servant" (Rom. 1:1; Phil. 1:1; Titus 1:1).
3. A short descriptive phrase, indicating the source of his apostleship or servanthood: "of Christ Jesus" (missing only in 1 Thess. 1:1 and 2 Thess. 1:1).
4. The mention of cosenders by name and title, typically "brother" (1 Cor. 1:1; 2 Cor. 1:1; Gal. 1:2; Phil. 1:1; Col. 1:1; 1 Thess. 1:1; 2 Thess. 1:1; Philem. 1).

Paul's consistent way of beginning his letters, therefore, is with a sender formula that stereotypically exhibits the following form: "Paul, an apostle of Christ Jesus, and so-and-so, our brother."

Interpretative Significance

The knowledge of how Paul typically writes the sender formula makes it possible to identify letter openings where the apostle has altered his words in some way. Once these unique letter openings have been identified, then the key question to be answered is this: Are these changes in the form of a given sender formula simply fortuitous and the innocent result of inconsistencies in Paul's writing style, or are these deviations in form conscious and deliberate and thus potentially significant for providing clues to Paul's intent in the letter? That the second of these two scenarios is the correct answer will be clearly demonstrated in the sample texts examined below.

ROMANS 1:1–6

When the sender formula in the letter opening of Romans (1:1–6) is compared to the same epistolary convention in Paul's other letters, its unique features become immediately apparent. Instead of the brief expression that he typically uses, "Paul, an apostle of Christ Jesus, and so-and-so, our brother," one finds a sender formula that has been expanded in an unparalleled manner:

[1]Paul, a servant of Jesus Christ, called to be an apostle, set apart for the gospel of God, [2]that which was promised beforehand through his prophets in the Holy Scriptures, [3]the gospel concerning his Son, who was from the seed of David according to the flesh, [4]who was appointed Son of God in power according to the Spirit of holiness, from the resurrection of the dead, our Lord Jesus Christ, [5]through whom we have received grace and apostleship for the obedience of

faith among all the gentiles for the sake of his name, [6]among whom you also are, the called of Jesus Christ.

Paul's self-introduction in Rom. 1:1–6 exhibits at least six unique features: (1) its great length; (2) its failure to mention any cosender(s); (3) its use of three titles instead of the expected one in verse 1; (4) its description of the gospel in verse 2; (5) in verses 3–4, its use of confessional material, liturgical forms that originated in the worship of the early church but were incorporated by Paul into his letters; and (6) the presence of additional comments in verses 5–6. Each one of these unique features can be explained as revealing Paul's larger purpose in the epistolary framework of the letter. He wishes to present himself in the opening (and in the thanksgiving and the closing) to his unknown readers in Rome as their divinely appointed apostle whose gospel (which he goes on to "preach" to them in the body of the letter) ought to be accepted.[2]

1. *Great length*. The sender formula consists of some 103 words—about eight times longer than is typically found in Paul's other letters. This suggests that Paul is very much concerned with the way he presents himself to the believers in Rome. The apostle is in the rare (at least for him in his extant letters) and difficult position of writing to Roman house churches that not only do not know him personally (since he neither founded these Roman congregations nor has he even visited them: see 1:10, 13; 15:22) but also churches who have heard slanderous things about his gospel (Rom. 3:8, "Why not say—as we are being slanderously reported as saying and as some claim that we say—'Let us do evil that good may result?' Their condemnation is just!"; see also 6:1). Paul, therefore, opens his letter with a greatly expanded sender formula by which he can introduce both himself and his gospel in a manner that likely will win the acceptance of his unknown and skeptical audience in Rome.

2. *Omission of cosender(s)*. Paul's purpose—presenting himself to his unknown readers in Rome as their divinely appointed apostle whose gospel should be accepted—accounts for Paul's failure to include the names of any cosenders. That this omission is not coincidental is suggested by the fact that the majority of Paul's letters (eight out of thirteen) include the names of cosenders. This omission is confirmed by the realization that Timothy, his closest associate and one who is identified in the apostle's other letters as a cosender (2 Cor. 1:1; Phil. 1:1; Col. 1:1; 1 Thess. 1:1; 2 Thess. 1:1), was with Paul at the time of writing (Rom. 16:21a), as were seven other leading Christians from Achaia (16:21b–23). It seems clear, therefore, that Paul omits any

---

2. For a fuller development of this proposed purpose in the epistolary framework of Romans, see Weima 1994b; also Jervis 1991.

mention of cosenders in order to draw the attention of his Roman readers to himself and, as the rest of the letter opening indicates, to his gospel. Commenting on the omission of any cosender, James Dunn (1988a: 7) observes, "We may assume therefore that Paul wanted to present himself in his own person to these largely unknown congregations, as (the) apostle to the Gentiles (cf. 11.13), and with the subsequent exposition of the gospel understood very much as his."

3. *Use of three titles.* The same concern also accounts for Paul's use of not one title to describe himself, as he does in all his other letter openings except for the opening to Titus, but three: "a servant of Christ Jesus, called to be an apostle, set apart for the gospel of God" (v. 1). Paul's apostolic role and his divine calling to preach the gospel are stressed both by the number of titles used and his choice of epithets. The first epithet, "a servant [lit., "slave"] of Christ Jesus," likely echoes an OT designation in the Septuagint ("servant/slave [of the Lord]") given to those who were called by God to perform special tasks of leadership: Abraham (Ps. 105:42); Moses (2 Kings 18:12); Joshua (Judg. 2:8); David (2 Sam. 7:5; Pss. 78:70; 89:3); the prophets (Amos 3:7; Zech. 1:6); and the psalmist (Pss. 27:9; 31:16). It also echoes the stereotyped phrase "servants of God" used in other writings of Paul's day to refer to divinely inspired prophets (e.g., 1QpHab 2.8–9; 7.5; 1QH 1.3; 2 Esd. [*4 Ezra*] 1:32; 2:1, 18). Paul therefore presents himself as one who stands in a long line of those who have been appointed by God to carry out a special mission among his people. As Joseph Fitzmyer (1992: 228–29) observes: "Paul would thus be implying that his ministry and service put him in the line of such venerable 'slaves' of Yahweh in the OT."

The second epithet, "called to be an apostle," has a similar authoritative function. The only other sender formula to use this same epithet is 1 Cor. 1:1, in a letter where Paul feels the need to stress his apostolic status to a Corinthian church that was leaning toward a rejection of him as an authoritative apostle whom they ought to obey (see Fee 1987: 4–10). The verb "called" involves the use of the so-called divine passive: the unspoken but not-so-subtly implied agent of Paul's call to be an apostle is God. Consequently, any rejection of Paul's apostolic status by the Roman churches would involve not merely a rejection of Paul but also a rejection of God, who has called him to this special role. Even though the congregations in Rome do not know Paul personally, they should nevertheless accept him as a "called apostle" whose gospel message bears the authority of God himself.

Paul's divine commission is driven home in the third epithet: "set apart for the gospel of God." Once again, Paul skillfully employs the use of the divine passive: the unspoken agent who has "set apart" the apostle for a special task is God. Paul's choice of the verbal phrase "set apart," especially in light of its use in Gal. 1:15–16 (God set Paul apart from birth and called him to preach his Son among the gentiles), likely alludes to the vocational call given to the OT prophets (Isa. 49:1; Jer. 1:5: so, e.g., Käsemann 1980: 6; Elliott 1990: 72; Schreiner 1998: 33). When this notion of being "set apart" is seen in light of the two previous epithets, it appears that Paul is claiming, before his Roman readers, an authority enjoyed by the prophets: "Such a designation again implies a self-designation of Paul as one in line with great prophetic fore-bearers in OT history" (Fitzmyer 1992: 229). Where this prophetic activity of Paul manifests itself most clearly is in his proclaiming "the gospel of God." Here for the first time we see the intimate connection between the themes of "apostleship" and "gospel"—correlated themes that will appear again and again in the epistolary framework of the Romans letter. The apostle, therefore, presents himself as one who, in the tradition of the prophets of old, has been divinely appointed by God to preach the gospel.

4. *Description of the gospel.* The sender formula in Paul's other letter openings typically ends at this point, and the apostle proceeds to the recipient formula. Here in Romans, however, Paul continues his lengthy self-introduction with a description of the gospel that he has been set apart to preach: "that which was promised beforehand through his prophets in the Holy Scriptures" (v. 2). Contrary to the slanderous claims about Paul that some in Rome have heard (Rom. 3:8; also 6:1), his gospel does not involve radical new teachings but is the same message previously proclaimed by the prophets and recorded in the sacred writings. In colloquial terms, Paul's gospel does not involve some new-fangled ideas about spirituality but the same "old-time religion" that was proclaimed by the OT prophets. The apostle will prove this point to his readers later in the body of the letter, which contains well over half of all the OT references found in his extent correspondence.

5. *Confessional material.* If the Roman Christians had any lingering doubt about the legitimacy of Paul's apostleship and the trustworthiness of his gospel, in the following verses such suspicion would surely be removed by the apostle's strategic citation of what quite likely is confessional material: "the gospel concerning his Son, who was from the seed of David according to the flesh, who was appointed Son of God in power according to the Spirit of holiness, from the resurrection of the dead, our Lord Jesus Christ" (vv. 3–4). By quoting a creed or hymn that the Christians in Rome know and perhaps recite themselves in worship, Paul effectively demonstrates that he shares with them a common gospel.

The situation would be similar to that of a guest preacher who, when visiting a congregation skeptical (as he has heard) about his orthodoxy with respect to Jesus's resurrection, calculatingly chooses to open the service thus: "I greet you today in the name of Jesus Christ, who on the third day rose again from the dead, ascended into heaven, and now sits at the right hand of God." In the preacher's greeting the congregation would immediately recognize a reference to the Apostles' Creed and, as a result of his deliberate citation of confessional material, not only be more assured about his orthodoxy but also more willing to continue listening to him for the rest of the service. Most commentators believe Paul is citing a creedal formulation here, but even if he is not, Paul's defining his gospel in terms of Jesus being "his [God's] Son," "the seed of David," "the Son of God," and "our Lord Jesus Christ" would reassure the Roman readers as to the orthodox nature of his message.

6. *Additional comments.* Paul continues his expanded sender formula with some additional comments that not only further validate his apostleship and gospel but also take the added step of placing the Roman believers within the sphere of his divine commission and message. These additional comments open with a relative clause: "through whom we received grace and apostleship" (v. 5a). This is the only instance in all of Paul's sender formulas where he makes a second assertion of his apostleship (see also v. 1), thereby emphasizing once again to the Roman readers his divine calling to be an apostle. Furthermore, since the antecedent of the relative clause is "our Lord Jesus Christ" (v. 4b), Paul establishes a direct line of authority for his apostleship from Christ to himself.

The apostle further asserts that his Christ-authorized apostleship is "for the obedience of faith among all the gentiles for the sake of his name, among whom you also are, the called of Jesus Christ" (vv. 5b–6). The logic of Paul's argumentation here is clear and not very subtle.

> First Premise: "I have received apostleship from Christ to preach the gospel among the gentiles."
>
> Second Premise: "You believers in Rome are gentiles."
>
> Conclusion: "I, therefore, have a divine responsibility to share my gospel with you."

Although Paul does not explicitly state this conclusion, it would have been readily apparent to his Roman readers (du Toit 1989: 194). Especially in the context of Paul's intent manifested in the many other changes he has made to his sender formula, this is a not-so-veiled attempt by Paul to place the Roman Christians under the authority of his apostolic calling and gospel. Hence Douglas Moo (1996: 53) comments on the clause "among whom are you also" (v. 6a): "The purpose of this remark [is] to show the Roman Christians that they belong within the sphere of Paul's apostolic commission. Paul is sent to 'all the gentiles'; and the Romans are 'among the gentiles.' They are thereby subject to his authority."

The sender formula in the letter opening of Romans provides not only important clues for the purpose of the letter as a whole but also a compelling initial illustration of both the validity and value of the method of epistolary analysis. Paul has masterfully expanded the typical form of his sender formula in such a way that the correlate themes of apostleship and gospel are highlighted. With his very first words, Paul presents himself to his unknown readers in Rome as their divinely appointed apostle whose gospel, which he will soon "preach" to them in the body of the letter, ought to be accepted.

GALATIANS 1:1–2A

Another sender formula that Paul has expanded in significant ways is Gal. 1:1–2a:

> [1]Paul, an apostle not from men nor through a man but through Jesus Christ and from God the Father, who raised him from the dead, [2]and all the brothers and sisters with me.

The first two of the four formal elements that make up this epistolary convention are as expected: the name is "Paul" and the title is "apostle." However, the third and fourth elements—the short descriptive phrase indicating the source of Paul's apostleship, as well as the mention of cosenders by name and title—have been altered in three ways: (1) the simple phrase "of Christ Jesus" as the source of Paul's apostleship has been embellished to read "not from men nor through a man but through Jesus Christ and from God the Father"; (2) the description of God is qualified by a likely creedal confession that he is the one "who raised him [Jesus] from the dead"; and (3) Paul chooses not to identify any cosenders by name but instead refers in an all-encompassing way to "*all* the brothers and sisters with me." All three changes are hardly accidental but part of Paul's larger goal in the letter to stress the divine origin of his apostleship and thus also the legitimacy of his circumcision-free gospel.

The situation that Paul faces in the Galatian churches to whom his letter is addressed can be reconstructed as follows. The Galatian churches consist of predominantly gentile Christians who were evangelized by Paul, probably during his first missionary journey, but then came under the influence of "Judaizers": Jewish Christians from Judea who claimed to represent the teachings and authority of James, Peter, John, and the other apostles. These Judaizers attacked not only Paul's gospel but also Paul's apostleship, the authority lying behind his gospel. Their attack on Paul to the churches in Galatia quite likely went something very close to this:[3]

> Why do you accept Paul's version of the gospel? Who is Paul anyway? He is nothing but an apostle-wannabe! Was he a disciple of Jesus? No! Did he spend three years with Jesus, learning accurately the truth of the gospel? No! *We* represent the real apostles—James, the brother of Jesus; Peter, the head of Jesus's disciples; and John, the disciple to whom Jesus was closest. *We* know the real gospel that these beloved apostles got firsthand from Jesus. Paul got his gospel only secondhand from these beloved apostles when he spent a brief time with them in Jerusalem after he belatedly became a believer in Jesus. Paul didn't tell you, did he, about the severe damage he did to the church before that time? No, he conveniently forgot to mention how much he persecuted our fellow brothers and sisters in Judea. And despite the terrible harm that he did, the beloved apostles were kind to Paul and forgave him for all that he had done to hurt the church. They graciously even allowed him to preach the gospel. But Paul was so eager to build himself up by getting lots of gentiles to become Jesus-followers that he compromised the truth of our faith! He is pushing a law-free and circumcision-free gospel that goes way beyond what the beloved apostles had taught him. *We* proclaim the authoritative teachings of the beloved apostles James, Peter, and John. Don't be misled by a second-rate apostle like Paul!

In the Galatians letter, therefore, Paul needs to defend the divine origin of his apostleship—not because he has a big ego and vainly wants everyone to acknowledge what an important church leader he is, but because Paul knows that the acceptance of his gospel message is intimately connected with the acceptance of his apostleship. If there are any doubts among the Galatian Christians about Paul's status as a full-fledged, divinely appointed apostle, then they may also have doubts about the trustworthiness and authority of his gospel message. As Francois Tolmie (2005: 34) explains, "The basic charge lodged against Paul is clear: his apostleship does not have divine authorization, and there is therefore no need to accept his version of the gospel."

In such a context, then, it is hardly surprising that Paul opens the body of his letter with an emphatic assertion about the divine origin of his gospel as well as his apostleship, which undergirds that gospel. As the author of the letter, Paul is free to begin his correspondence with whatever subject he wants, typically the subject that he deems most needed by the recipients. It is significant, therefore, that as the very first point of the letter body, Paul

---

3. The following is based on a mirror reading of Paul's lengthy autobiographical defense in Gal. 1:11–2:14.

emphatically asserts, "For I want you to know, brothers and sisters, that the gospel which was preached by me is not a gospel according to man; for I did not receive it from man nor was I taught it [from man], but it came through a revelation from Jesus Christ" (Gal. 1:11–12).

Paul, knowing that this will be the first main point he will soon make in the letter body, skillfully adapts the letter opening to assert the very same thing. Thus he delivers a preemptive strike in the sender formula (and, as we will see below, also in the greeting formula of 1:3–5), which anticipates the main strike against his opponents that will be delivered in the letter body. All three unique features of Gal. 1:1–2a noted above, modifications of the expected form of the sender formula, can be explained as the result of Paul anticipating the defense of his apostleship and his gospel message in the letter body.

1. *Embellished source of Paul's apostleship*. The first and most obvious way that Paul stresses the divine origin of his apostleship[4] is by employing an antithetical ("not *x* but *y*") statement. Instead of following his title "apostle" with the expected phrase "of Christ Jesus," Paul states more fully and emphatically "not from men nor through a man but through Jesus Christ and from God the Father." This use of an antithetical statement adds emphasis not only because it is longer—it takes more words to make the same point—but even more so because by first expressing the point negatively and then expressing it positively, the statement reaches a climactic conclusion. Paul's statement about the divine origin of his apostleship achieves even greater emphasis, however, by not merely including a single negative that is contrasted with a single positive, as is normally done in antithetical statements, but by including two negatives ("not from men nor through a man") that are contrasted with two positives ("but through Jesus Christ and from God the Father").

The form of this antithetical statement with its two negatives and two positives perhaps ought to be identified more precisely as a *chiasm* (so Bligh 1969: 62; Betz 1979: 39; Longenecker 1990: 5)—a literary device sometimes used by Paul and other biblical writers (for more on this literary device, see discussion in chap. 4). This chiasm can be outlined as follows:

A "not from men
  B nor through a man
  B′ but through Jesus Christ
A′ and [from] God the Father"[5]

4. Schütz (1975: 114) observes that here Paul's "polemic is scarcely veiled."
5. The presence of a chiasm would explain two peculiar features of Paul's words. First, it would account for the unusual word order in which Paul begins with "Jesus Christ" and then follows with "God the Father" (Gal. 1:1), which is a reversal of the apostle's practice when

There is the very real danger that modern readers will treat the two references to "Jesus Christ" and "God the Father" as merely formulaic and thus not directly related to Paul's overriding concern in this letter opening to stress the divine origin and authority of his apostolic status. This concern is manifest first in Paul's use of the preposition "through" before "Jesus Christ," which alludes to Paul's apostolic call *through* Jesus Christ on the road to Damascus—an allusion that Paul makes explicit a few verses later at the beginning of the letter body: "*through* a revelation of Jesus Christ" (1:12). As James Dunn (1993: 27) observes: "His [Paul's] primary concern was evidently to emphasize that even the *mediation* of his apostolic authority was direct from heaven." Paul's concern to stress the divine origin and authority of his apostolic status is manifest second in his reference to God as "Father." Such a paternal identification evokes the notion of God as the begetter of and thus also authority over all creation; it also evokes the authority that a father had, in the patriarchal culture of Paul's day, over his wife, children, and members of his household, both slaves and freed persons. Thus Dunn (1993: 27) is again right to observe: "[Paul's] concern was rather to call on the authority which both words [God and Father] so powerfully evoked. His appeal was to nothing less than the highest authority conceivable, the God who is Father (of all). *That* was the source of his authority as apostle."

2. *Creedal description of God.* Paul chooses to identify God not only as "Father" but also as the one "who raised him [Jesus] from the dead." An identical or very similar clause occurs elsewhere both in Paul and in other NT writings (Rom. 4:24–25; 8:11; 10:9; 1 Cor. 6:14; 15:15; 2 Cor. 4:14; 1 Thess. 1:10; Acts 3:15; 4:10; 1 Pet. 1:21), suggesting that this may well be a confession or creedal statement of the early church (so, e.g., Mussner 1977: 46; Cook 1992: 515; Dunn 1993: 28; Martyn 1997: 84–85; Tolmie 2005: 35–37). Such a possibility is strengthened by Paul's use of confessional material a few verses later (1:4a; see discussion of this text below under "The Greeting Formula").

Why does Paul quote a creedal statement at the opening of his Galatians letter? The answer is that it adds weight to his words and so strengthens his relationship to his readers. The description of God as the one "who raised him from the dead" is not something that only Paul believes but instead is a

---

mentioning the two persons of God together (Rom. 1:7; 1 Cor. 1:3; 2 Cor. 1:2; Eph. 1:2; Phil. 1:2; 1 Thess. 1:1; 2 Thess. 1:1, 12; 1 Tim. 1:2; 2 Tim. 1:2; Titus 1:4; Philem. 3). Second, the presence of a chiasm would account for the use of the single preposition "through" before the pair "Jesus Christ" and "God the Father"; instead, the preposition "from" used in the A line ("not from men") ought to be implied in the corresponding A′ line ("and [from] God the Father").

statement of faith that he has in common with his Galatian readers. It will be harder for the Christians in Galatia to reject Paul's apostleship and his gospel when he shares with them the same key confession that God raised Jesus from the dead.

Yet there presumably are several creedal statements that Paul has in common with the Galatian readers that he could use to strengthen his relationship with them. Why does Paul quote this particular confession? Half the answer is suggested by his purpose at work in the chiasm in Gal. 1:1. There Paul underscores the *divine* origin of his apostleship in response to his Judaizing opponents, who claim that his apostleship derives from human authorities, perhaps church leaders in Antioch or Jerusalem, and that it has been mediated by a specific person, perhaps James, Peter, or Barnabas. Paul skillfully defends the legitimacy of his apostolic status not only by alluding to his Damascus road encounter with Jesus ("not from men nor through a man but through Jesus Christ") but also by citing a confession clearly affirming that his apostolic-grounding encounter with Jesus was with the *resurrected* Jesus. One key criterion in selecting an apostolic leader to replace Judas was that the person be a "witness to his [Jesus's] resurrection" (Acts 1:22). When Paul's authority as an apostle was questioned by the Corinthians, who were more willing to show deference to Peter than to the founder of their church, Paul defended the legitimacy of his apostleship by similarly appealing to his encounter with the resurrected Jesus (1 Cor. 9:1, "I am an apostle, am I not? I have seen Jesus, our Lord, haven't I?"). Paul does the same thing later in the First Letter to the Corinthians, highlighting how his apostleship is grounded in the fact that the resurrected Jesus appeared to him too, just like all the other apostles (1 Cor. 15:8). Paul also closely connects his apostleship with Christ's resurrection in the expanded introduction of himself to his unknown and skeptical Roman readers (Rom. 1:1–6). The Judaizers in Galatia may claim to represent the authoritative teachings of James, Peter, and John, but Paul will not take a backseat to these so-called pillars of the church (Gal. 2:6, 9). Paul's status as a full-fledged, authoritative apostle is grounded in his divine call "from God the Father" and mediated "through Jesus Christ"—the Jesus Christ whom (as declared in a creedal statement that the Galatian readers themselves affirm) God "raised . . . from the dead."

Yet there is likely also a second half of the answer to why Paul quotes this particular confession dealing with Christ's resurrection. In the apostle's way of thinking, the resurrection signals the end of the "present evil age" (Gal. 1:4a) and the beginning of the "new creation" (Gal. 6:15; see also Isa. 26:19; Ezek. 37:1–14; Dan. 12:1–3; *2 Bar.* 20.2). Throughout the Galatian letter, Paul will stress Christ's death on the cross and his subsequent resurrection since this key redemptive event means that the old age, which was characterized by circumcision and other expressions of obedience to the law, has come to an end, and the new age of the Spirit, in which neither circumcision nor uncircumcision counts for anything (5:6; 6:15), has begun. At the opening of the letter, Paul's addition of a creedal confession about God's raising Jesus from the dead, therefore, is a not-so-subtle reminder to the Galatians that "the time has fully come" (4:4) and the eschatological age has begun. All of this has powerful implications for the central issues to be discussed in the rest of the letter. As Douglas Moo (2013: 69) notes: "Paul, therefore, alludes here to what will become the key theological argument of the letter: in Christ, God has inaugurated a new age in salvation history, a situation that 'changes everything'—including especially the evaluation and application of the law." Thomas Schreiner (2010: 75) similarly observes:

> One of the major themes of the letter emerges here. The Galatians were turning back the clock in salvation history by submitting to circumcision and the Mosaic law. Since Jesus has been raised from the dead, believers are no longer under the Mosaic covenant. Once again Paul anticipates one of the central themes of the letter (the fulfillment of God's eschatological promises).[6]

3. *All-encompassing reference to cosenders*. The third way that Paul has adapted the sender formula so that it more effectively persuades the Galatians readers to accept both his apostleship and his gospel involves his all-encompassing reference to cosenders. Paul departs from his normal practice by choosing not to identify any cosenders by name but instead he comprehensively refers to "all the brothers and sisters with me." The presence of the adjective "all" is unique in Paul's sender formulas and important. If Paul had omitted this word and instead simply said "the brothers with me," he might, as Richard Bauckham (1979: 65) has argued, have chosen this "vague phrase" because it "covers his embarrassment in not being able to ask his partner [Barnabas] to endorse the letter" after the painful incident narrated in Gal. 2:11–13. The addition of the adjective "all," however, suggests that Paul, far from being embarrassed, is confident and bold: he asserts that *all* the believers with him acknowledge his authoritative status as an "apostle not from men nor through a man but through Jesus Christ and from God the Father." The implied but barely veiled challenge is that the Galatians should join "all the brothers and sisters with me" and similarly acknowledge the divine origin of Paul's apostleship. James Dunn is among those "alert" commentators who see the persuasive force of Paul's all-encompassing reference to cosenders

---

6. See also Cook 1992: 514–15; Witherington 1998: 74.

(see also, e.g., Longenecker 1990: 5; Witherington 1998: 74; Tolmie 2005: 34; Schreiner 2010: 75):

> But the immediate mention of "*all* brothers" here, at the very beginning, is probably a not too subtle attempt to underscore the support that Paul had for the position he was going to maintain in what followed. Although he was making strong claims for himself and his authority as apostle, claims disputed at least in their implications by some among the churches in Galatia, he was writing with the *unanimous* support of those among (or along with) whom he was now ministering. (Dunn 1993: 29, emphasis in original)

The prepositional phrase "with me" is also significant. Paul not only expands the cosenders to include "all the brothers and sisters" but also stresses the close relationship that all these believers have with him: they are "with me." The word order in the Greek text highlights this close relationship even more emphatically: "all the with-me brothers and sisters." Paul, therefore, is by no means a marginalized, second-rate leader whom the Galatians can ignore but a full-fledged apostle who enjoys both divine authority and widespread ecclesiastical backing.

The sender formula in Galatians provides another illustration of both the method and the exegetical payoff of epistolary analysis. The careful examination of Gal. 1:1–2a makes it impossible to claim that the changes in the form of this epistolary convention are due to mere chance or are innocent variations in Paul's writing style. Instead, the evidence shows that Paul has skillfully adapted the sender formula in three ways so that it more persuasively asserts the divine origin of his apostolic status. The Galatian readers should acknowledge the divine authorization of Paul's apostleship and so also accept the circumcision-free and law-free version of the gospel that he is about to defend in the body of the letter.

1 Thessalonians 1:1a

The two sender formulas that we have examined thus far are striking for the extensive and skillful way that Paul has expanded the form of this epistolary convention. The third formula, from 1 Thess. 1:1a, by contrast is so short and simple that it hardly seems noteworthy: "Paul and Silas and Timothy." Nevertheless, this brief sender formula allows us to comment on two things: first, the significance here of Paul's omission of the expected title "apostle"; second, and more important, Paul's practice and purpose of including cosenders. The central thesis of this book is that Paul's epistolary practices are never accidental but relate in some way to his purposes in the letter as a whole. This in turn suggests that Paul's inclusion of cosenders, however insignificant such a habit may appear to be, similarly has an important function in the apostle's persuasive strategy.

Every letter of Paul, except for two, includes a title in the sender formula, and of these letters every one but two uses the title "apostle." The absence of this title in his First Letter to the Thessalonians (and also in 2 Thessalonians) is, therefore, conspicuous. A likely explanation for this omission is that, in contrast to several other letters (esp. Romans, 1 and 2 Corinthians, and Galatians), Paul's apostleship was not an issue with the Thessalonian congregation, and so in the letter opening he has no need to assert his authoritative status. Paul mentions his apostleship only once in his two letters to the Thessalonians (1 Thess. 2:7), and this single instance serves not to stress his authority but to demonstrate the opposite point: that he did not, in a self-serving and heavy-handed manner, assert his right as an apostle to be supported financially by the Thessalonian congregation but that he self-sacrificially worked with his hands to provide his own support rather than become a burden to them. In many other churches, however, Paul faced questions and even outright challenges to his authority, and so in the letter opening he justifiably asserts his privileged position as an apostle, alongside others who were "brothers," as in 1 Cor. 1:1, "Paul, called to be an *apostle* of Christ Jesus by the will of God, and Sosthenes our *brother*"; 2 Cor. 1:1, "Paul, an *apostle* of Christ Jesus by the will of God, and Timothy our *brother*." But since Paul enjoys a very warm and positive relationship with the Thessalonians, in the sender formula he has no need to highlight his distinctive title as an apostle. As Leon Morris (1959: 47) puts it, "To the Thessalonians he is just 'Paul.' There is no need to protest his position to these good friends."

A second feature about the sender formula in 1 Thess. 1:1a that requires more than just a brief comment—because the issue is more complicated and more important than is typically recognized—is Paul's inclusion of cosenders, Silas and Timothy. In *all* of Paul's letters, three questions pertaining to the issue of cosenders need to be answered in order to properly understand his inclusion of Silas and Timothy in the sender formula of 1 Thess. 1:1a: (1) Was the practice of including cosenders common among ancient letter writers or a unique feature of Paul's letter-writing style? (2) What role, if any, did cosenders play in the composition of Paul's letters? And finally, (3) if, as I will argue below, Paul emerges as the ultimate or real author of the letter, why did he choose to include the names of cosenders?

1. *Is the inclusion of cosenders a common or rare practice?* The practice of naming other people in the letter opening as cosenders was clearly not common in the ancient world. There are examples of this epistolary phenomenon,

but they appear to be the exception, not the rule. The Roman statesman Cicero distinguishes two types of letters that he has received from his friend Atticus, "both those which you have written jointly with others and those in your own name" (*Att.* 11.5.1), though the off-handed manner in which Cicero makes this distinction suggests that he is not so surprised by the existence of a multiauthored letter. Randolph Richards (1991: 47n138; 2004: 34) found no examples among the extant letter collections of Cicero,[7] Seneca, and Pliny the Younger and only six examples among 645 papyrus letters from Oxyrhynchus, Tebtunis, and Zenon in Egypt. Michael Prior (1989: 38) was able to track down 15 papyrus letters with multiple named senders, which he recognizes as only "a tiny proportion of all the extant papyrus letters." Jeffrey Reed (1997: 184n120) claims to have found 83 instances of cosenders in just one corpus of papyrus letters yet still admits that the mention of another person in the sender formula "is unquestionably rare." It also ought to be recognized that no letter writer in the NT except Paul names other people with himself in the opening of the letter. All this serves to sharpen the contrast with Paul's practice where the majority of his letters—8 out of 13—*do* include a reference to cosenders. As Samuel Byrskog (1996: 247) observes, "The mention of co-sender(s) in the prescripts [of Paul's letters] is an unusual, and therefore probably intentional, epistolographic feature."

2. *What role did the cosenders play in writing Paul's letters?* The phenomenon of co*senders* must not be equated with the phenomenon of co*authors*. In other words, just because Paul frequently included the names of others in the sender formula does not necessarily mean that these named cosenders played an equal or even minor role in the actual composition of the letter. In the Letter to the Galatians, for example, Paul's extensive use of the first-person singular "I" (38 times) and the very personal and heated tone of the correspondence make clear that his cosenders, "all the brothers and sisters with me" (Gal. 1:2a), did not actually help him write it. The same conclusion may be drawn from other letters where cosenders are named. First Corinthians 1:1 lists the name of Sosthenes in the sender formula, but the voice of this cosender disappears in the rest of the letter where the first-person singular ("I") occurs some 75 times. Philippians 1:1 lists Timothy as a cosender, but the 52 occurrences of "I" in this relatively short letter, combined with the intensely personal nature of the correspondence, strongly implies that Timothy, although a cosender, was not a coauthor. The Letter to Philemon names Timothy as a cosender, but again the 17 occurrences of "I" in this briefest of Paul's extant letters—along

---

7. Richards failed to note a few instances where Cicero did include family members as cosenders: *Letters to Family* 14.14, 18; 16.1, 3, 4, 5, 6, 11.

with the many references to intimate details about Paul's life and his relationship to both the slave owner, Philemon, and his slave, Onesimus—lead one to conclude that Paul is the true and single author of this correspondence. When the five letters where Paul does not include any reference to others in the sender formula (Romans, Ephesians, 1–2 Timothy, Titus) are added to these examples, there is compelling evidence for Paul's practice of writing letters in which he is the real or sole author, even if cosenders are included. In other words, there is no need to change the way Christians have typically identified Paul's letters and start referring to "The Letter of Paul and Sosthenes to the Corinthians," "The Letter of Paul and Timothy to the Philippians," and so on (as advocated by Prior 1989: 39).

The strongest evidence that cosenders were also coauthors and *did* play an active role in the writing of a letter is found in the sender formulas of both 1 and 2 Thessalonians. Not only are these letters identified as coming from "Paul and Silas and Timothy," but there is also the widespread use of the first-person plural ("we") in the rest of the letter. This has caused some to conclude that Silas and Timothy played an active role in the composition of the letter. The situation is likened to that of a group project in which all three individuals contribute to the subject matter, organizational structure, and perhaps even the vocabulary of the letter. Jerome Murphy-O'Connor (1995: 19), for example, asserts that "the mention of those associated with Paul in the address should be explained in terms of the letter; that is, he selected them to play a role in the creation of the epistle as coauthors. It seems obvious that the recipients of such letters would have taken the 'we' at face value as referring to the senders." Randolph Richards (2004: 33) boldly states: "We[8] are arguing that Paul's letters were a team project," though he immediately adds, "but not a team of near-equals. Paul was the leader and the dominant voice; the others were his disciples."

Against this scenario, however, are not only the important observations made above about Paul's other letters that do and do not include cosenders, but also additional evidence from 1 Thessalonians. There are three instances in the letter where the text shifts significantly to the first-person singular, suggesting that the first-person plurals in the letter ought to be read not *literally* but *literarily*. The first instance is 2:18, where Paul's desire to revisit the Thessalonians is originally expressed in the plural ("We wanted to come to you") but then clarified with a personal interjection in the singular ("in fact, I, Paul, wanted to do so more than once"). The second occurrence is

8. It is worth raising the question to whom the plural "We" refers: to Richards alone or to a team of coauthors?

the *inclusio*[9] formed between 3:1–2 and 3:5: the expression containing a first-person plural ("Because we could no longer contain it, . . . we sent Timothy . . . in order to comfort you concerning your faith") is restated and clarified by an expression containing a first-person singular ("Because I could no longer contain it, I sent [Timothy] in order to learn about your faith"). The third occasion is 5:27, where the letter closes with a strong exhortation given in the singular: "I cause you to swear an oath by the Lord that this letter be read to all the brothers." A similar shift from the plural "we" to the singular "I" occurs twice in 2 Thessalonians (see 2:5 and 3:17).

If cosenders Silas and Timothy did have an active role in the composition of the letter, their participation could have been communicated easily with a statement such as "The three of us appeal to you that . . . ," or "Silas, Timothy, and I send greetings." No such clear indication of multiple authorship is found in 1 Thessalonians or any of Paul's other letters. Thus the conclusion of Samuel Byrskog (1996: 249) in his detailed study of cosenders, coauthors, and Paul's use of the first-person plural is justified: "Although the co-senders probably were important discussion partners of Paul, there is not much evidence to suggest that they actively composed the letters together with him."

3. *Why did Paul include cosenders?* If, as the evidence suggests, Paul is the sole author of his letters, including 1 Thessalonians, why has he included Silas and Timothy as cosenders? That Paul's epistolary practices are never accidental but relate in some way to his persuasive strategy suggests that the mention of cosenders has a similarly persuasive function. This seems to be confirmed by the one letter where Paul's purpose in including cosenders is quite transparent: in the sender formula of Galatians, he made the cosenders as comprehensive as possible by identifying them as "all the brothers and sisters with me" in order to not-so-subtly claim widespread ecclesiastical support for his apostleship and his gospel.

A persuasive function for the inclusion of cosenders reveals the naiveté of those who see this epistolary practice as "a matter of courtesy" (Morris 1959: 46): Paul graciously mentions the names of those with him when he begins to write—a polite but meaningless act. This proposed "courtesy" function for listing cosenders is further undermined by the several instances where people mentioned in the closing greetings were clearly with Paul at the time of his writing, yet the apostle fails to include their names as cosenders.

---

9. An *inclusio* is a literary device by which a key word, phrase, or sentence is repeated at the beginning and ending of a literary unit to mark the unit's boundaries. See further discussion of this literary device in chap. 4.

For instance, Timothy was with Paul when he wrote Romans (Rom. 16:21), but the apostle does not include him as a cosender; Aquila and Prisca were both with Paul when he wrote 1 Corinthians (1 Cor. 16:19), but the apostle does not include them as cosenders; Epaphras, Mark, Aristarchus, Demas, Luke, and Justus were all with Paul when he wrote to Philemon (Philem. 23–24) and to the Colossians (Col. 4:10–14), but the apostle does not include any of them as cosenders. It would obviously be wrong to conclude that Paul offended these fellow believers by not including them in the sender formula.

Another proposed function that must be rejected is the idealized view of those who see in Paul's inclusion of cosenders evidence of the apostle's modesty. Richards (2004: 33), for example, claims that mentioning cosenders involves "lowering oneself" and that this is "one of the many ways Paul differed from the epistolary elite of society. Unlike their letters, Paul's were not intended as examples of the author's skill." However, Paul's comprehensive reference in Galatians to "all the brothers and sisters with me" hardly seems evidence of the apostle's humility; quite the opposite, he boldly claims the backing and ecclesiastical support of *all* those with him. Furthermore, Paul's frequent and careful distinction in the sender formula between his title as an "apostle" and that of the cosender who is a "brother" (1 Cor. 1:1; 2 Cor. 1:1a; Gal. 1:1–2a; Col. 1:1; Philem. 1a) suggests that Paul's practice of naming others in the letter opening does not stem first and foremost from his modesty.

Also misguided is the view that Paul's reference to cosenders functioned as a commendation of the letter carrier. William Doty (1973: 30), for example, argues that "the persons mentioned by name [in the sender formula] were often the trusted persons who were transmitting the letters and whose authority the addressees were to acknowledge." The mention or recommendation of a letter carrier, however, typically occurred not in the opening but in the closing section of the letter (C.-H. Kim 1972), and this appears to be Paul's practice elsewhere (Rom. 16:1–2; Eph. 6:21–22; Col. 4:7–9).

Yet another proposed function for the inclusion of cosenders is that the named individual could fulfill the legal requirement of Deut. 19:15 that any testimony would be considered valid only if it was supported by two or more witnesses. Luther Stirewalt (2003: 42–44) cites several examples of this practice from Jewish official letters and additionally claims that Paul was very familiar with this requirement for witnesses (see 2 Cor. 8:16, 22; 12:16–18; 13:1). Stirewalt (2003: 44) concludes, "A convincing accounting for the use both by Paul and by the secular writers is to identify co-senders as personnel who were informed participants in the letter-event and who supplied the requirements for witness to the written message."[10] This proposed authenticating function is attractive not just because of the evidence forwarded by Stirewalt but also because it agrees with the broader persuasive function that this rare epistolary practice clearly has for Paul in Gal. 1:1–2a: the naming of individuals who can testify to the truth of what Paul writes surely makes his letters more persuasive. Nevertheless, this view suffers from the fact that Paul most often cites only *one* person as a cosender, but at least *two* witnesses are required since the apostle cannot serve as a witness to what he himself has written (Byrskog 1996: 248–49).

The most likely reason for including cosenders is that the named individuals enjoy a special relationship with the addressees of the letter and that the presence of these named individuals with Paul adds weight to the apostle's words, thereby enhancing the letter's overall persuasive force. Paul includes the names of Silas and Timothy in the sender formula of 1 Thess. 1:1 because both individuals have played a key role in the Thessalonian congregation— Silas in the establishing of the church (Acts 17:1–10) and Timothy in the subsequent strengthening of the church (1 Thess. 3:1–5). The inclusion of these two men as cosenders, therefore, *gives further weight or authority to Paul's letter*: it not only shows the Thessalonians that the apostle is well informed about the current situation in their congregation from the report of the recently returned Timothy (1 Thess. 3:6–10) but also shows that Paul and these other two leaders agree about the recipients' required and expected response to their present circumstances (so also Wanamaker 1990: 68). In his First Letter to the Corinthians, Paul names Sosthenes as cosender no doubt because of his former membership and leadership position in their community (Acts 18:17). As Richard Hays (1997: 15–16) observes: "If he [Sosthenes] was a notable Corinthian convert who had suffered for the gospel, he might have been a person of some influence among the Corinthian Christians. Thus, though he is not mentioned again in the text, his appearance in the salutation perhaps *lends some additional weight to the appeals* that Paul will make throughout the letter" (emphasis added). Also in the letters of 2 Corinthians, Philippians, Colossians, and Philemon, Timothy is listed as cosender, presumably because of his past work, personal connection, and/or positive reputation in these congregations.

My examination of Paul's use of cosenders in 1 Thess. 1:1 and in his other letter openings has led to an admittedly tentative proposal about its

10. About Paul's reference to Timothy as a cosender in Phil. 1:1, Moisés Silva (2005: 39) similarly states, "We may then recognize that the apostle, by joining Timothy's name to his, calls upon his coworker as a *corroborating witness* of the truths he expounds" (emphasis added). See also Furnish 1984: 104.

function. The rarity of this epistolary practice in other letters of that day and that Paul nowhere spells out the reason why he names others in the sender formula means that any proposed function must remain an open question. Nevertheless, the evidence concerning Paul's use of cosenders does clearly support the central thesis of this book, namely, that Paul is a gifted letter writer who skillfully adapts the epistolary conventions of his day so that they more effectively support his persuasive purposes, and that consequently the method of epistolary analysis is an important hermeneutical key for properly interpreting his letters. As Sean Adams (2010: 44) observes:

> Paul did not randomly include people in his letters as co-senders, but strategically integrated them within his letters. . . . Paul selected from the people who were with him the most appropriate and those who had a strong relationship to the people in the place where the letter was being sent. Paul did not create the multiple sender form in the Greek letter, but utilized this convention to bolster the weight of the letter.

The Recipient Formula

Formal Analysis

The second epistolary convention in Paul's letter openings is the recipient formula. This follows the precedent established in other letters of this time, except, as noted above, occasionally in letters of petition where the sender is appealing for help to a person of a higher rank and the letter writer honors the recipient by putting that person's name first. The recipient formula in Paul's letters consists of two formal elements (see table 2.2: The Recipient Formula):

Table 2.2: The Recipient Formula

Letter	Recipient	Descriptive Phrase
Rom. 1:7	To all those in Rome	who are loved by God and called to be holy
1 Cor. 1:2	To the church of God that is in Corinth	to those who have been made holy in Christ Jesus, called to be holy, together with all those who in every place call on the name of our Lord Jesus Christ, both their Lord and ours
2 Cor. 1:1b	To the church of God that is in Corinth with all the holy ones who are in the whole of Achaia	
Gal. 1:2	To the churches of Galatia	

Letter	Recipient	Descriptive Phrase
Eph. 1:1	To the saints who are in Ephesus	and are faithful in Christ Jesus
Phil. 1:1	To all the saints who are at Philippi, with the overseers and deacons	in Christ Jesus
Col. 1:2	To the saints and faithful brothers and sisters at Colossae	in Christ
1 Thess. 1:1	To the church of the Thessalonians	in God the Father and the Lord Jesus Christ
2 Thess. 1:1	To the church of the Thessalonians	in God our Father and the Lord Jesus Christ
1 Tim. 1:2	To Timothy	my true child in the faith
2 Tim. 1:2	To Timothy	my beloved child
Titus 1:4	To Titus	my true child in a common faith
Philem. 1–2	To Philemon and Apphia and Archippus and the church in your house	our beloved fellow worker our sister our fellow soldier
James 1:1	To the twelve tribes in the Dispersion	
1 Pet. 1:1–2	To the exiles of the Dispersion in Pontus, Galatia, Cappadocia, Asia, and Bithynia	who have been chosen and destined by God the Father and sanctified by the Spirit to be obedient to Jesus Christ and to be sprinkled with his blood
2 Pet. 1:1	To those	who have received a faith as precious as ours through the righteousness of our God and Savior Jesus Christ
2 John 1–2	To the elect lady and her children	whom I love in the truth, and not only I but also all who know the truth, because of the truth that abides in us and will be with us forever
3 John 1	To the beloved Gaius	whom I love in truth
Jude 1	To those	who are called, who are beloved in God the Father and kept safe for Jesus Christ

1. The designation of the recipient as either "church" or "saints," along with the name of the city or region where the congregation is located (1 Cor. 1:2; 2 Cor. 1:1; Gal. 1:2; Eph. 1:1; Phil. 1:1; Col. 1:2; 1 Thess. 1:1; 2 Thess. 1:1). In letters addressed to an individual (even though the

larger church community is still in view), just the name of the person is listed (1 Tim. 1:2; 2 Tim. 1:2; Titus 1:4; Philem. 1b–2).

2. A brief descriptive phrase that positively describes the readers' relationship to God and/or Christ, such as "in God (our) Father and the Lord Jesus Christ" (1 Thess. 1:1; 2 Thess. 1:1) or "in Christ Jesus" (1 Cor. 1:2; Phil. 1:1). In letters addressed to an individual, a positive description of the reader's relationship to Paul is given: "my true child in the faith" (1 Tim. 1:2); "my beloved child" (2 Tim. 1:2a); "my true child in a common faith" (Titus 1:4a); "our beloved fellow worker" (Philem. 1b).

The second element of the recipient formula sounds very formulaic and perfunctory to our modern Christian ears, and so we can easily miss the commendatory aspect of this brief descriptive phrase. But when Paul, for example, describes his Thessalonian readers as those who are "in God (our) Father and the Lord Jesus Christ" (1 Thess. 1:1; 2 Thess. 1:1), the believers in that city would naturally be pleased to hear their church founder acknowledge in this public way that they do indeed have a living and active relationship with both God and Jesus. They would be more willing to listen to what the praise-giving Paul was about to say in his letter and so live according to their God/Christ-relationship that the apostle has invoked.

Interpretive Significance

1 CORINTHIANS 1:2

The recipient formula of 1 Cor. 1:2 (see also 2 Cor. 1:1) stands out among the extant occurrences of this epistolary convention in Paul's letters. There is a subtle but significant change in the first formal element: the designation of the recipient is listed not as the "church in Corinth" or the "church of the Corinthians" but rather as the "church *of God* that is in Corinth." There is also a major expansion of the second formal element. Instead of a brief descriptive phrase that positively describes the readers' relationship to God and/or Christ, there is a lengthy identification of the Corinthian readers that far exceeds that found in any other recipient formula: "to those who have been made holy in Christ Jesus, called to be holy, together with all those who in every place call on the name of our Lord Jesus Christ, both their Lord and ours."

The "alert" reader who interprets 1 Corinthians following the method of epistolary analysis will expect to find that these variations in Paul's normal approach have been designed to address the specific situation in Corinth and to anticipate some of the key ideas that the apostle will develop later, in the body of the letter. Four truths expressed in Paul's changes to this recipient formula are all particularly relevant to the circumstances of his Corinthian readers: (1) the Corinthian church belongs to God; (2) the Corinthians are the church of God only because of the work of God and Christ in their lives; (3) the Corinthians must live a holy life; and (4) the Corinthians constitute just a small part of the universal church.

1. *The Corinthian church belongs to God.* In contrast to Paul's earlier letters to the Thessalonians, where Paul addressed his correspondence "to the church *of* the Thessalonians *in* God" (1 Thess. 1:1; 2 Thess. 1:1), here the apostle writes "to the church *of* God *in* Corinth." That this is not an accidental or insignificant change is supported by two facts: first, Paul similarly identifies the Corinthian church in his second letter to them as "the church *of God*"; and second, he uses the possessive description "of God" in none of his other recipient formulas addressed to a church. Paul's emphasis that the church belongs first and foremost to God is especially relevant for a Corinthian church whose members are divided over their loyalty to whichever church leader they believe proclaims the gospel in an impressive or "wise" way (1 Cor. 1:10–4:21): some are saying they are "of Paul" while others are claiming to be "of Apollos" or "of Cephas" (1:12). Already long ago the early church father John Chrysostom interpreted Paul's remarks in 1:2 as a claim that the church is the possession "not of this person or that person but of God" (*Hom. 1 Cor.* on 1:2). In the recipient formula, Paul's emphasis on the church not belonging to any individual leader or group within the Corinthian church but is instead "the church *of God*" anticipates a similar claim in the body of the letter. Paul will later assert that he and Apollos are "fellow workers *of God*" and that the congregation in Corinth is a "field *of God*" and a "building *of God*" (3:9). All three references to the possessive description "of God" are emphasized by the Greek word order. Paul further reminds his Corinthian readers that "you are the temple *of God*" (3:16) and that "you are of Christ, and Christ is *of God*" (3:23).

2. *The Corinthians are the church of God only because of the work of God and Christ in their lives.* The explicit mention of God in the possessive description "of God," along with two implicit references to God elsewhere in the recipient formula, ought to be recognized along with the other multiple references to God found in the opening and thanksgiving sections of 1 Corinthians. There is a heavy concentration of references to both God and Christ in the brief nine verses that make up the beginning of this letter: fourteen references are to God,[11] and eleven references are

---

11. There are six explicit references to God: 1 Cor. 1:1 ("called . . . by the will of God"); 1:2 ("church of God"); 1:3 ("from God our Father"); 1:4 (2×: "I give thanks to God . . . the grace

to Christ.[12] In light of these impressive statistics, Gordon Fee's observation (1987: 36) about the thanksgiving (1:4–9) is equally true also of the opening (1:1–3): "The whole of the thanksgiving is God-orientated and Christ-centered. Everything comes *from God* and is given *in Christ Jesus*" (emphasis in original).

What accounts for this theocentric and christocentric emphasis? The answer lies in the problem of pride at work in the Corinthian church. By Paul's own admission, they were a gifted congregation who had been "enriched in every way, in all your speech and knowledge" (1:5), with the result that "you are not lacking any spiritual gift" (1:7). But as the rest of the letter reveals, their giftedness was accompanied by an attitude of pride and boasting. They thought of themselves as already spiritually filled so that they lacked nothing, as rich in the gifts of the Holy Spirit, and as already in the triumphant position of kings (4:8). They viewed themselves as wise, strong, and in a position of honor (4:10). Simply put, they were full of themselves. Paul will confront this proud and boastful congregation with the harsh reality that they are not as great or special as they think: "For who sees anything special in you?" (4:7a). Paul also will remind them that all their abilities in speech and knowledge, which they view with such pride, are actually gifts from God made accessible to them only through their relationship to Christ: "What do you have that you did not receive? If then you received it, why do you boast as if it were not a gift?" (4:7b). The opening and the thanksgiving sections, therefore, anticipate Paul's later argument against Corinthian pride and already assert the important principle that all the congregation's gifts come *from God* and are theirs only because of their relationship *to Christ*.

---

of God"); and 1:9 ("God is faithful"). There are also eight implicit references to God. Six are in multiple occurrences of the divine passive, where the unspoken agent of a verb or noun in the passive voice is assumed to be God. Thus, in the recipient formula of 1:2, when Paul describes his Corinthian readers as both "those who have been made holy" and "called to be holy," the unspoken but obvious actor who made the Corinthians holy and who called them to be holy is God. Four uses of the divine passive also appear in the thanksgiving section: God is the implied actor in the grace that was "given" to the Corinthian church (1:4), in their "being enriched" in all their speech and knowledge (1:5), in their having Paul's testimony about Christ "confirmed in you" (1:6), and the one through whom the Corinthians "were called" (1:9). The final two implicit references to God involve the relative pronoun of 1:8—God is the one "*who* will sustain" the Corinthians until the end of time when Christ returns—and he is also the referent of the personal pronoun in the phrase "*his* son, Jesus Christ, our Lord" (1:9).

12. There are nine explicit references to Christ: 1:1 ("an apostle of Christ Jesus"); 1:2 (2×: "made holy in Christ Jesus . . . the name of our Lord Jesus Christ"); 1:3 ("from the Lord Jesus Christ"); 1:4 ("in Christ Jesus"); 1:6 ("testimony about Christ"); 1:7 ("the revelation of our Lord Jesus Christ"); 1:8 ("the day of our Lord Jesus Christ"); and 1:9 ("the fellowship of his Son, Jesus Christ, our Lord"). Christ is also implied in the two possessive pronouns "both their Lord and ours" in 1:2, as well as in the personal pronoun in the prepositional phrase "in him" in 1:5.

Viewed just by itself, the recipient formula with its three references to God (one explicit and two implicit) and its four references to Christ (two explicit and two implicit) may not seem so significant. However, when seen in light of the clear theocentric and christocentric focus found elsewhere in the letter opening and thanksgiving, the multiple references to God and Christ in the recipient formula are an important part of Paul's strategic plan for correcting the false pride at work in the Corinthian church by getting them instead to view their gifts as coming from God via their relationship to Christ.

3. *The Corinthians must live a holy life.* Paul's focus in the sender formula on holiness can be easily missed in many English translations, which often use the words "sanctified" and "saints" to render the two occurrences in this verse of the same root word in Greek. It is better, then, to translate the apostle's double description of the Corinthians as "those who have been made *holy* in Christ Jesus, called to be *holy*." Paul stresses the theme of holiness not just by repeating the key word "holy" in each phrase but also by using a rarer and more emphatic verb tense (the perfect) in the first occurrence of this term. And although not explicit, Paul's previous identification of the Corinthian congregation as "the church *of God*" also evokes the theme of holiness, since the congregation must ensure that its conduct matches the holy character of the God to whom they belong ("Be holy because I, the LORD your God, am holy": Lev. 11:44, 45; 19:2; 20:7; 22:32; 1 Pet. 1:16). Both occurrences of "holy" involve an implicit reference to God: God is the unnamed agent who has made them holy and who has called them to be holy. There is, therefore, a strong sense of obligation expressed: God has not only caused them in the past to be holy; he also continues to call them in the present to be holy. Holy living for the Corinthian readers, then, is not merely Paul's preference but also a requirement of God.

This emphasis on holy living is especially relevant for members of the Corinthian church who were failing to live distinctly holy lives—lives that showed in clear and tangible ways that they had been "set apart" from the world and from their former sinful ways and were now devoted to God. In many ways, their conduct failed to match the holiness of their God: the divisions in the church and their desire to have the gospel preached in a rhetorically impressive manner (1:10–4:21), their tolerance of a sexual relationship between a congregational member and his stepmother (5:1–13), their lawsuits in secular courts (6:1–11), their engaging the services of prostitutes (6:12–20), their idolatrous participation in cultic meals (8:1–11:1), their discrimination of the poor at Lord's Supper meal celebrations (11:17–34), and their use of spiritual gifts to build up themselves individually instead of building up the larger body of Christ (12:1–14:40). Such conduct is contrary to God's call for the Corinthians to be holy. Paul clearly has adapted the typical or expected form of his recipient formula so that it now highlights, among other things, the theme of holy living. As Gordon Fee (1987: 32) observes, Paul's decision to repeat the word "holy" in 1:2 is "hardly accidental. . . . Paul's concept of holiness regularly entails observable behavior. That will be particularly the case in this letter, which is addressed to a community whose 'spirituality' and 'higher wisdom' have been largely divorced from ethical consequences. Thus at the outset his readers are singularly identified as the 'church of God, *sanctified* in Christ Jesus.'"

4. *The Corinthians constitute just a small part of the universal church.* In his expansion of the recipient formula, the fourth truth that Paul conveys to the Corinthians is that they ought to view themselves not individually but as members of the larger, collective body of Christ. The apostle communicates this truth by not-so-subtly joining his Corinthian readers "with all those who in every place call on the name of our Lord Jesus Christ." Paul further stresses this universalizing reference by adding, at the very end of the sentence, the awkward phrase "both their Lord and ours." This phrase is tautological since it adds nothing new in terms of content; nevertheless, it functions rhetorically to add emphasis to what has already been said (see Belleville 1987: 17). Confirmation that this is indeed a conscious concern of the apostle specifically for the Corinthian congregation is found in the recipient formula of his later letter to them where he similarly locates his readers within the broader church community: "To the church of God that is in Corinth, with *all* the holy ones who are in the *whole of Achaia*" (2 Cor. 1:1b).

Paul's point that the Corinthians constitute just a small part of the universal church is deliberately directed at the congregation's specific situation. As David Garland (2003: 29) observes, "The letter betrays that an attitude of superiority had crept into the church at Corinth and was destroying their solidarity. By linking them with 'all those who call upon the Lord in every place' and underscoring that it is 'their [Lord] and ours,' Paul sounds a universal note that undermines their independent streak and egotism." The Corinthian Christians need to realize, as Anthony Thiselton (2000: 74) pointedly puts it, "They are not the only pebble on the beach."

By reminding the Corinthians of this truth at the beginning of the letter, Paul foreshadows a similar argument he will make several times in the body of the letter, where he will justify his exhortations on how the Corinthians ought to live by referring to the wider church community: "This is my rule in all the churches" (7:17b); "Give no offense to Jews or Greeks or to the church of God" (10:32); "We have no other practice, nor do the churches of God" (11:16); "Or do you despise the church of God?" (11:22); "As in all the churches of the holy ones" (14:33); "Did the word of God originate from you, or are you the only ones it has reached?" (14:36); "As I directed the churches of Galatia" (16:1). The Corinthians are also indirectly reminded of the broader church of which they are a part by the two confessions that Paul quotes concerning the Lord's Supper (11:23–26) and Christ's resurrection (15:3b–5). Finally, the universalizing reference in the recipient formula also sets up the Corinthian readers to accept Paul's challenge in 16:1–4 that they contribute money as part of the apostle's collection from his gentile churches for the needy Jewish believers in Judea (Garland 2003: 29). If the Corinthian believers see themselves as an integral part of a network of faith communities located throughout the Mediterranean world, they will be more likely to view distant Jesus-followers in Judea as fellow members of the same widespread church and help them out financially.

Galatians 1:2b

Although the recipient formula of 1 Cor. 1:2 is striking for its length (expanding what is normally a brief descriptive phrase that positively describes the readers' relationship to God and/or Christ), the recipient formula in Gal. 1:2b is noteworthy for the opposite. It is only five words long (four words in Greek). Paul completely omits the expected positive phrase. Instead of identifying his Galatian readers with an affirming statement like "in God (our) Father and the Lord Jesus Christ" (1 Thess. 1:1; 2 Thess. 1:1) or "in Christ Jesus" (1 Cor. 1:2; Phil. 1:1), Paul says nothing. He tersely and tellingly writes only "To the churches of Galatia."

The reason for Paul's omission lies in his uncertainty whether his Galatian converts have been convinced by his Judaizing opponents that both Paul's apostleship and his gospel are suspect, with the result that his readers' status of still being "in God our Father and the Lord Jesus Christ" is now in doubt. Many commentators not only mention the brevity of the recipient formula in Galatians but also correctly interpret this change from Paul's typical letter-writing practice as evidence of the apostle's deep concern over the spiritual health of his readers. Richard Longenecker (1990: 6), for example, observes: "Paul's address in Galatians is exceedingly brief, without the epithets and compliments found in the addresses of all his other letters. . . . This rather matter-of-fact address serves to signal Paul's agitation and indignation over the situation faced and to set a tone of severity that permeates the entire letter."

What is missed by virtually all commentators, however, is the powerful contrast that is created by means of Paul juxtaposing his omission in the recipient formula in 1:2b with his expansion of the immediately preceding sender formula in 1:1–2a. We have observed (above) how Paul skillfully embellishes his sender formula so that his apostleship has both divine authority ("not from men nor through a man but through Jesus Christ and from God the Father") and widespread ecclesiastical backing ("and all the brothers and sisters who are with me"). This divine authority and broad church support enjoyed by Paul is set in sharp relief to the weak position of his readers, who are simply identified as "the churches of Galatia." As Philip Tite (2010: 87–88) explains:

> By not supplying any expansions for the *adscriptio* . . . Paul effectively negates the authority of the recipients while offering a formal and abrupt tone to the prescript. The misbalance between the expansions in the *adscriptio* and the *superscriptio* is shocking and places the sender in a privileged position in contrast to the recipients: Paul has divine authority and ecclesial support, whereas the Galatian Christians have no authority or backing worth mentioning.

The "misbalance" that Paul creates is not so much "shocking" as it is indicative of the apostle's impressive epistolary skill. He faces the daunting task of winning his Galatian converts back to "the truth of the gospel" (2:5, 14) that he originally preached to them. The prospect of success, however, is severely compromised by the painful reality that his readers in Galatia seem to be under the spell of Judaizing opponents who have waged an effective campaign to undermine the legitimacy of his apostleship and thereby also the accuracy of his gospel. Before Paul defends both his apostleship and his gospel in the body of the letter, the apostle begins by expanding the sender formula and abbreviating the recipient formula in such a way that his divine authority and widespread ecclesiastical support are powerfully affirmed, while the position and backing of his Galatian readers (and the Judaizers who are adversely influencing them) are seriously undermined. In the letter opening, Paul skillfully adapts two epistolary conventions to set himself up as a divinely authorized apostle who enjoys the support of the broader church and who therefore ought to be heeded in the rest of the letter.

The Greeting Formula

Formal Analysis

The third and final epistolary convention in Paul's letter openings is the greeting formula (see table 2.3: The Opening Greeting Formula).

Table 2.3: The Opening Greeting Formula

Letter	Greeting	Recipient	Divine Source
Rom. 1:7b	Grace and peace	to you	from God our Father and the Lord Jesus Christ.
1 Cor. 1:3	Grace and peace	to you	from God our Father and the Lord Jesus Christ.
2 Cor. 1:2	Grace and peace	to you	from God our Father and the Lord Jesus Christ.
Gal. 1:3–5	Grace and peace	to you	from God our Father and the Lord Jesus Christ, who gave himself for our sins in order to rescue us from the present evil age, according to the will of our God and Father, to whom be the glory forever and ever. Amen.
Eph. 1:2	Grace and peace	to you	from God our Father and the Lord Jesus Christ.
Phil. 1:2	Grace and peace	to you	from God our Father and the Lord Jesus Christ.
Col. 1:2b	Grace and peace	to you	from God our Father.
1 Thess. 1:1b	Grace and peace.	to you	
2 Thess. 1:2	Grace and peace	to you	from God our Father and the Lord Jesus Christ.
1 Tim. 1:2b	Grace, mercy, and peace		from God the Father and our Lord Christ Jesus.
2 Tim. 1:2	Grace, mercy, and peace		from God the Father and our Lord Christ Jesus.
Titus 1:4b	Grace and peace		from God the Father and Christ Jesus our Savior.
Philem. 3	Grace and peace	to you	from God our Father and the Lord Jesus Christ.
James 1:1b	Greetings!		
1 Pet. 1:2b	Grace and peace be multiplied.	to you	
2 Pet. 1:2	Grace and peace be multiplied	to you	in the knowledge of God and of Jesus our Lord.
2 John 3	Grace, mercy, and peace	will be with us	from God the Father and from Jesus Christ the Father's Son, in truth and love.
Jude 2	Mercy, peace, and love be multiplied	to you.	

Letter	Greeting	Recipient	Divine Source
Rev. 1:4b–5	Grace and peace	to you	from him who is and who was and who is to come, and from the seven spirits before his throne, and from Jesus Christ the faithful witness, the firstborn of the dead, and the ruler of the kings on earth.

This convention consists of three formal elements:

1. The greeting: "grace and peace."
2. The recipient: "to you."
3. The divine source: "from God our Father and the Lord Jesus Christ."

The greeting "Grace and peace" sounds very familiar to the ears of contemporary Christians because this is the greeting that opens virtually all of Paul's letters (a slightly expanded form—"grace, mercy, and peace"—is found in 1 Tim. 1:2 and 2 Tim. 1:2) and the letters of other NT writers (1 Pet. 1:2; 2 Pet. 1:2). This greeting would have sounded unfamiliar and unique, however, to both Paul's gentile Christian readers and his Jewish Christian readers. It differs from the common infinitive greeting that typically opened Greek letters of their day: *chairein*, which literally means "Rejoice!" but has the colloquial sense of "Greetings!"[13] It also differs from the greeting found in the few Jewish letters that survive from that time period.[14]

Since neither Hellenistic nor Jewish letters provide an exact parallel to Paul's opening greeting formula, "Grace to you and peace," it is difficult to determine with certainty the origin of the apostle's salutation. The explanation that seems most likely and has won the most support is that the apostle has taken the expected secular or Greek greeting *chairein* and "Christianized" it by using the similar sounding Greek word *charis*, which means "grace." Both words not only sound similar but are also linguistically linked, which causes Sean Adams (2010: 47) to comment, "This similarity is beyond chance and suggests that Paul was adapting his letter greeting from the traditional *chairein* form." In Paul's adapting the secular greeting *chairein* into the Christian term *charis*, or "grace," Gordon Fee (2009: 17) sees "a marvelous example of Paul's 'turning into gospel' everything he sets his hand to." Paul then adds to this Christianized greeting the expected Jewish greeting "peace" (i.e., *shalom*). This was the opinion already of Tertullian (AD 160–220), who significantly

---

13. For examples of this greeting in Greek papyrus letters, see Exler 1923: 24–40, 42–44, 50–56; Weima 1994a: 29–30, 36. For examples in the NT, see Acts 15:23; 23:26; James 1:1; 2 John 10, 11.
14. For more on the opening greeting in Jewish letters, see Weima 2014: 70–71.

refs to Paul's adding "peace" to his opening greeting as "a formula which the Jews still use. For to this day they still salute each other with the greeting of 'peace'" (*Against Marcion* 5.5.1; cited by Thiselton 2000: 63). Paul's combining of "grace and peace" results, therefore, in a new and distinctive greeting that is truly inclusive of both his gentile Christian and Jewish Christian readers.

Paul's change of the secular "Greetings" (Greek *chairein*) to the new, Christianized salutation "Grace" (Greek *charis*) may be slight in sound but is significant in sense, for the newly minted greeting of "Grace" evokes the crucial role of the divine in the readers' salvation. Grace is the supreme gift of God's undeserved favor given to the readers by virtue of their relationship with Christ. The Jewish greeting "Peace" similarly evokes the work of God in the readers' lives. Peace here involves not the Greek sense of the absence of conflict but the Jewish notion of wholeness—a restoration of the fellowship and harmony that before the fall characterized humankind's relationship with God, with one another, and with the creation (see Rom. 2:10; 8:6; 14:17; Eph. 6:15; W. Foerster, *TDNT* 2:402–8). The apostle's combination of "grace and peace," then, demonstrates his skill in not merely borrowing from the epistolary conventions of his day but also cleverly adapting these conventions. Paul's gifted revision of the traditional greeting formula results in "as rich a greeting as can be imagined: a prayer which recognizes God as the source of the enabling ('grace') to live in mutually productive and beneficial harmony ('peace')" (Dunn 1993:23).

Paul also adds to his new greeting the divine source of grace and peace: "from God our Father and the Lord Jesus Christ." This supplementary clause reflects the theological perspective of the apostle, who acknowledges the crucial role of the divine—both God and Christ—not just in providing the gifts of grace and peace to the readers but also in being the ultimate cause of their salvation. This juxtaposition of "the Lord Jesus Christ" and "God our Father" likewise reflects the high Christology that would have been an important part of Paul's missionary preaching and that he can now safely assume was accepted by his readers. As Geoffrey Wilson (1975) states, "That such a construction could be used without comment not only implies the writer's belief in the deity of Christ, but also takes the reader's acknowledgment of it for granted" (cited by Morris 1991: 192). Jon Weatherly (1996: 212) similarly observes: "Paul, who was steeped in Jewish monotheism, attributes such gifts ["grace and peace"] to both God and Jesus with absolute ease and naturalness. Such is possible for him because he regards Jesus as fully divine."

Finally, the opening greeting formula serves an important literary function in framing the boundaries of the letter. The phrase found in the letter opening—"*grace* to you and *peace* from God our Father and our Lord Jesus Christ"—is repeated in reverse or chiastic order in the letter closing, first in the peace benediction (1 Thess. 5:23, "May the God of *peace* . . .") and then, after some other closing conventions, in the grace benediction (5:28, "The *grace* of our Lord Jesus Christ . . ."). The sender formula brings the letter opening to a definitive close in a comparable way that the corresponding peace benediction and grace benediction mark out the letter closing and so bring Paul's correspondence to a definitive close.

Interpretive Significance: Galatians 1:3–5

One greeting formula stands out from the others because of the way Paul has greatly expanded it. In Gal. 1:3–5, after the expected words "Grace to you and peace from God the Father and our Lord Jesus Christ," the apostle adds the following: "who gave himself for our sins in order to rescue us from the present evil age, according to the will of our God and Father, to whom be the glory forever and ever. Amen." The greeting is one of the epistolary formulas that is least frequently adapted in Paul's letters (only the closing grace benediction is more formally consistent), which makes this addition in the Galatians opening even more conspicuous. Paul's embellishment of the greeting formula consists of three things: (1) confessional material on the redemptive work of Christ; (2) a statement about the divine will and fatherhood of God; and (3) a concluding doxology. As we have seen in the other examples from the letter openings that we have studied thus far, here too this expansion is hardly fortuitous but instead stems from Paul's conscious attempt not just to prepare his Galatian readers for key arguments that he will make in the body of the letter but also to win their acceptance of these key arguments.

1. *Confessional material on the redemptive work of Christ.* The expanded material focuses not merely on what Christ has done ("who gave himself")—a clear reference to his death on the cross—but also stresses the redemptive significance of his death ("for our sins in order to rescue us from the present evil age"). Paul may well be quoting from an early Christian confession,[15] just as he already has done a couple of verses earlier in his expansion of the sender formula (see the fuller discussion [above] of the expression in Gal. 1:1b, "who raised him from the dead"). If so, this adds weight to the apostle's words, since he is reminding his readers of truths that they cannot easily dismiss as

---

15. See also Gal. 2:20; Rom. 4:25; 8:32; Eph. 5:2, 25; 1 Tim. 2:6; Titus 2:14. Commentators who view this expansion as confessional material include Bruce 1982: 75; Longenecker 1990: 7; Cook 1992: 515; Martyn 1997: 85–88; Smiles 1998: 69; Vouga 1998: 19; and Bryant 2001: 120–23.

the esoteric claims of their founder, whom some in their midst are disparaging as a second-rate apostle with a defective gospel message; rather, such a confessional reminder about the redemptive work of Christ is the very same truth that the Galatian readers themselves affirm in their corporate worship and that they have in common with the apostle and others in the early church. Paul's use of this confessional or traditional material "binds" his Galatian readers to him and allows the apostle "to achieve a common understanding as a potential ground for an agreement before proceeding to controversial issues later" (Tolmie 2005: 36).

Paul's reference to the death of Christ ("who gave himself") here in the greeting formula of the letter opening foreshadows the central role that the topic of Christ's crucifixion plays throughout the Galatian letter. As Vincent Smiles (1998: 69) helpfully notes: "In this letter it is the death of Christ that provides the main springboard for Paul's arguments against the Judaizers." After a lengthy autobiographical section in which Paul defends the divine origin of his apostolic status (1:11–2:14), he then defends the gospel message that is at the heart of his apostleship—a gospel that the Galatians have subsequently replaced with "another gospel" (1:6) advocated by the Judaizers. Paul opens the defense of his gospel (2:15–21) by highlighting the death of Christ on the cross. The expanded words of the greeting formula about Christ "who gave himself" anticipate Paul's claim that Christ "gave himself for me" (2:20) and that "Christ died" (2:21). It is only through Christ's death on the cross, and not through obedience to the law, that a person is justified (2:15–16). Paul has "been crucified with Christ" (2:20), and this is the only way one can secure a right relationship with God—not through the law or one aspect of the law such as circumcision.

The centrality of Christ's redemptive work on the cross is also highlighted in the immediately following section in the letter body. Paul rebukes his readers in 3:1 by exclaiming: "O foolish Galatians! Who has bewitched you, before whose eyes Jesus Christ was clearly portrayed as having been crucified?" In his mission-founding preaching to the Galatians Paul had so clearly proclaimed Christ crucified that he cannot understand how they could fail to appreciate the significance of Christ's death on the cross for the issue at hand. The apostle again refers to the redemptive work of Christ on the cross in 3:13, portraying Christ as the cursed one who "hanged on a tree" and so "redeemed us from the curse of the law." The cross and Christ's death are clearly implied in 4:5, where Paul refers to God sending his son "to redeem those who were under the law." More explicit is 5:11, where Paul speaks of "the stumbling block of the cross." Preaching the necessity of circumcision might well free Paul from persecution, but it would nullify the saving significance of Christ crucified. In the body of the letter, a final reference to Christ's redemptive death occurs in 5:24, which states that "those who belong to Christ Jesus have crucified the flesh with its passions and desires."

In light of the way Paul foreshadows the redemptive work of Christ in the expansion of the opening greeting formula and then stresses this same subject throughout his argument in the body of the letter, it is not surprising that the apostle also highlights the cross in the letter closing (6:11–18). Paul takes up the pen from his secretary and brings the letter to a close in his own hand, where he creates a series of four sharp contrasts between his opponents in Galatia and himself. What is most significant for our purposes is how in each of these contrasts the key theological issue at stake distinguishing the position of Paul from that of his opponents is the cross, thereby echoing the emphasis on the redemptive work of Christ on the cross found throughout the letter body and foreshadowed in the expansion of the greeting formula. The four contrasts between Paul and his opponents, all of which are centered on the cross of Christ, are outlined in the following table:[16]

Contrast	Opponents	versus	Paul
Motive 1	Boast in the circumcision of the Galatians (6:12, 13)	C	Boasts only in the cross of Christ (6:14)
Motive 2	Avoid persecution for the cross (6:12)	R	Accepts persecution ("marks of Jesus") for the cross (6:17)
External	Compel the Galatians to be circumcised (6:12, 13)	O S	Claims circumcision and uncircumcision do not matter (6:15)
Theological	Live in the "world" (6:14) under its powers	S	Lives in the "new creation" (6:15) under the lordship of Christ

Thus far I have briefly traced how Paul emphasizes the redemptive work of the cross throughout the letter body in Galatians and how he skillfully stresses this theme again in the letter closing. I have done so in order to demonstrate that Paul's expansion of the greeting formula in 1:4a is hardly accidental but deliberately foreshadows a key theme that he will develop later, in both the body and closing sections of the letter. Several commentators have rightly recognized that Paul's addition in 1:4a concerning Christ—"who gave himself for our sins in order to rescue us from the present evil age"—"strikes the keynote of the epistle" (Lightfoot 1881: 73), "strikes the first chord in a theme which reappears at various points throughout the letter" (Dunn 1993: 34), "serves as one of the topic sentences for the whole of the letter" (Martyn 1997: 90), "signals a central theme of the entire letter" (Schreiner 2010: 76),

---

16. For a full explanation of these contrasts, see Weima 1993; 1994a: 161–74.

or "anticipates the argument of the letter" (Moo 2013: 71). The results of my analysis, however, are perhaps best summarized by Longenecker (1990: 10):

> To this standard, though enriched opening, Paul adds what appears to be a portion of an early Christian confession (v. 4), which speaks of Christ's work and the purpose of that work for mankind's salvation. In so doing, he highlights a further important theme in the letter—i.e., the full sufficiency of Christ's work for mankind's salvation, apart from any works of the Mosaic law.

2. *Divine will and fatherhood*. After his confessional assertion about the redemptive work of Christ, Paul adds that Christ's giving of himself in order to rescue humanity from this present evil age was an action that happened "according to the will of our God and Father." That Paul frequently refers to "the will of God" (Rom. 1:10; 12:2; 15:32; 1 Cor. 1:1; 2 Cor. 1:1; 8:5; Eph. 1:1, 5, 9, 11; 6:6; Col. 1:1, 9; 4:12; 1 Thess. 4:3; 5:18; 2 Tim. 1:1) might lead to the assumption that this expression was merely a pious platitude or empty cliché for the apostle, as the saying "God willing" is for many people today. Paul, however, viewed his world as a place where things never happen by fate or luck but rather where God is in control and has a clear plan for the redemption of the world. Not surprisingly, then, the apostle reminds his Galatian readers that the act of Christ giving himself for their sins to rescue them from the present evil age is part of that overarching plan. In so doing, Paul raises the stakes in his debate with his Galatian readers. For if they continue to insist on circumcision and other expressions of obedience to the law as a requirement for salvation, they not only deny the sufficiency of Christ's redemptive work on the cross, but they also go against the divine will of God, who ordained this redemptive work.

Paul exerts still further pressure on his readers by adding yet another reference—the third one in the letter opening—to God as "Father." In the patriarchal culture of that day, the father had virtually unlimited authority over his wife, children, and all the members of his household. Both Greco-Roman and Jewish sources emphasize the hierarchical relationship of father to family members, often with language that jars the egalitarian spirit of our modern age. Aristotle states, for example, "The father is a kind of god to his children, a full head and shoulders above, and rightly so, for the father is a king" (*Pol.* 1.12.3; see also *Nic. Eth.* 8.11.2). Plutarch similarly locates parents on a hierarchical scale in which they are second in rank only to the gods: "Both Nature and the Law, which uphold Nature, have assigned to parents, after the gods, first and greatest honor" (*Frat. amor.* 7.479F). Jewish writers were influenced by the fifth commandment, to honor one's parents—a commandment that establishes the authority of parents and especially that of the "father [who is] head of the house" (Philo, *Names* 217). Thus, for the Galatians to reject Paul and his gospel is tantamount not only to going against the divine will of God but also the authority of God as their Father. One of the rare voices to recognize the persuasive force of Paul's addition "according to the will of our God and Father" is James Dunn (1993: 37):

> It will have been no accident, then, that Paul thus rounds off his opening paragraph with his focus once again on God and with a third reference to God as Father in the same sentence. It is his way of underscoring his conviction to his Galatian readers that what was at stake in their dispute was nothing less than the will and purpose of God for his world, and that Paul's gospel looked to no other source and no other validation.

3. *Doxology.* Paul brings his significant expansion of the greeting formula to a close in Gal. 1:5 with a doxology—an expression that ascribes glory to God ("to whom be the glory forever and ever")—and an affirmatory response ("Amen"). The doxology should not be identified narrowly as an epistolary formula, since it does not originate in letters or occur exclusively in letters. Instead, it is viewed more broadly as a liturgical form that Christian writers like Paul and others incorporate in their correspondence. In chapter 4, I will examine in greater detail the doxology, along with other liturgical forms often found in letters. For now I simply note that the doxology has a concluding function: it brings the preceding discussion to a climactic close. This is how the doxology always functions in Paul's letters, marking the end of either a section of the letter body (Rom. 11:36; Eph. 3:20–21; 1 Tim. 1:17; 6:16), the letter as a whole (Rom. 16:27; Phil. 4:20; 2 Tim. 4:18) or, as is the case only here, the letter opening (Gal. 1:5).

The presence of a doxology and an affirmatory response here in the greeting formula are entirely understandable from a theological point of view. The preceding references to the redemptive significance of Christ's work on the cross and how this act is in keeping with the will of God naturally lead Paul to give glory to God. The ascribing of glory to God also follows logically from the thoroughly theocentric character of Paul's overall theology. The final "Amen" (lit., "[It is] true!") similarly can be viewed as Paul's automatic yet genuine affirmatory response to the redemptive work through Christ that God has willed.

The presence of a doxology and the affirmatory response "Amen" are also understandable, however, from Paul's strategy of persuasion. These two elements place added pressure on the Galatian readers to submit to the apostle's assertions about the sufficiency of Christ's redemptive work on the cross and how this is in accordance with the will of their God and Father. The doxology creates a worship-like setting in which the readers are confronted not merely with Paul but with God and are encouraged to join the apostle in responding to what God has done in Christ by saying "Amen" and thereby affirming Paul's just-stated assertions. As Louis Martyn (1997: 106) observes:

> Having quoted and interpreted a confession the Galatians may be using in their current worship (1:4), and having pronounced a doxology to God (1:5a), Paul brings the Galatians climactically into God's presence by inviting them to utter the word "Amen." It is a signal of his conviction that his own words can and will become the active word of God, because God will be present as the letter is read to the Galatians in their services of worship. One might even say that by using the word "amen," Paul intends to rob the Galatians of the lethal luxury of considering themselves observers. With him, they stand in God's presence. Fundamentally, then, they are dealing with God, not merely with Paul (1:6).

Philip Tite (2010: 88–89) similarly recognizes the persuasive force of Paul's addition of the doxology and concluding "Amen":

> This liturgical expansion is an emphatic device that reinforces Paul's position: it is not grounded on human authority, but upon divine activity. . . . The liturgical closing "Amen" shuts down any possible debate on this matter, thereby leaving the readers with an authoritative and unquestionable voice to contend with as the letter swiftly moves into its polemical barrage.

The pressure-inducing character of Paul's words in Gal. 1:5 may perhaps be better understood and more fully appreciated in light of an analogous experience I had at an academic meeting of evangelical scholars many years ago. On this particular occasion a biblical scholar gave a paper with which I had several strong disagreements. Before opening up the session for questions and further discussion, this scholar closed his address by inviting all those there to stand and sing the well-known doxology "Praise God from Whom All Blessings Flow." This is not a normal way for a scholar to end an academic paper, even in evangelical circles. In fact, this has never happened to me ever again in my almost thirty years of attending scholarly conferences. That action of closing his paper with the singing of the doxology, however, was not only rare but also had a strong persuasive effect. First, I felt pressure to stand and sing along with others the words of the doxology, because how could a genuine Christian not want to join others in giving glory to God? Second, I felt pressure not to publically question the claims of the speaker in his paper, because to question the speaker after the singing of the doxology—an act that seemed to "baptize" his paper with God's divine approval—seemed very much like one was questioning God himself. In a somewhat similar fashion, Paul's closing doxology, though no doubt genuine, "baptizes" his preceding claims about the sufficiency of Christ's redemptive death on the cross in a way that makes it harder for his Galatian readers to reject, especially if they join the apostle in the natural response of "Amen" to God's salvific work through Christ.

3

The Thanksgiving

Even "alert" readers of Paul's correspondence often see the third and final epistolary convention of the letter opening—the greeting formula ("Grace to you and peace from God our Father and the Lord Jesus Christ")—and expect the apostle now to have completed the opening pleasantries and to begin the body of the letter, where he takes up the real issues about which he is primarily concerned. Although this expectation is understandable, it is wrong and can easily lead to a misinterpretation of Paul's content. His customary pattern is not to move directly from the letter opening to the body of the letter but instead to insert a "thanksgiving" section between them. The thanksgiving section is a distinct epistolary unit in Paul's letters in which he gives thanks to God for the believers to whom he is writing. It derives its name both from the verb with which it opens ("I/We give thanks") and its general content. To understand better the meaning and significance of any specific thanksgiving section in Paul's letters, it is necessary first to examine this epistolary unit more broadly in terms of its source, form, and function.

Source

Is Paul's custom of including a thanksgiving section in his letters a standard practice in ancient letter writing that he borrows and adapts, or is it a new literary convention that he himself created? The former position is supported by the presence of ancient letters that open in a way similar to

Paul's correspondence by expressing words of thanksgiving to the gods. For example, a third-century BC letter begins:

> Toubias to Apollonios, greeting. If you are well and if all your affairs and everything else is proceeding according to your will, *many thanks to the gods*; we also are well, always remembering you, as I should. (P.Cair.Zen. 59076; White 1986: 39)

Almost a century later (168 BC), in a letter from an angry wife to her wandering husband over his failure to return home, we similarly find an expression of thanks to the gods near the opening of the correspondence:

> Isias to Hephaiston, greeting. If you are well and your other affairs turn out in like fashion, it would be as if I have been continually praying to the gods (I myself and the child and all in the household are continually thinking of you).[1] When I received your letter from Horos, in which you make clear that you are safe in the Serapeum in Memphis, *I gave thanks to the gods* immediately that you are well, but I am disgusted that you have not come home, when all the others who had been secluded there have come back. (P.Lond. 42; White 1986: 65)

A second-century AD letter, from a new recruit of the Roman legion who had just completed a dangerous sea journey to Italy, written to his father provides yet another parallel:

> Apion to his father and lord, Epimachos, very many greetings. Before all else I pray that you are well and that you may prosper in continual health, together with my sister and her daughter and my brothers. *I give thanks to the lord Serapis* [an Egyptian god] because, when I was endangered at sea, he rescued me immediately. (*BGU* 423; White 1986: 159–60)

At first blush these parallels seem impressive and convincing: Paul, by opening his letters with a note of thanksgiving, appears to be borrowing from a common epistolary practice of his day.[2] Nevertheless, Paul's thanksgivings differ from expressions of thanks to gods found in common letters of his day in at least three ways. First, in terms of content, Paul's thanksgivings deal with the spiritual rather than physical well-being of his recipients. Second, in terms

---

1. This line was added by Isias after the letter was completed—an afterthought in order to reassure her husband that she still loved him, despite the strident tone of her words in the rest of the letter.

2. The majority of scholars have adopted this position, influenced heavily by the pioneering work of Schubert, who concluded that "the papyri convincingly attest a wide-spread conventional use of an epistolary, religious or non-religious, introductory thanksgiving" (1939: 180).

of form, Paul's thanksgivings are much longer and formally complex than the short and simple expressions of thanks found in other letters of his day. Third and most important, in terms of frequency, virtually all of Paul's letters include a thanksgiving section, but the vast majority of Greco-Roman letters do not.

Which, then, of the two positions about the source of the Pauline thanksgiving is correct? Is Paul indebted to the letter-writing practice of his day, or is he inventing a new epistolary convention? The answer is by no means obvious and certain. One can never prove literary dependence, and the parallels between the expressions of thanks in Paul's letters and in Greco-Roman letters are not nearly as frequent as they are often assumed to be.[3] Nevertheless, the parallels are not rare but occur with sufficient frequently to justify the likelihood that Paul is borrowing and adapting an optional epistolary convention of his day.[4]

Form

When the thanksgiving sections of Paul's surviving letters are viewed together side-by-side, they reveal a common form or basic structure that typically consists of five distinct units.[5]

Statement of Thanksgiving

The thanksgiving opens with the main verb "I/we give thanks" and the identification of the one to whom thanksgiving is directed: "to [my] God." The

---

3. After reviewing the motif of thanksgiving in the letters of both Paul and secular writers of his time, McFarlane (1966: 11) concludes, "In the face of the overwhelming evidence of the majority of letters, which simply do not contain at any position such a statement, clause, or phrase, we can hardly speak of the thanksgiving period as part of the 'standard Hellenistic epistolary form.'" In a more recent extensive survey of the vocabulary of thanksgiving in ancient letters, Arzt (1994: 37) similarly concludes, "Because of the lack of references within the large number of Greek papyrus letters we may conclude that an 'introductory thanksgiving' never existed as a set phrase." See also Arzt-Grabner 2010: 143–49, 157.

4. See esp. Reed 1996, who responds directly to the important studies of Arzt (1994) and Collins (2010).

5. The formal analysis of the Pauline thanksgiving section presented here follows the fivefold structure proposed by Jervis (1991: 86–109). The first to examine the form of this epistolary unit was Schubert (1939), who proposed that there are two basic types of thanksgiving, one being formally more complex than the other. Despite the importance of Schubert's groundbreaking work and its widespread acceptance (see esp. O'Brien 1977), his formal analysis suffers from a couple of weaknesses. First, the two proposed formal types do not account for the structure of *all* the Pauline thanksgivings, thereby requiring Schubert to identify yet a third ("mixed") type. Second, and more significant, Schubert focused his attention only on the initial parts of the thanksgiving section, ignoring to a large extent the relatively consistent structure and function of the concluding parts.

visual image of himself that Paul evokes in the first part of the thanksgiving is of the apostle pointing his finger straight up toward heaven, as he directs his thanksgiving to God, the one whom he views as the ultimate source of the spiritual gifts evidenced in the lives of his readers.

Manner of Thanksgiving

There are several different ways in which one could potentially express thanksgiving to God: through song, confessional statements, or some other creative activity. Paul's preferred manner of expressing thanks to God is through prayer. Thus his thanksgivings typically contain some reference to "remembering/making mention of you all in my prayers." The visual image of himself that Paul evokes in this second part of the thanksgiving is of the apostle on his knees, passionately praying to God on behalf of his readers (see Eph. 3:14, "I kneel in prayer to the Father").

Cause of Thanksgiving

Every thanksgiving includes one or more causal constructions (often involving verbs of "hearing" or "learning") that give the reason for Paul's thanksgiving. Although Paul's theocentric perspective requires him to direct his thanksgiving to God, the apostle is not hesitant to acknowledge the praise-worthy actions of his readers. The visual image of himself that Paul evokes in this third part of the thanksgiving is of the apostle no longer pointing his finger toward heaven but now toward his readers, as he acknowledges what God is doing in and through their lives.

Explanation

This section usually modifies the preceding causal unit and so serves either to explain more fully the just-stated cause for Paul's thanksgiving or to provide additional reasons for giving thanks. The visual image of Paul pointing his finger at his readers continues, as the apostle publically acknowledges the positive way his readers are living out their faith.

Prayer Report

Paul sometimes concludes his thanksgiving with a report of what he specifically prays for regarding his addressees. This fifth unit should not be confused with the second unit, even though both involve prayer. The difference between the two units can be illustrated in the difference between a dad saying to his college-aged son, "Mom and I are praying for you," versus "Mom and I are praying that you will study hard, make good friends, and use well the intellectual gifts that God has given you." In the first case, the son simply knows that his parents are praying for him; in the second case, the son knows in summary form the specific content of his parents' prayer on his behalf. In Paul's thanksgivings, therefore, the second unit shares with the readers simply the fact of Paul praying for them, while the fifth unit lets the readers know very clearly what specific things the apostle is praying will happen in their lives. Once more Paul conjures up in his readers' mind the image of their apostle on his knees in prayer to God for their well-being.

The thanksgiving section of Phil. 1:3–11 illustrates well all five of the units typically found in this epistolary convention:

Table 3.1: Five Units Typically Found in the Thanksgiving Section

1. *Statement of Thanksgiving*	[3]I thank my God
2. *Manner of Thanksgiving*	every time I remember you, [4]constantly praying with joy in every one of my prayers for all of you
3. *Cause of Thanksgiving*	[5]because of your sharing in the gospel from the first day until now. [6]I am confident of this, that the one who began a good work among you will bring it to completion by the day of Jesus Christ.
4. *Explanation*	[7]It is right for me to think this way about all of you, because you hold me in your heart, for all of you share in God's grace with me, both in my imprisonment and in the defense and confirmation of the gospel. [8]For God is my witness, how I long for all of you with the compassion of Christ Jesus.
5. *Prayer Report*	[9]And this is my prayer, that your love may overflow more and more with knowledge and full insight [10]to help you to determine what is best, so that in the day of Christ you may be pure and blameless, [11]having produced the harvest of righteousness that comes from Jesus Christ for the glory and praise of God.

Not all of Paul's thanksgivings, of course, follow this five-part structure perfectly; some of them deviate from this structure in significant ways. It would be wrong, therefore, to conclude that Paul had a form of the thanksgiving fixed firmly in his mind and that he slavishly followed this form in all his letters. As David Pao (2010: 119) observes: "Paul is not a prisoner to an epistolary form, even a form that he himself creates." Nevertheless, the freedom with which Paul expresses his thanksgiving to God is not a random or unreflective process. The fivefold structure of the Pauline thanksgiving is sufficiently established with the result that, when one or more of these formal units is missing or altered in a significant manner, such a change in the expected form may well be due to the specific epistolary situation and reflect Paul's particular purposes at work in the letter. In other words, exactly what we observed in the previous chapter with respect to the letter opening is also true here: changes in the expected form of Paul's thanksgiving are not due to chance or mere stylistic variation but are conscious, deliberate, and therefore exegetically significant in providing important clues to the apostle's intentions in the text.

Function

It is crucial to consider the function(s) that the thanksgiving plays in the persuasive strategy of Paul. The question naturally arises as to why the apostle does not move directly to the body of the letter but instead chooses to preface this material with an expression of thanks to God about his readers. Why not cut to the chase, save time and energy, and immediately get to the heart of the matter? What does Paul gain or accomplish by not immediately addressing the main concerns raised in the letter body and instead first articulating a word of thanks to God concerning his letter recipients? The answer to this question lies in recognizing three important functions of Pauline thanksgivings in support of his broader persuasive strategy.

Pastoral Function

The thanksgiving has first a pastoral function: it reestablishes Paul's relationship with his readers by means of a positive expression of gratitude to God for their faith, hope, and love. The letter is typically the first communication that Paul has had with a given church since his original mission-founding ministry among them. It is important, therefore, for the apostle to reconnect with his readers if he wants them not only to accept his letter but also to obey his exhortations contained in it. The thanksgiving also reveals Paul's deep pastoral concern for his readers as evidenced by his comments in units 2 (the manner of thanksgiving) and 5 (the prayer report) indicating that he regularly prays for them. It is harder for the apostle's readers to dismiss his exhortations when they have an image of Pastor Paul on his knees, praying on their behalf.

The purpose and importance of this pastoral function may become clearer with a modern analogy. Suppose I am about to write a letter to a former student of mine named George, who graduated from my seminary some six months earlier and is now serving as pastor of a church located in another part of the country. I know George fairly well because not only has he been in four of my courses, but he also was in my small mentoring group for the whole three years of his seminary studies. Although I have not had any contact with George since he graduated and started his first pastorate, I recently visited his church's website and listened to a few of his latest sermons. There I discovered, to my great disappointment and concern, that he has been advocating some teachings about the end times that I had strongly rejected both in my classes with George and in some of our mentoring discussions. From a biblical perspective, the issue at hand is not a minor or unclear one, and so I have determined to write to him about this matter. How, then, should my letter to George begin?

It would certainly be efficient to raise the issue immediately at the beginning of the document: "Dear George: I am deeply disappointed to learn from your recent sermons that you are advocating from the pulpit teachings about the end times that are not biblical and that were clearly taught differently during your student days here at seminary!" But while such a strategy would involve an economy of words and space, it would be neither very pastoral nor likely to convince George to preach differently. It would be much more appropriate and persuasive to begin this way: "Dear George: I hope that you and your family are doing well and getting adjusted to the demands of full-time ministry. I give thanks to God for the three years that we spent together here at seminary and for the rich spiritual gifts that he has given you. I also have been praying for you, asking God to give you insight into the truth of his word. To that end I hope that you will allow me to raise a concern about your latest sermons on the end times that I listened to online."

If Paul began his letters by immediately moving from the letter opening to the body of the letter, where he proceeds to raise the key concerns or problems at work in the church, his readers would judge his approach in dealing with them as abrupt and perhaps even offensive. After all, they lived in a day when virtually every letter began with the health wish—a stereotyped expression that conveyed the writer's concern for the well-being of the letter recipients (e.g., "If you are well and if your other affairs are well, it would be as I wish").[6] But Paul included his thanksgiving not merely to enhance the persuasive force of his letter. He did so because he genuinely was thankful to God for his divine work in the hearts and lives of his readers. Paul did so because he also genuinely cared about his spiritual children and prayed to God about them. As Paul himself observed, even more difficult for him than the physical sufferings he endured because of his ministry—the imprisonments, floggings, stonings, shipwrecks, robberies, sleeplessness, hunger, thirst—was

---

6. The prevalence of the health wish can be seen in that it occurs in all three of the ancient letters cited at the beginning of this chapter.

his "anxiety for all the churches" (2 Cor. 11:28). The thanksgiving allows Paul
the pastor powerfully to convey to his readers his deep gratitude to God for
them as well as his genuine care and concern for them.

Exhortative Function

Second, the thanksgiving has an exhortative function: even though Paul
is expressing his thankfulness to God, there is an implicit, or at times even
an explicit, challenge for the letter recipients to live up to the praise that the
apostle is giving them in his words of gratitude.[7]

This function involves persuasion through praise, since people typically
respond to the praise that others have of them by desiring to live up to that
praise. For example, imagine that I begin my seminary class one day by saying:
"I give thanks to God for you students—for the way you always arrive on time
to class, how you faithfully complete all the assignments, how you ask such
great questions, and how you even laugh at my corny jokes!" Not only would
my students feel good about themselves for the praise that I have just given
them, and not only would they feel well-disposed to me for praising them in
such a complimentary manner, but they would also implicitly feel pressure to
live in a way that justifies that praise—to continue coming to class on time,
completing all the assignments, asking great questions, and laughing at the
jokes. Thus, for example, when Paul gives thanks to God for the Christians
in Colossae "because we have heard of your faith in Christ Jesus and of the
love that you have for all the saints on account of the hope stored up for you in
heaven" (Col. 1:4–5a), this places implicit pressure on the Colossian believers to
continue to exhibit in their lives this kind of praiseworthy faith, love, and hope.

In those thanksgivings where Paul includes the fifth and final formal
unit—the prayer report (2 Thess. 1:11–12; Phil. 1:9–11; Col. 1:9–14; also
Rom. 1:10b)—the challenge is no longer implicit but explicit, since his readers know from the content of the apostle's prayer exactly what he expects
from them. There is nothing subtle or hidden about Paul's desires for the
Colossian church when he closes his thanksgiving to this church with the
following lengthy prayer report:

[9]This is why, ever since the day we first heard about you, we have not stopped
praying for you and asking that you may be filled with the knowledge of God's
will in all spiritual wisdom and understanding, [10]so that you may lead lives
worthy of the Lord and may please him in every way: by bearing fruit in every

---

7. Schubert (1939: 26, 89) stated that the Pauline thanksgiving is "implicitly or explicitly
paraenetic" (see also O'Brien 1977: 141–44, 165, 262–63).

good work; by growing in the knowledge of God; [11]by being strengthened with all power according his glorious might so that you may have great endurance and patience; and by joyfully [12]giving thanks to the Father, who has qualified you to share in the inheritance of his people in the kingdom of light, [13]since he has rescued us from the dominion of darkness and brought us into the kingdom of the Son he loves, [14]in whom we have redemption, the forgiveness of sins. (Col. 1:9–14)

Foreshadowing Function

Third, the thanksgiving has a foreshadowing function: it looks ahead to the main topics that will be taken up in the body of the letter. In modern movie jargon, it is a "preview of coming attractions" (Witherington 2006: 52). It would be overstating the case to say that Paul's thanksgiving is like a modern-day "Table of Contents," spelling out in a comprehensive and precise sequential order all the topics to be addressed in the document. Yet it would be understating the case to deny that Paul is an extremely skilled letter writer: he knows ahead of time the issues he will be addressing in the body of the letter and thus effectively foreshadows those issues already in the thanksgiving section. As Peter O'Brien (1977: 15) observes: "We note in these [thanksgiving] periods an epistolary function, i.e., to introduce and indicate the main theme(s) of the letters."

This foreshadowing function explains why Paul's thanksgiving sections can be difficult passages for preachers and Bible teachers who are searching for a single theme or one key idea at work in the whole passage that will give coherence to their sermon or hold together their class lesson. Such a search will prove frustrating because Paul's thanksgivings are introductory: he is not yet addressing at length and in detail any single topic or one particular problem at work in the church but presenting several key issues in a preliminary way, thereby setting the stage for the rest of the letter to come.

The thanksgiving, however, anticipates not only the central themes and key issues to be developed in the body of the letter but also the nature of the relationship that exists between Paul and the church as well as the overall tone of his correspondence to them. As Paul Schubert (1939: 77) recognized in his groundbreaking study: "Each thanksgiving not only announces clearly the subject matter of the letter, but also foreshadows unmistakably its stylistic qualities, the degrees of intimacy and other important characteristics." The thanksgiving reveals whether Paul enjoys a "warm and fuzzy" relationship with his readers (1 and 2 Thessalonians; Philippians) or if feelings between the apostle and his readers are cool (1 Corinthians) or even downright frosty (Galatians). Such knowledge of the letter's context revealed in its form (in this case, the thanksgiving section) is crucial to an accurate interpretation of the letter's content.

Summary

The thanksgiving has at least three important functions in aiding the persuasive strategy of Paul: a pastoral function, an exhortative function, and a foreshadowing function. The multiple purposes of this epistolary unit is affirmed by the conclusion of O'Brien's monograph-length study of Paul's thanksgivings:

> Paul's introductory thanksgivings have a varied function: epistolary, didactic and paraenetic, and they provide evidence of his pastoral and/or apostolic concern for the addressees. In some cases one purpose may predominate while others recede into the background. But whatever the thrust of any passage, it is clear that Paul's introductory thanksgivings were not meaningless devices. Instead they were integral parts of their letters, setting the tone and themes of what was to follow. (O'Brien 1977: 263)

Let's now turn to a detailed exegetical examination of relevant passages in Paul's letters in order to demonstrate that the apostle's thanksgivings are indeed "not meaningless devices" but "integral parts of their letters."

Interpretative Significance

1 Thessalonians 1:2–10

The primary purpose for engaging in an epistolary analysis of 1 Thess. 1:2–10 is to illustrate and validate the claims made earlier in this chapter about the form and function of Paul's thanksgiving sections. In this section I demonstrate how the knowledge of both formal and functional features of a thanksgiving helps one to grasp more fully and accurately what Paul is writing to the Thessalonian readers.

FORM OF THE PASSAGE

The thanksgiving of 1 Thess. 1:2–10 consists of four main clauses in the original Greek text: verses 2–5, 6–7, 8, and 9–10. The first main clause (vv. 2–5) is the thanksgiving proper and exhibits the pattern that is consistent with the form found in Paul's other thanksgivings: first, the "statement" of thanksgiving: "We give thanks to God always concerning you all" (1:2a); second, the "manner" of thanksgiving: "by making mention of you in our prayers" (1:2b); and third, the "cause" of thanksgiving, which here involves two causes: "because we constantly remember" (1:3) and "because we know" (1:4). The three remaining main clauses (vv. 6–7, 8, 9–10) function as the fourth unit of a thanksgiving—the "explanation"—and serve to elaborate on the cause for Paul's words of gratitude to God.[8] The thanksgiving lacks the fifth and final unit—a prayer report, which is sometimes found at the close of this epistolary section (see 2 Thess. 1:11–12; Phil. 1:9–11; Col. 1:9–14; also Rom. 1:10b).

A consideration of these grammatical and epistolary features, along with the content of the passage, leads to the following outline of 1:2–10:

Statement of Thanksgiving	[2]We give thanks to God always concerning you all,
Manner of Thanksgiving	by making mention of you in our prayers,
Cause of Thanksgiving	because we constantly [3]remember your work of faith and labor of love and steadfastness of hope in our Lord Jesus Christ before our God and Father, [4]because we know, brothers and sisters loved by God, your election, [5]namely, that our gospel was not among you in word alone but also in power—both in the Holy Spirit and much conviction, as you know what kind of men we were among you because of you;
Explanation	[6]and you on your part became imitators of us and of the Lord, receiving the word in much affliction with joy that comes from the Holy Spirit, [7]so that you became an example to all the believers in Macedonia and in Achaia. [8]For from you the word of the Lord has echoed forth not only in Macedonia and Achaia, but [also] in every place your faith toward God has gone forth, so that we have no need to say anything. [9]For they themselves report concerning us what kind of visit we had among you, and how you turned to God from idols in order to serve a living and true God [10]and to wait for his Son from the heavens, whom he raised from the dead, Jesus, the one who rescues us from the coming wrath.

Function of the Passage

All three proposed functions of the thanksgiving section can be seen in this passage.

1. *Pastoral function.* The pastoral function is evident first in the apostle's opening statement that he gives thanks to God "concerning you *all*" (1:2a). This prepositional phrase may well have a polemical thrust, so that Paul here gives thanks "not only for his faithful supporters, but [also] for the idle, fainthearted,

---

8. The presence of the explanatory conjunction "for" at the beginning of both v. 8 and vv. 9–10 indicates that the ideas of these verses are closely connected and thus further support the explanation just given in vv. 6–7.

weak (5:14), and the ones who actually oppose him" (Wiles 1974: 180; so also Marshall 1983: 50; Weatherly 1996: 36; Fee 2009: 20). Although there is an obvious danger in reading too much into the occurrence of the adjective "all," only one other Pauline thanksgiving includes this word as modifying "you" (Rom. 1:8; contrast with 1 Cor. 1:4a; Phil. 1:3a; Col. 1:3; 2 Thess. 1:3a; Philem. 4a), so its presence here cannot be easily dismissed as being merely "formulaic" (so Richard 1995:45) or "simply part of the liturgical style of this section of the letter" (Malherbe 2000: 106). Furthermore, the addition of "all" would certainly be in keeping with Paul's practice elsewhere of adapting the thanksgiving section so that it foreshadows issues addressed later in the letter. Finally, the intensity of Paul's deep love for the Thessalonian believers, evident in various ways throughout the letter,[9] provides further indirect evidence that the addition of "all" to the opening statement of thanksgiving may well be a deliberate attempt by the apostle to convey his pastoral affection and concern for *all* the believers in Thessalonica, including those who, later in the letter, will come under rebuke and may have been opposed to Paul and his appointed leaders in the church.

If the pastoral function of the thanksgiving is only subtly expressed by the prepositional phrase "concerning you all," it is more overtly conveyed in Paul's subsequent claim that he gives thanks to God "by making mention of you in our prayers" (1:2b). Here the plural reference to "prayers" evokes, in the readers' mind, an image not of a dictatorial leader but a caring pastor who meets daily with his coworkers, Silas and Timothy, to pray and thank God for the blessings evident in the lives of the converts in Thessalonica. The depth of Paul's pastoral concern for his Thessalonian readers is further conveyed by the frequency of his intercessory prayers for them—a frequency indicated not only by the surrounding adverbs "always" and "constantly" but also by the verb choice, "making mention," which stresses the ongoing or continuous nature of the apostle's intercessory prayers.[10]

The pastoral function of the thanksgiving section stems from Paul's need in all his letters to reestablish his relationship with his readers such that they are open to hear and heed his words in the body of the letter. This need is even greater, however, in his first letter to the Thessalonians, where Paul spends the first half of his correspondence (2:1–3:13) defending the integrity of his

9. E.g., Paul refers to them as "brothers and sisters" fourteen times in this short letter, portrays his relationship to them as like that of "a nursing mother taking care of her own children" (2:7) and like "a father with his children" (2:11), and declares that he cares for them individually (2:11, "each one of you").

10. The present tense of the participial clause "making mention" (*mneian poioumenoi*, 1:2), in distinction from the aorist tense, is emphatic and expresses the ongoing nature of the action.

motives and conduct (for a fuller justification of this often disputed point, see Weima 1997a; 2014: 121–25). Non-Christians in Thessalonica—the "fellow citizens" (2:14) of believers—not only oppressed and harassed members of the church but also raised questions about the integrity of its founder, Paul. They claimed that the apostle was no different from the wandering philosophers or traveling teachers, who were the "used-car salesmen" of that day and had a notorious reputation for being interested solely in winning human praise and financial gain. These non-Christians in Thessalonica also used Paul's failure to return to the city and its church for a second visit to raise further doubts about the genuineness of his motives and love for the Thessalonian believers. Although the Christians in Thessalonica had not bought into these charges, Paul—concerned for a young church separated from its spiritual father and under heavy social pressure to resume its former pagan practices—felt the need to answer these accusations. The seriousness of the situation is seen in Paul's devoting the first half of the letter to defending himself, both his past conduct during the mission-founding visit (2:1–16) and his current inability to return (2:17–3:10). At the outset of the letter, the pastoral function of the thanksgiving section in 1:2–10, therefore, is of great importance in reassuring his new Thessalonian converts of the genuineness of his feelings toward them. The apostle wants his readers to know that "Pastor Paul" truly cares about them and that he cares about them *all*.

2. *Exhortative function.* The exhortative function manifests itself in the third formal unit of the thanksgiving, which states the cause of Paul's thanks to God: "because we constantly remember your work of faith and labor of love and steadfastness of hope in our Lord Jesus Christ before our God and Father" (1:2b–3). By letting his Thessalonian readers know it is their faith, love, and hope that cause him to direct thanksgiving to God, the apostle implicitly places pressure on them to continue to conduct themselves in ways that live up to such thanks-inducing faith, love, and hope.

The exhortative function of the thanksgiving is also at work in the fourth unit of the thanksgiving, the "explanation," where Paul lists three additional causes of thanksgiving. The apostle specifically cites their (a) exemplary life (1:6–7, "and you on your part became imitators of us and of the Lord, receiving the word in much affliction with joy that comes from the Holy Spirit, so that you became an example to all the believers in Macedonia and in Achaia"), (b) their evangelistic activity (1:8, "For from you the word of the Lord has echoed forth not only in Macedonia and Achaia, but in every place your faith toward God has gone forth, so that we have no need to say anything"), and (c) their conversion (1:9, "For they themselves report . . . how you turned to God from idols in order to serve [lit., "to be a slave to"] a living and true God").

By spelling out these specific further reasons why he gives thanks to God for the Thessalonian believers, Paul subtly but persuasively encourages them to continue imitating their founding pastors (who are themselves imitating Christ Jesus; see also 1 Cor. 11:1), sharing the gospel message even with those who live far beyond the walls of their city, and living radically changed lives that are characterized by absolute service—a different kind of "slavery"—to the one and only true God.

The exhortative function of the thanksgiving section in 1 Thess. 1:2–10 can be summarized this way: Paul's extended praise of the Thessalonians' *present* conduct carries with it the implicit expectation that such behavior should continue in the *future*.

3. *Foreshadowing function.* Paul's literary skill is especially evident in the impressive way he constructs the thanksgiving of 1:2–10 so that it anticipates the major themes or key issues of the letter and functions as a "preview of coming attractions." In this thanksgiving, indeed, the "alert" reader detects all four major topics that will be taken up in the body of the letter, two in the first half (2:1–3:13) and two in the second half (4:1–5:22; see table 3.2: Outline of 1 Thessalonians): (a) the defense of Paul's integrity (2:1–16, 17–20; 3:6–10); (b) the concern over persecution endured by the Thessalonians (3:1–5; 3:6–10); (c) the exhortations to proper conduct (4:1–12; 5:12–22); and (d) the comfort concerning the fate of believers—both deceased and living—at Christ's return (4:13–18; 5:1–11).

Table 3.2: Outline of 1 Thessalonians

Opening (1:1–10)	Defensive Function (2:1–3:13)	Exhortative Function (4:1–5:22)	Closing (5:23–25)
Letter opening (1:1)	Paul defends his past conduct in Thessalonica (2:1–16)	Pleasing God in sexual conduct and brotherly/sisterly love (4:1–12)	Letter closing (5:23–25)
Thanksgiving (1:2–10)	Paul defends his present absence from Thessalonica and comforts the persecuted (2:17–3:10)	Comfort concerning deceased Christians at Christ's return (4:13–18)	
	Transitional prayers (3:11–13)	Comfort concerning living Christians at Christ's return (5:1–11)	
		Exhortations on congregational life and worship (5:12–22)	

a. *Defense of Paul's integrity.* I have already noted (above) Paul's need to defend his integrity in 1 Thessalonians. Non-Christians in Thessalonica, the "fellow citizens" (2:14) of the believers, were raising questions about the moral character of the infant church's founder, Paul, claiming that he was no different from the wandering philosophers or traveling teachers of that day who had a notorious reputation for being interested solely in securing people's praise and purse. Paul anticipates the lengthy defense he will make at the beginning of the letter body (2:1–16, 17–20; 3:6–10) by already asserting his integrity in the thanksgiving: "Our gospel was not among you in word alone but also in power—both in the Holy Spirit and much conviction, as you know what kind of men we were among you because of you" (1:5).

If we compare the thanksgiving section in 1 Thessalonians with the thanksgiving sections of Paul's other letters, we can highlight the unique character of this verse. In all other thanksgivings Paul focuses primarily *on his readers* and his thanksgiving to God for *them*, yet here in 1:5 the apostle also focuses heavily on *himself* and the righteous character of *his* activity among them. Or to pick up the image developed earlier in this chapter: after Paul's points his finger vertically up to heaven and identifies God as the recipient of his thanksgiving, then he normally points his finger horizontally at his recipients and lists specific things they are doing that cause him to give thanks to God. Here in 1:5, however, Paul does something unusual in a thanksgiving section: he points his finger back to himself, drawing attention to how he conducted himself during his mission-founding visit to Thessalonica.

One ought to be struck, however, not just by the mere presence of this rare self-reference in a thanksgiving section but also by the prominent location (before the additional causes of thanksgiving in 1:6–10), the length, and the defensive tone of this verse. For in 1:5a, in addition to using an antithetical construction ("not *x* but *y*") that adds emphasis to his words, Paul here deviates from his typical manner of referring to the gospel and employs the personal pronoun "our,"[11] thereby stressing the crucial role that he and his fellow missionaries have played in the Thessalonians' conversion. As Abraham Malherbe (2000: 110) notes: "Paul draws attention to his part ("*our*") in the proclamation of the gospel." Paul also feels the need to use not one but three nouns ("power," "Holy Spirit," and "much conviction") to highlight the sincere nature of his preaching activity among them. But even this is not enough, apparently, to make his point. Thus he adds a comparative clause (1:5b, "as you know what kind of men we were among you because of you") by which he appeals to the Thessalonians' firsthand knowledge of his and his coworkers' exemplary conduct among them. When all these unique features

11. Thus "our gospel": the personal pronoun "our" or "my" with "gospel" occurs only in six of sixty occurrences of this noun in Paul's letters.

of 1:5 are recognized, it becomes clear that Paul in 1 Thessalonians is very much concerned with defending his integrity and already here in 1:5 anticipates the lengthy defense that he will present at the beginning of the letter body (2:1–16, 17–20; 3:6–10).

For a second time later in the thanksgiving section, Paul foreshadows the defense of his integrity in 1:9a: "For they themselves report concerning us what kind of visit we had among you." As in 1:5, here too the apostle points his finger away from the Thessalonians and the positive things they are doing that cause him to give thanks to God and instead points his finger back to himself in order to highlight the honest and sincere way that he and his coworkers conducted themselves during their mission-founding visit to Thessalonica. Paul's use of the striking term "visit" (*eisodos*)—a word not used in any of his other letters—makes it certain that 1:9a is intended to anticipate Paul's lengthy defense in the letter body, since the opening verse of that defense contains his only other use of the term "visit": "For you yourselves know, brothers and sisters, about our visit [*eisodos*] to you, namely, that it was not insincere" (2:1).[12]

The point the apostle makes is clear: there is a widespread report of the genuine character of his original visit to Thessalonica. In an age where traveling philosophers and wandering orators frequently entered a city with self-serving motives and deceptive deeds (see Winter 1993), people throughout Macedonia, Achaia, and even beyond recognized that Paul's mission-founding visit to Thessalonica exhibited none of these vain and dishonest practices. In this way, Paul not only further defends himself in anticipation of his lengthy apology in the letter body but also strengthens his relationship with his original readers by reminding them of the crucial role that he played in their conversion.

b. *Concern over persecution endured by the Thessalonians.* A second major topic of 1 Thessalonians to be located in the first half of the letter body concerns the persecution that the Thessalonians were enduring for their newfound faith. This topic emerges briefly in 2:14–16 (esp. 2:14, "For you yourselves, brothers and sisters, became imitators of the churches of God in Christ Jesus that are in Judea, because you indeed suffered the same things from your own fellow citizens as they also did from the Jews") yet is addressed at greater length

12. The foreshadowing function of 1:9a is unfortunately hidden in many leading translations. This is because they wrongly render the key term *eisodos* as "reception" or "welcome" (e.g., NIV 1984: "what kind of reception you gave us"; NRSV, NIV 2011: "what kind of welcome we had among you") and so mislead the contemporary reader into believing that the emphasis here is on the Thessalonian believers and their warm reception of the missionaries and the gospel. The word, however, means "entrance" or "visit" and clearly refers to the activities of Paul along with his fellow missionaries and not that of the Christians in Thessalonica. For a fuller discussion of this translation error, see Weima 2014: 107–8.

in 3:1–5, where Paul's stated goal in sending Timothy back to Thessalonica is "in order to strengthen you and comfort you concerning your faith, so that no one may be shaken by these afflictions" (3:2b–3a). The importance of this topic of persecution is indicated by the fact that, when Timothy finished his ministry in Thessalonica and returned to Paul, it is one of the two things about his report that comforted Paul: "But Timothy has now come to us from you and has brought good news about your faith and love" (3:6). In other words, Paul was comforted by both the Thessalonians' "faith," meaning their ongoing faith in God and in Jesus despite facing strong opposition from their fellow citizens (2:14), and the Thessalonians "love," their continued love for Paul despite the accusations made against his integrity. There is also additional evidence in both Thessalonian letters and elsewhere that believers in Thessalonica were encountering open hostility and opposition for their faith (see also 1 Thess. 2:2; 2 Thess. 1:4–7; 2 Cor. 8:1–2; Acts 17:5–7, 13).

In light of the importance of Paul's concern in the first half of the letter over the persecution endured by the Thessalonians, it is not surprising that this topic is foreshadowed in the thanksgiving section: "and you on your part became imitators of us and of the Lord, receiving the word in much affliction with joy that comes from the Holy Spirit, so that you became an example to all the believers in Macedonia and in Achaia" (1:6–7). Not only does the phrase "receiving the word in much affliction" anticipate well the discussion of persecution in 3:1–5 and 3:6–10, but there is also a significant verbal parallel between the combination of "and you became imitators, . . . receiving the word" (1:6–7) and the same combination in 2:13–14 ("you received the word, . . . you became imitators"). The Thessalonians' joyful reception of the gospel in spite of much affliction has had a formative influence on the Christians located in their region since the imitators have now become the imitated. This is high praise indeed. For though Paul often uses the language or idea of imitation, nowhere else does he state that a particular church has served as an inspiring "example" for believers in other locations (1:7). Such praise, therefore, not only foreshadows the later discussion about persecution but also reaffirms the close relationship between the apostle and his church (pastoral function) and encourages the Thessalonians to persevere in the face of adversity (exhortative function).

c. *Exhortations to proper conduct.* A third major topic of the letter body that is anticipated in the thanksgiving section concerns proper conduct. As affirming and upbeat as Timothy's report to Paul about the Thessalonians was (3:6), it nevertheless also included several issues of concern in the church—issues that caused the apostle to pray most earnestly and repeatedly that God would allow him to return to Thessalonica and "complete the things that are lacking in [their] faith" (3:10). Since Paul is not able to do this in person, he does it instead by sending this letter. In response to Timothy's report, the topics that the apostle takes up in the second half of the letter fall into two broad categories: exhortation to proper conduct (4:1–12; 5:12–22) and comfort concerning the fate of believers, both deceased and living, at Christ's return (4:13–18; 5:1–11).

The topic of proper conduct is foreshadowed in the thanksgiving section, though in a more general and imprecise way than the other major topics of the letter. Paul lists the conversion of the Thessalonians as an additional cause of his thanksgiving to God: "how you turned to God from idols in order to serve a living and true God" (1:9b). The first half of this statement ought to be connected with the already-highlighted topic of persecution, since the total renunciation of all pagan deities by the Thessalonian believers and their exclusive worship of no god except the God of Israel has deeply wounded public sensibilities, led to charges that they are "atheists," and aroused the resentment and anger of their fellow citizens. The second half of this statement, however, anticipates Paul's concern in this letter with their proper conduct: the purpose of their conversion is "to serve a living and true God." Conversion, then, involves not merely a mental change in which one's thinking and beliefs are radically altered; it also involves a lifestyle change in which one's conduct and behavior are profoundly transformed. Conversion involves not merely a verbal acknowledgment of the living and true God; it also involves an outward demonstration of devotion to God. The Thessalonians' turning to God from idols ought to show itself in concrete ways in their conduct as they "serve" (Greek, lit., "to serve as a slave") him in an absolute manner and seek to do his will. In this way, the goal of the Thessalonians' conversion foreshadows the concern for proper moral conduct found later in the letter body (4:1–12 and 5:12–22).

d. *Comfort concerning the fate of believers at Christ's return.* The fourth major topic of the letter deals with comfort concerning the fate of believers at Christ's return, both those deceased (4:13–18) and those living (5:1–11). Paul's extended and pastoral discussion of this subject in the body of the letter is anticipated both at the beginning of the thanksgiving section and at its end. The thanksgiving opens with Paul's giving thanks for the Thessalonians' "steadfastness of hope in our Lord Jesus Christ" (1:3). In light of the end-time concerns that permeate this letter, as well as the explicit reference to Christ's return in 1:10, it is clear that Paul is referring not merely to a *general* hope that the Thessalonians have in the person and work of Christ but to their very *specific* hope in Christ's imminent return from heaven to bring about their deliverance. The thanksgiving closes with a more explicit foreshadowing of the topic of Christ's return: "to wait for his Son from the heavens" (1:10a).

Two additional clauses at the end of the thanksgiving section similarly look ahead in a very specific way to eschatological material treated in the letter body. First, there is the reference to Jesus's resurrection: "whom he raised from the dead" (1:10b). At first glance the presence of this additional clause is surprising, since its mention of the resurrection seems to interrupt the strong end-time theme found in both the immediately preceding clause and the immediately following clause:

End-Time Theme	to wait for his son from the heavens (v. 10a)
Resurrection	whom he raised from the dead (v. 10b)
End-Time Theme	who rescues us from the coming wrath (v. 10c)

A modern editor reading this letter of Paul might well be tempted to delete this middle clause with its reference to Jesus's resurrection in order to keep the apostle's argument focused on the single subject of Christ's return. However, rather than being a mere "afterthought" (Wanamaker 1990: 87) or "awkward addition" (Furnish 2007: 49), this middle clause (1:10b) skillfully anticipates Paul's eschatological discussion in 4:13–18, where the apostle grounds his words of comfort by first appealing to Jesus's resurrection: "For since we believe that Jesus died and *rose again*, so, through Jesus, God will bring with him those who have fallen asleep" (4:14). Apparently Paul is such a skilled letter writer that he not only knows ahead of time the topics that he will later treat in the letter body and foreshadows these topics in the thanksgiving; the apostle also knows ahead of time an argument that he is going to use in treating these topics and even foreshadows this argument in the thanksgiving.

Second, the very final clause of the thanksgiving (1:10c) provides yet additional evidence of this section's foreshadowing function. The reference here to the final judgment ("Jesus, the one who rescues us from the coming *wrath*") anticipates a similar reference to salvation from future wrath through Christ's work in 5:9 ("For God has destined us not for *wrath* but for the obtaining of salvation through our Lord Jesus Christ") as part of Paul's attempt to comfort the Thessalonians with regard to those believers who are alive at Christ's return (5:1–11).

1 Corinthians 1:4–9

Next I turn to an epistolary analysis of the thanksgiving section found in Paul's first surviving letter to the Corinthians (the apostle's earlier letter to them has been lost: cf. 1 Cor. 5:9 ["I wrote to you in my letter"] with 5:11 ["but now I am writing"]). Once again, the goal of this analysis is to illustrate and validate the claims made earlier in this chapter about the form and function of Paul's thanksgiving sections and how, in important ways, the knowledge of these epistolary features aids accurate interpretation of the apostle's letters.

FORM OF THE PASSAGE

The thanksgiving of 1 Cor. 1:4–9 is shorter than most of Paul's other thanksgivings, especially for a letter that ranks as the second longest of the apostle's writings. The brevity of this epistolary unit almost certainly stems from the "cool" nature of Paul's relationship with the Corinthian church (despite a lengthy, eighteen-month ministry in their city) and the deep concerns he has about these believers. His brief thanksgiving consists of two main clauses: verses 4–8 and verse 9.

The first main clause (1:4–8) follows the pattern found in a relatively consistent manner in Paul's other thanksgivings, though there are two noteworthy omissions. This epistolary section opens with the first expected element, the "statement" of thanksgiving: "I give thanks to my God always concerning you" (1:4a). The "manner" of thanksgiving that normally comes next is missing: one searches in vain for some statement where Paul refers to his intercessory prayers on behalf of the Corinthian believers. Instead, the thanksgiving moves directly into the third element, stating two "causes" for his thanksgiving to God: "because of the grace of God that has been given to you in Christ Jesus" (1:4b) and "because in everything you have been enriched in him in all speech and in all knowledge" (1:5). The first causal statement provides a general reason for giving thanks: God's grace given to the Corinthian church; the second causal statement specifies two manifestations of that grace exhibited by the believers in Corinth: speech and knowledge.[13] The fourth element usually appearing in Paul's thanksgivings is the "explanation," and this is found in 1:6–8, where the apostle either elaborates on the just-mentioned causes of thanksgiving and/or lists additional causes of thanksgiving.

The second main clause (1:9) involves a unique formal feature: Paul brings his thanksgiving to a close not as he frequently does, with a prayer report (2 Thess. 1:11–12; Phil. 1:9–11; Col. 1:9–14; also Rom. 1:10b), but with a type of benediction: "Faithful is God, through whom you were called into the fellowship of his Son, Jesus Christ our Lord." As Peter O'Brien (1977: 130) observes, "The apostle rounds out the passage with a confirming climax, in words not unlike a concluding benediction."

---

13. The conjunction *hoti* that opens this clause is explanatory: so, e.g., Findlay 1900: 759–60; O'Brien 1977: 116; Fee 1987: 38; Schrage 1991: 114; Thiselton 2000: 90.

A consideration of these grammatical and epistolary features, along with the content of the passage, leads to the following outline of 1:4–9:

Statement of Thanksgiving	⁴I give thanks to my God always concerning you,
Manner of Thanksgiving	—
Cause of Thanksgiving	because of the grace of God that has been given to you in Christ Jesus ⁵and because in everything you have been enriched in him in all speech and in all knowledge,
Explanation	⁶because the testimony about Christ has been guaranteed in you ⁷so that you are not lacking in any spiritual gift while you eagerly wait for the revelation of our Lord Jesus Christ, ⁸who will indeed guarantee you until the end as blameless on the day of our Lord Jesus Christ.
Concluding Benediction	⁹Faithful is God, through whom you were called into the fellowship of his Son, Jesus Christ our Lord.

FUNCTION OF THE PASSAGE

As in 1 Thess. 1:2–10, so also here in 1 Cor. 1:4–9 all three proposed functions of the thanksgiving section in Paul's letters generally can be observed.

1. *Pastoral function.* The thanksgiving serves to convey to the Corinthian church the ongoing care and concern that Paul has for them in spite of all their problems that he will address in the body of the letter. Just as parents who are about to rebuke their child for some misconduct will preface their reprimand with the words "We want you to know that Dad and Mom love you very much," so also Paul prefaces his lengthy rebuke of his spiritual children in Corinth by letting them know that he genuinely cares for them, as evidenced by his giving thanks to God for them. This pastoral function of the thanksgiving is recognized by O'Brien (1977: 136): "By reporting his actual thanksgiving Paul showed his concern for them and his desire to build them up and encourage them in spite of the strong words that might follow. Indeed his 'ability' to give thanks to God for a congregation which had erred in so many ways was evidence of his deep pastoral care." Roy Ciampa and Brian Rosner (2010: 61) similarly observe: "The positive and confident statements in the thanksgiving, which are so startling in a letter that deals with so many serious faults in the congregation, serve a pastoral purpose, communicating Paul's genuine concern and care for the church." This pastoral function of the thanksgiving aids the persuasive force of the letter, since the Corinthians are more likely to accept Paul's rebuke and obey his exhortations if they believe that the apostle's feelings for them are sincere and deep.

But though this thanksgiving conveys to the Corinthians the genuineness of Paul's affection for them, a comparison of his words here with the thanksgivings in his other letters reveals that this epistolary unit is not as fulsome, warm, and intimate. As noted above, the apostle's thanksgiving is shorter than normal, and it focuses on what God has done for the Corinthians rather than what they themselves are doing. Also significant in this regard are the omissions in the expected form of the thanksgiving: the absence of any reference to Paul's constant remembrance or prayers for the Corinthian church (second element) and the lack of any prayer report (fifth element). The prayer report is also missing in other thanksgivings, including the one in 1 Thessalonians—a church with whom Paul was clearly pleased and enjoyed a close relationship—and so one must be careful not to draw a conclusion too quickly from the absence of this formal element in 1 Corinthians. The reference to Paul's constant prayers for his readers, however, is an element found in all of the apostle's other thanksgivings, and so its absence here in 1 Cor. 1:4–9 is significant. As Linda Belleville (1987: 19) points out, "There are several aspects about the Corinthian thanksgiving period that indicate a strained relationship. 1 Corinthians contains the only thanksgiving which does not include a reference to constant remembrance or intercession for the church addressed."

Nevertheless, the growing tension between Paul and the Corinthian church, though real and reflected in the thanksgiving, is not so great that this epistolary unit loses its pastoral function. Paul may not provide the Corinthians with an image of him on his knees constantly praying on their behalf, but the apostle does conclude his thanksgiving with an image of him as their caring pastor standing with his hands raised high as he bestows on them a benediction and reassures them that the God who called them into a saving relationship with his Son, Jesus Christ, is "faithful" (1:9).

2. *Exhortative function.* Although the thanksgiving of 1:4–9 contains no explicit commands, its stated reasons for giving thanks to God puts pressure on the Corinthian church to continue such thanks-inducing activities. In this way, the thanksgiving also has an exhortative function. There are three ways in which the thanksgiving section implicitly calls on the Corinthian church to change the way in which they think of themselves: Paul gives thanks that they are—and so also ought to continue to be—a church (a) gifted by God through Christ, (b) focused on the future, and (c) called into community (Fee 1987: 36; Hays 1997: 17). Here the apostle's focus is less on the external conduct of the Corinthians than on their internal self-perception. Paul knows that the way people act is intimately connected with the way people think. Thus, before addressing in the letter body (in no less than sixteen chapters)

the Corinthians' problematic behaviors, in the thanksgiving section he takes up the wrong thinking that lies behind their sinful conduct. In colloquial terms, Paul exhorts the Corinthians to reframe their identity—to think of themselves in three specific ways.

a. *A church gifted by God through Christ.* The first area where the Corinthians need to reframe their identity concerns how they view their spiritual gifts. A superficial reading of Paul's reason for giving thanks to God leads to a very positive evaluation of the Corinthian believers: "namely, in everything you have been enriched in him in all speech and in all knowledge, . . . so that you are not lacking in any spiritual gift" (1:5, 7a). Such words, no doubt, initially would "seem apt and pleasing to those members of the Corinthian church who prided themselves on precisely these aspects of their spiritual experience: the possession of privileged knowledge and the ability to speak with spirit-endowed eloquence, including speaking in tongues" (Hays 1997: 18). But a more careful reading of these words, and especially of Paul's opening causal statement, reveals the problem that the apostle is addressing: "because of the grace of God that has been given to you in Christ Jesus" (1:4b). The apostle gives thanks not for anything that the Corinthians have done but rather for what God has done.

Comparing this cause of giving thanks to the same element in all of his other thanksgivings highlights the uniqueness of Paul's words to the Corinthians. In all of the apostle's other thanksgivings, he is not hesitant to use the personal pronoun "your" when giving thanks for what his readers have done:

Table 3.3: The Use of "Your" in Paul's Thanksgivings

Rom. 1:8b	because *your* faith is proclaimed in all the world
Phil. 1:5	because of *your* fellowship in the gospel
Col. 1:4	because we have heard of *your* faith in Christ Jesus and of the love that you have for all the saints
1 Thess. 1:3	because we constantly remember *your* work of faith and labor of love and steadfastness of hope
2 Thess. 1:3	because *your* faith is growing abundantly
Philem. 5	because I hear of *your* love and faith

Paul's words to the Corinthians, by comparison, involve a subtle but significant difference, because he identifies the cause of his thanksgiving as what God has done rather than what the Corinthians have done: "because of the grace of God which has been given to you in Christ Jesus" (1:4b). As Ann Jervis (1991: 98) indicates, "The thanksgiving period of 1 Cor. 1:4–9 is distinctive vis-à-vis Paul's other letters because of its lack of mention of any cause for thanks originating in the Corinthian community itself. Rather, Paul's cause for thanks is exclusively rooted in God's grace to the Corinthians." Peter O'Brien (1977: 137) states more pointedly: "In this thanksgiving there was no mention paid to the achievements of the Corinthians—and with good reason!" The visual image of himself that Paul evokes is of the apostle deliberately pointing his finger not horizontally at his readers but rather vertically up to heaven as he gives thanks to God—not to them!—for the gift of grace that God has given to the Corinthians.

In this thanksgiving, Paul's attempt to get the Corinthian church to view itself as gifted by God through Christ can also be seen in the way he emphasizes the work of both God and Christ. In the previous chapter's study of Paul's letter openings, I drew attention to how he adapts and expands the recipient formula in 1 Cor. 1:2 by including three references to God and four references to Christ in order to stress to the Corinthians that they are not their own masters but are instead the church *of God* and that this is possible only because of the work of God and Christ in their lives. Paul continues this theocentric and christocentric emphasis in the thanksgiving, where this relatively short epistolary unit contains no less than nine more references to God[14] and six more references to Christ.[15] Contemporary readers may well miss these references due to their overfamiliarity with biblical texts and doctrinal affirmations about God and Christ, but these references would likely catch the attention of the Corinthian church (at least the apostle hopes they will). Paul saturates the opening and thanksgiving sections of 1 Corinthians with references to God and to Christ because he wants to drive home the truth that all the gifts that the Corinthians wrongly view with pride actually came from God and were given to them only because of their relationship to Christ. This means that there is no justification for any pride or boasting; there is only reason to give thanks to God, who is the giver of these gifts through his Son, Jesus Christ. As Paul will explicitly ask them later in the body of the letter:

14. Three references to God are explicit: "I give thanks to my God" (1 Cor. 1:4); "because of the grace of God" (1:4); "Faithful is God" (1:9). Six references to God and his activity are implicit but still clear. There are four uses of the divine passive, where God is the implied actor: in the grace that was "given" to the Corinthian church (1:4), in their "being enriched" in all their speech and knowledge (1:5), in their having Paul's testimony about Christ "guaranteed in you" (1:6), and the one through whom the Corinthians "were called" (1:9). God is the likely figure implied in the relative pronoun of 1:8—God is the one "*who* will guarantee" the Corinthians until the end of time when Christ returns—and he is also the referent of the personal pronoun in the phrase "*his* Son, Jesus Christ our Lord" (1:9).

15. Each verse of the thanksgiving includes a reference to Christ: "in Christ Jesus" (1:4), as implied by the personal pronoun in the prepositional phrase "in him" (1:5), "testimony about Christ" (1:6), "the revelation of our Lord Jesus Christ" (1:7), "the day of our Lord Jesus Christ" (1:8), and "the fellowship of his Son, Jesus Christ, our Lord" (1:9).

"What do you have that you did not receive? And if you received it, why do you boast as if it were not a gift?" (4:7).

b. *A church focused on the future*. The second area where the thanksgiving section implicitly exhorts the Corinthian church to reframe its identity deals with their failure to be focused on the future. The pride that the Corinthians feel over their spiritual gifts has made them complacent. They have no sense for the urgency of the gospel—that the gospel has to be both preached and properly lived out because on one future day Jesus Christ will be coming back in judgment. Instead, the Corinthian Christians are complacent with their present situation, smugly believing that from a spiritual perspective they have "arrived"—that there is nothing more for them to do or accomplish as followers of Jesus Christ.[16]

Paul seeks to correct such errant thinking by encouraging the Corinthian church to become more focused on the future. He accomplishes this with no less than three references in his brief thanksgiving to the time of the end:

> while you eagerly wait for the revelation of our Lord Jesus Christ
>   (1:7b)
> who will indeed guarantee you until the end as blameless (1:8a)
> on the day of our Lord Jesus Christ (1:8b)

The presence of an end-time reference in a Pauline thanksgiving is not surprising, since the apostle on a number of occasions brings this epistolary unit to a close with an eschatological note (see also Phil. 1:10; 1 Thess. 1:10; 2 Thess. 1:7–10). O'Brien (1977: 124) refers to "the customary eschatological climax of the introductory thanksgivings." A few scholars have argued that these end-time references function to mark the shift from the end of the thanksgiving section to the beginning of the letter body (Sanders 1962; Roberts 1986). The presence of not one or even two but *three* end-time references, however, is unparalleled in Paul's thanksgivings and thus is unlikely to be fortuitous. Instead, this unique feature stems from Paul's attempt to address the problem of complacency that is the logical consequence of their false pride. As Ben Witherington (1995: 89) observes about 1:7: "This reference to the future, to Christ's appearing, reminds them that even with all their gifts they are not yet complete. What they have is only good enough for the interim." Richard Hays (1997: 18–19) similarly comments about all three end-time references:

16. Some commentators have identified the Corinthians' false way of thinking as "overrealized eschatology": the belief that events expected to occur or be "realized" in the future, such as the outpouring of God's Spirit and the resurrection, have already taken place in some real or even full way (see, e.g., Thiselton 1977–78: 510–26; Fee 1987: 12).

"The Corinthians, if they were listening carefully, may have heard all this talk of waiting and preparation for judgment as a sobering corrective to their enthusiastic spiritual experience in the present. That, of course, is precisely Paul's aim."

c. *A church called into community.* The third area where the thanksgiving section implicitly exhorts the Corinthian church to reframe its identity concerns their relationship with fellow members. The Christ-followers in Corinth were badly divided. The division was partly rooted in the Corinthians' loyalties to different Christian leaders, some of whom seemed more rhetorically impressive (and thus "wise") than others (chaps. 1–4). The division also stemmed from tension between rich and poor, with the wealthy members of the church discriminating in a variety of ways against the poorer members (e.g., 11:17–34).

Paul knows that if this badly divided congregation in Corinth is to act differently, then it first needs to think of itself differently—namely, as a church called into community both with Christ and with one another: "Faithful is God through whom you were called into the fellowship of his Son, Jesus Christ our Lord" (1:9). The key term here is the Greek word *koinōnia*, which means "fellowship" or "close relationship" (BDAG 552.1). With whom do the Corinthians have this fellowship or close relationship? Although the text explicitly refers to the intimate relationship that believers have with Jesus Christ, this close fellowship is not limited to him alone: it also involves a fellowship with all those who similarly have a relationship to Jesus Christ. Believers cannot have a *koinōnia* relationship with Christ without also having a similar relationship with fellow Christ-followers. David Garland (2003: 33) observes: "All Christians are in Christ Jesus together, and none can imagine themselves to be self-sufficient, self-ruling, or detached from other Christians." Or as Garland (2003: 37) more simply puts it: "Common-union with Christ creates common-union with other Christians."

Paul not so innocently states that the Corinthians "were called" into fellowship or community both with Christ and with each other. This occurrence of the divine passive (i.e., God is the implied agent of the passive construction) not only strengthens the work of God that is emphasized throughout this brief epistolary unit, but it also places pressure on the Corinthian readers to accept Paul's implicit exhortation to unity. The notion of viewing themselves as a community of believers who share a common relationship to Christ cannot be merely dismissed as a Pauline preference that can be either embraced or rejected. Rather, "fellowship" is a divine calling that must be obeyed—a calling from God himself to the kind of fellowship or community existence that is incompatible with division.

3. *Foreshadowing function*. There is an understandable overlap between the exhortative and foreshadowing functions in 1 Cor. 1:4–9, since the three ways in which the thanksgiving section implicitly calls on the Corinthian church to change the way they think of themselves are, as demonstrated above, all closely connected to key issues taken up (later) in the body of the letter. Yet there are additional ways in which this thanksgiving anticipates subsequent discussions in the correspondence, and these will be highlighted briefly here.

The cause of Paul's thanksgiving to God is specifically identified as "the grace of God" (1:4). The uniqueness of this reference is likely missed by modern readers who assume that Paul, who always begins his letters with a grace greeting and always ends them with a grace benediction and whose gospel message clearly stresses grace, is simply reflecting that emphasis here. However, this is the only one of the apostle's thanksgivings that grounds his note of thanks in grace. The uniqueness of this sole reference to grace is thrown into sharper relief when contrasted with Paul's typical practice of giving thanks for one, two, or all three elements of the triad "faith," "love," and "hope."

The explanation for this solitary appearance of "grace" is that it foreshadows the topic of spiritual gifts dealt with in a general way in many places of the letter and discussed specifically at length in chapters 12–14. The key to this explanation lies in recognizing that the Greek word used here, *charis*, does not have its common general meaning of "God's undeserved favor" but its rarer narrow sense of "grace gift/gifts"—what are commonly referred to as "spiritual gifts" or the "gifts of the Holy Spirit." This latter, more narrow sense is confirmed by the second occurrence of the same root word later in the thanksgiving, where Paul states in 1:7 that the Corinthians "are not lacking in any spiritual gift" (*charismata*). The Corinthians are using these grace gifts not for "the common good" (12:7) and the "building up" of the body of believers (14:3, 4, 5, 12, 17, 26) but instead to enhance their own standing and prestige. In the thanksgiving Paul anticipates this problem by grounding his thanks in "the grace of God"—something that is unmerited by the Corinthians and "given" to them by God, with the result there is no justification for pride and boasting, as well as the resulting problems of complacency and division within the church.

Paul chooses to highlight in the thanksgiving two specific "grace gifts" or "spiritual gifts": he acknowledges that the Corinthians have been enriched "in all speech" and "in all knowledge" (1:5). Roy Ciampa and Brian Rosner (2010: 64) point out, "These two terms occur many more times in this letter than in Paul's other letters. Their appearance in the thanksgiving obviously anticipates later discussions in the book." The first gift of "speech" (*logos*) foreshadows the lengthy discourse of chapters 1–4. This first major section

of the letter body reveals that the divisions in the Corinthian church stem
from whether Paul is impressive enough in his "speech"—whether the apostle
presents the gospel with the kind of persuasive words and eloquent arguments
that their non-Christian neighbors would find "wise" and not "foolish." The
reference to "speech" in the thanksgiving section, then, looks ahead to Paul's
argument in the opening chapters of the letter body. As Linda Belleville (1987:
20) rightly observes:

> Paul focuses in chapters 1–4 on the false value the Corinthians have placed on
> gifting in "speech." Four times he emphasizes that his preaching and teaching
> did not come with persuasive words or eloquent speech so as not to detract
> from the message itself (1:17; 2:1, 4, 13). Twice "speech" and "power" are con-
> trasted (4:19, 20). Four times in these chapters Paul also attacks the attitude of
> arrogance and boasting that has resulted in their valuing "speech" above the
> message (1:29, 31; 3:21; 4:7).

The reference to "speech" in the thanksgiving section, however, may also
foreshadow spiritual speech such as tongues and prophecy (so Garland 2003:
33), which are treated at length in chapters 12–14.

The second gift of "knowledge" (*gnōsis*) is another grace gift that the Corinthian believers overemphasize and misuse. This is most clearly seen in Paul's
lengthy response to the Corinthians' question about eating meat sacrificed to
idols (8:1–11:1). The apostle opens that discussion by first quoting a likely
claim of the Corinthians, "We all have knowledge" (8:1a), and then asserting
in response to their claim the important corrective that "knowledge puffs up
but love builds up" (8:1b). The Corinthians justified their participation in
cultic meals by appealing to their "knowledge" that "no idols in the world
really exist" and that "there is no God but one" (8:1–6; see also 8:7, 11). Thus
Paul is being a bit ironic when he later in this same discussion begins a new
argument as part of his lengthy response with the statement: "I do not want
you not to know . . ." (10:1). A similar rebuking tone ought to be heard in
the rhetorical question that he asks them no less than ten times, "You know,
don't you, that . . . ?" (3:16; 5:6; 6:2, 3, 9, 15, 16, 19; 9:13, 24), affirming on
the one hand that they do have knowledge (the Greek text clearly indicates
that Paul expects a yes answer to his questions) but also signaling on the other
hand that their knowledge is imperfect because it does not result in proper
holy living. The Corinthians' preoccupation with and misemployment of
the gift of knowledge as well as of speech explain Paul's assertion that both
gifts are only temporary blessings in contrast to love: "Love never ends. As
for prophecies [a gift of speech], they will come to an end; as for tongues

[another gift of speech], they will cease; as for knowledge, it will come to an end" (13:8; see also 13:1–2, where tongues, prophecy, and knowledge need to be accompanied by love). The reference to being enriched "in all knowledge" in the thanksgiving, therefore, clearly looks ahead to later discussions of this spiritual gift in the letter body.

The three eschatological references in the thanksgiving (1:7b, "while you eagerly wait for the revelation of our Lord Jesus Christ"; 1:8a, "who will indeed guarantee you until the end as blameless"; 1:8b, "on the day of our Lord Jesus Christ") have already been noted and explained above. Here we need only observe how these end-time references further illustrate the foreshadowing function of the thanksgiving section, anticipating how throughout the whole letter Paul tries to get his Corinthian readers to view their present (and typically sinful) conduct in light of the future (3:13–15, 17; 4:5; 5:5; 6:13–14; 7:26–31; 11:27, 32; 15:24, 51–56; 16:22). As Gordon Fee (1987: 36) puts it, "The second emphasis [in 1:4–9] is eschatological. They lack no spiritual gift, but they have not yet arrived. They *await* the revelation (v. 7). Christ will establish them so that they *will be blameless* on the Day of the Lord (v. 8). This eschatological tension between their present giftedness (spirituality) and the final glory will emerge again in this letter (e.g., 4:8–13; 13:8–13)."

Finally, the reference to how God has called them into "fellowship" or community both with Christ and with each other (1:9) has been discussed fully above. Also discussed fully was how this theme anticipates the problem of division taken up especially in chapters 1–4 but elsewhere in the letter as well. The foreshadowing function of this part of the thanksgiving is recognized by Richard Hays (1997: 19): "Thus, when Paul concludes his thanksgiving by reminding the Corinthians that they have been called into Christ's *koinōnia*, he is sounding a theme whose manifold variations he will continue to play from beginning to end in this letter."

The thanksgiving of 1 Cor. 1:4–9 does not address *directly* all the topics discussed in the letter body. There is no explicit reference to matters such as the Corinthian church's toleration of sexual sin in their fellowship (5:1–13; 6:12–20), public lawsuits between congregational members (6:1–11), issues connected with marriage (7:1–40), and so on. In this sense the thanksgiving of 1:4–9 is not as comprehensive as its counterpart in 1 Thess. 1:2–10, where Paul foreshadows not only all four of the major topics of the letter but even an argument used in the treatment of one of these major topics. Nevertheless, the thanksgiving of 1 Cor. 1:4–9 does touch on all the topics of the letter *indirectly* because Paul has chosen to address in this epistolary unit not the wrong conduct of the Corinthian church but the wrong thinking that lies behind such conduct. Consequently, every issue in the letter is either corrected or affirmed by the Corinthians' right perception of themselves as a church gifted by God through Christ, focused on the future, and called into community both with Jesus Christ and with each other.

Galatians 1:6–10

The method of epistolary analysis involves an awareness of both the form and function of the various letter-writing conventions used by Paul as well as the conviction that deviations in the apostle's expected form and epistolary practice are never fortuitous but deliberate and thus exegetically significant. Although this truth has already been well-demonstrated in our analysis of the thanksgiving section in 1 Thessalonians and 1 Corinthians, the unique situation of Paul's Letter to the Galatians also deserves comment.

FROM "AMEN" TO "ANATHEMA"

In the preceding chapter, we observed how in Galatians Paul has skillfully adapted all three of the epistolary conventions typically found in the letter opening—the sender, recipient, and greeting formulas—to defend two closely connected things: the divine origin and authority of his *apostleship* and the legitimacy of his circumcision-free *gospel*. What should come next in keeping with his epistolary practice elsewhere is the thanksgiving section, where Paul typically presents an image of himself with his finger pointed straight up to heaven as he gives thanks to God for his Galatian readers. What's more, since Paul has expanded the greeting formula (1:3–4) by adding a doxology (1:5) and thus ending the letter opening with his finger already pointed up to heaven as he brings glory to God, it would be natural for the apostle to continue this posture by following his expected pattern of giving thanks to God. Even if Paul is unhappy with the believers in Galatia and unable to find in them anything commendatory, he could have chosen to do what he did in his letter to the Corinthians, namely, thank God for *his* divine work in the lives of the Galatians rather than recognize anything that they, the readers, are doing themselves. It is, therefore, quite unexpected to hear next not "I give thanks" but "I am astonished" and to see how in the one short paragraph that follows (1:6–10), Paul goes from the doxological "Amen" (1:5) to the twice-threatened curse "anathema" (1:8–9; Das 2014: 99):

> [6]I am astonished that you are so quickly deserting the one who called you by the grace of Christ and are turning to a different gospel—[7]not that there is another gospel; only there are some who are confusing you and wanting to pervert the gospel of Christ. [8]But even if we or an angel from heaven should

preach a gospel to you contrary to the gospel we preached to you, let that person be accursed [*anathema*]! [9]As we have said before, so I also now say again: if anyone preaches a gospel to you contrary to what you received, let that person be accursed [*anathema*]! [10]Am I now trying to win the approval of people, or of God? Or am I seeking to please people? If I were seeking to please people, I would not be Christ's slave.

Most modern scholars are struck by the change here in Paul's epistolary practice and recognize that his omission of the thanksgiving section is neither accidental nor insignificant but an important part of his persuasive strategy. The failure of Paul to give thanks to God for his Galatian readers reveals the depth of his concern for his converts in Galatia, and it alerts his original readers to the dangerous circumstances in which they have placed themselves. Douglas Moo (2013: 75) states: "While we must exercise caution in inferring too much from unusual formal features (esp. if Galatians is the first letter Paul wrote), it seems justified to conclude, with most commentators, that Paul is signaling his extreme distress at the situation of the Galatian Christians." Ben Witherington (1998: 80) views Paul's rebuke of 1:6–10 to be a "splash of cold water in the face of the audience to get their attention and wake them up to what their situation really was and to the fact that they needed to take action to correct the situation." Frank Matera (1992: 48–49) observes:

> The omission of a thanksgiving derives, in part, from the situation which Paul faced in Galatia. Because the Galatians were in the process of abandoning the God who called them and were embracing a different gospel, there was little reason for Paul to commend their faith. . . . The omission of the thanksgiving and its replacement by a statement of astonishment alerts the audience that the situation has reached crisis proportions. Paul does not bypass the thanksgiving in order to insult the Galatians but to signal that this is not an ordinary letter.

Did the Galatians Even Notice the Omitted Thanksgiving?

A few commentators have questioned not the reason why Paul omits the thanksgiving but whether the Galatian readers would have caught this omission such that the apostle's persuasive strategy would be effective. Robert Van Voorst (2010: 160–61) contends that "a thanksgiving period was not in fact customary in letters of the time, so that the Galatians in all likelihood would not have noted Paul's not giving thanks for them, much less viewed it as meaningful." Andrew Das (2014: 99n9) similarly states, "The Galatians, who were not familiar with Paul's other letters, would not have known what they were missing."

Two responses to this assertion ought to be made. First, although most letters of that day did not open with a thanksgiving, most did open with a health wish, a formula in which the writer expresses concern for the physical health and safety of the recipient(s), and also often a prayer report, a formula in which the writer prays for the well-being of the recipient(s). The rebuke section of 1:6–10 would seem to the Galatians a quite abrupt and harsh way to begin the letter in contrast to these expected and missing epistolary conventions. After conceding that it was not customary in Greek letters to include a prayer of thanksgiving and that the Galatians may well not have realized the absence of this specific epistolary convention, Francois Tolmie (2005: 39) nevertheless goes on to observe, "Numerous contemporary papyrus letters contain another element, namely, a report of the writer's prayer for the recipients at the beginning of the letter, and one may assume that his audience would have been familiar with this habit, and that its absence—if not taken as a direct rebuke—would, at least, have been strange to them."

Second, even if the readers in Galatia would not have noticed the omission of a thanksgiving, yet for today's readers this striking deviation from Paul's epistolary practice reveals the depth of the apostle's concern and his mindset when writing this letter, which in turn is helpful for a proper interpretation of the Galatians correspondence. Here, then, is a good illustration of an important aspect (mentioned briefly in the introductory chapter of this book) of the method of epistolary analysis: it involves the kind of comparative analysis—comparing all of Paul's letters together to discern not only his common epistolary practices but also the deviations from those practices— that was not possible for most of the apostle's original readers. In this way the modern reader can at times have a better window into authorial intent than the ancient reader had and see more clearly what Paul was attempting to communicate. The meaning of any biblical text is not limited by whether the audience would "get" what was written but also includes what the author, inspired by the Holy Spirit, was intending to say.

An analogy to this second response is provided by a possible echo of an OT text that Paul makes in 1:6 when he rebukes the Galatians for "quickly" (*tacheōs*) deserting God, who had called them in the grace of Christ. The apostle may well be alluding to the infamous golden calf incident when Israel "quickly" (Exod. 32:8 LXX, with the cognate form *tachy*; Deut. 9:12, 16; cf. Judg. 2:17) turned from the way that God had called them to live (so, e.g., Longenecker 1990: 14; Ciampa 1998: 71–77; T. Wilson 2004: 554–59). It is uncertain whether all or even most of the predominantly gentile readers in Galatia would have recognized this OT echo. Nevertheless, it is still helpful for modern readers to recognize what the original readers may have missed but what Paul intended, since it provides an important clue to how seriously the apostle viewed the situation in Galatia, namely, a situation so grave that it paralleled the apostasy of Israel during its wilderness wandering. In a similar way, the modern reader who engages in an epistolary analysis of Galatians can recognize in the omission of the thanksgiving what the original readers may have missed but what Paul intended and how the knowledge of this omission aids the right interpretation of the letter.

An Omitted or Replaced Thanksgiving?

Rather than saying that Paul *omits* the thanksgiving section, it is more accurate to say that he *replaces* the thanksgiving section. Several commentators rightly recognize that in Galatians the apostle deviates from his typical pattern of giving thanks to God for his readers but wrongly view him as immediately beginning the body of the letter with the rebuking words of 1:6. Timothy George (1994: 88–89), for example, writes, "Paul moved with great abruptness from the salutation into the body of the letter itself. As we have seen, the thanksgiving section that usually comes at this point in his letters is omitted in Galatians." Louis Martyn (1997: 107) similarly asserts, "Rather than turning at this point to the expected thanksgiving paragraph, he begins the body of the letter with a rebuke." Tom Schreiner (2010: 82) follows suit: "This expression of astonishment in terms of epistolary features may be construed as the opening of the rebuke section of the letter. The body of the letter commences here."

The flaw with this interpretation is Paul's use of the "disclosure formula" in 1:11 (see the fuller discussion of this epistolary convention in chap. 4). Elsewhere in Paul's letters this formula typically functions as a major transitional marker, signaling the shift from the end of the thanksgiving section to the beginning of the letter body (Rom. 1:13; Gal. 1:11; 2 Cor. 1:8; Phil. 1:12; 1 Thess. 2:1; a different epistolary convention, the appeal formula, marks the beginning of the letter body in 1 Cor. 1:10 and Philem. 8–9). That the body of the letter begins at 1:11 is confirmed by the address "brothers and sisters," which is another transitional marker commonly found in letters of that day (see further treatment of this literary device also in chap. 4).

The distinction between Paul *omitting* the thanksgiving in Galatians and his *replacing* it is not a mere semantic technicality but has an important consequence for how the paragraph of 1:6–10 ought to be identified and interpreted. This "rebuke" paragraph, like the thanksgiving section that it replaces, does not develop any of the letter's main arguments in any sustained way; this will happen later, in the body of the letter (1:11–6:10). Instead, this rebuke paragraph, again like the thanksgiving section that it replaces, is introductory in character, setting the stage for the rest of the letter to come. The anticipatory or preparatory character of 1:6–10 can be seen in how Paul raises multiple important points in this paragraph but does not advance any of them in an extended manner. As Francois Tolmie (2005: 44) observes:

> It is possible to identify [in 1:6–10] a large variety of notions which Paul seems to want to convey to the audience. . . . Developed in more detail, most of these notions can serve as powerful arguments or proofs; yet, Paul merely mentions or suggests most of them. The reason for this seems to be that it is not his primary intention at this stage to persuade the audience by means of individual rational arguments, but to combine all of this . . . to convey his negative feelings to them in such a way that they will reconsider what they are about to do. It is as if he is saying to them repeatedly: "Stop! You are on the wrong track! Don't do it!"

FUNCTION OF THE REBUKE SECTION

If, as I have argued above, the rebuke section of 1:6–10 is not the beginning of the letter body but the replacement paragraph for the omitted thanksgiving section and thus is preparatory for the rest of the letter to come, then this epistolary unit plausibly also has the same three functions of the thanksgiving section that it replaces.

1. *Pastoral function.* The pastoral function of 1:6–10 is the hardest of the three to see because it is conveyed quite differently than in other letters due to the seriousness of the situation in Galatia. Instead of the image of Pastor Paul on his knees praying for them, there is the image of Pastor Paul confronting them with shame-inducing words of astonishment. Although such words are difficult for the Galatian readers to hear, the words ultimately stem from the genuine care and concern that the apostle has for the church. As the writer of Proverbs puts it: "Better is open rebuke than hidden love; wounds from a friend can be trusted but an enemy multiplies kisses" (Prov. 27:5–6; cited by Hansen 1994: 34–35). Or as Jesus said to the Laodicean congregation, the most spiritually poor of the seven churches: "I rebuke and discipline those whom I love" (Rev. 3:19). And despite the cool tone of the letter opening and the strong words of the introductory rebuke section, the body of the letter does convey Paul's pastoral affection for his Galatian readers: nine times he refers to them as "brothers and sisters" (1:11; 3:15; 4:12, 28, 31; 5:11, 13; 6:1, 18), and one time he even identifies them as "my children, for whom I am again in the pain of childbirth until Christ is formed in you" (4:19). Finally, Paul's justified anger is directed less at his converts in Galatia than at his opponents

in that region: the apostle may be "astonished" at the converts (1:6), but the opponents who are leading Paul's converts astray he threatens with a curse of "anathema," not just once but twice (1:8–9).

2. *Exhortative function*. Paul in 1:6–10 is not merely venting or blowing off steam in order to get rid of his own frustration and anger over what is happening in the Galatian churches; rather, his words clearly have an exhortative function. Paul is calling on his readers to respond to his tough words by acting differently. But unlike his letters to healthier churches, where the thanksgiving involves "persuasion through praise," here in writing to the spiritually sick congregations of Galatia, there is "rectification through rebuke": pressure is placed on the readers to act in a way that avoids the shame of astonishing their founder Paul and coming under the divine judgment of a curse.

By letting his readers know the specific matters over which he is astonished—namely, their "deserting the one who called you by the grace of Christ" and their "turning to a different gospel" (1:6b)—Paul implicitly exhorts the Christians in Galatia to reexamine their relationship to the God who has called them and their need to return to the version of the gospel that he originally preached to them, which he later in the letter calls the "truth of the gospel" (2:5, 14). Similarly, by letting his readers know that "there are some who are confusing you and wanting to pervert the gospel of Christ" (1:7), Paul not only vilifies his opponents in Galatia and raises doubts in the readers' minds about the motives and behavior of such individuals, but he also implicitly exhorts the Christians there to distance themselves from these false leaders. Likewise, by declaring a twofold curse not just on his opponents but also on hypothetical angels from heaven and even on himself if he were to proclaim a gospel different from the one he first gave them (1:8–9), Paul not only indirectly claims divine authority (since God is the only one who can actually cause an individual to be cursed) but also raises the stakes to such a high level that the Galatians are forced to act. As Kjell Morland (1995: 15) points out:

> Such a curse cannot be overlooked once it has been uttered. The primary pragmatic aspect of the curse is that it puts before the Galatian churches a very serious choice: Either to accept the double anathema as a carrier of divine authority, and thus to isolate the opponents, or to reject it as false, and thus to question the authority of Paul himself. The curse claims to carry divine authority, and there it demands to be accepted as such. The only alternative is to reject it as false. Thus the situation cannot be as it was before in Galatia: Once the curse has been uttered, the churches are forced to choose between the authority of Paul and [that of] his opponents.

An exhortative function ought also to be seen in the closing verse of the rebuke section that replaces the thanksgiving. The two rhetorical questions of 1:10 ("Am I now trying to win the approval of people, or of God? Or am I seeking to please people?") and the concluding conditional clause ("If I were seeking to please people, I would not be Christ's slave") involve an implicit exhortation to the Galatian readers both to reject a false claim questioning the integrity of Paul's character and also to accept his authoritative status as a full-fledged, divinely called apostle. His opponents in the Galatian churches apparently accuse Paul of being a second-class leader who is so insecure about his status that he seeks the approval of others by compromising the gospel (i.e., by not requiring circumcision or other Jewish customs), thus making it easier for gentiles to become Christ-followers (see 5:11). Paul, however, repudiates the charge of being a people-pleaser and also claims to be "*Christ's slave*" (the word order in Greek emphasizes whose slave Paul is)—a title that, in the ears of early Christians, actually expresses his authority (Das 2014: 114). The authority inherent in Paul's "self-title" (see also Rom. 1:1; Phil. 1:1) stems from the fact that a slave's status was determined by that of the master (D. Martin 1990: 15–68). Since Christ's authority in the church is supreme, Paul as "Christ's slave" shares in his master's position of power such that the Galatian readers are pressured to acknowledge Paul's authoritative status. As James Dunn (1993: 51) helpfully states, "To be a slave of an important figure carried a certain status with it, so that 'slave of Christ' could also function in some degree as a claim to leadership."

The apostle's motivation here is not simply to feed his ego and to be acknowledged as important; rather, Paul knows of the intimate link between the messenger and the message. Thus the apostle hopes that, if the Galatians accept his authoritative status as "*Christ's* slave," they will also accept his gospel as genuine rather than submitting to the false version of the gospel presented by his opponents.

3. *Foreshadowing function.* The rebuke section of 1:6–10 also functions as a preview of what this letter is ultimately about: a defense of Paul's version of the gospel. Virtually all commentators miss this foreshadowing function in 1:6–10, either because they fail in a general way to approach Paul's letters by using the method of epistolary analysis or because they fail in a specific way to recognize that Paul has not merely omitted the thanksgiving section here in Galatians but has replaced it with a rebuke section that still has a foreshadowing function similar to that of a thanksgiving. A rare exception is Louis Martyn (1997: 107): "He [Paul] thus employs this rebuke paragraph to lay out the theme of the epistle, giving a forecast of the whole. And having done that, he provides in 1:10–6:10 supporting theses, arguments, and

conclusions, explicating what he has said about the term 'gospel' and about its counterfeit in 1:6–9."

a. *Defense of Paul's gospel*. Galatians fundamentally involves a defense of Paul's version of the gospel, which is foreshadowed in the rebuke section. Though brief, it contains multiple references to the noun "gospel" (*euangelion*) and the verb "to preach the gospel" (*euangelizomai*). The opening verse of this section expresses Paul's astonishment that his Galatian converts are so quickly deserting God and turning to "a different gospel" (1:6). He then immediately rejects the possible existence of such a competing gospel, claiming "not that there is another gospel" (1:7a). For the first time in the letter, Paul also identifies the presence of opponents who are "wanting to pervert the gospel of Christ" (1:7b). In keeping with the preparatory character of this rebuke section, Paul does not spell out precisely how these individuals were perverting the gospel, nor does he provide counterarguments to their claims; this will happen in the body of the letter. Instead, the apostle expresses what is perhaps the harshest rhetoric found anywhere in his letters as he not once but twice declares a curse not just on his opponents but also on anyone, including even himself, who preaches a different gospel: "But even if we or an angel from heaven should preach a gospel to you contrary to the gospel we preached to you, let that person be accursed [*anathema*]! As we have said before, so I also now say again: if anyone preaches a gospel to you contrary to what you received, let that person be accursed [*anathema*]!" (1:8–9). These multiple references to the noun "gospel" and the verb "to preach the gospel" in the rebuke section foreshadow and prepare the reader well for the extended defense of what Paul calls "the truth of the gospel" (2:5, 14)—a law-free, circumcision-free, and faith-based gospel—that will be given in the body of the letter.

b. *Condemnation of Paul's opponents*. The rebuke section of 1:6–10 also anticipates additional topics taken up later in the letter, topics closely connected to the central theme of defending Paul's version of the gospel. One of these related topics involves the apostle's opponents, who are advocating a competing gospel. Paul's reference to those "who are confusing you and wanting to pervert the gospel of Christ" (1:7b) looks ahead to his future references to these opponents given throughout the body of the letter: "Who has bewitched you?" (3:1); "They are zealously courting you but not for your good; they want to exclude you in order that you might zealously court them" (4:17); "You were running well; who hindered you from obeying the truth?" (5:7); "A little leaven leavens the whole batch of dough" (5:9), meaning that just a few of these opponents advocating a false gospel can negatively impact all the Galatian believers; "The one who is disturbing you will pay the penalty, whoever that person may be" (5:10); and "I wish that the ones who are troubling you would castrate themselves!" (5:12). The opponents are likely also in view in Paul's citation of Gen. 21:10 in Gal. 4:30: "But what does scripture say? 'Drive out the slave woman and her son, for the son of the slave woman will by no means inherit with the son of the free woman.'" Paul here is commanding the Galatian believers to throw out of their fellowship those advocating a false gospel.

In light of the foreshadowing reference to Paul's opponents in the rebuke section and the multiple references to them in the body of the letter, it is not surprising that the apostle also discusses them in the letter closing (6:11–18). Paul stresses their insincere, self-serving motives: they are advocating circumcision only (1) to build themselves up ("It is those who want to make a good showing in the flesh who are compelling you to be circumcised" [6:12a]; "but they want you to be circumcised in order that they might boast in your flesh" [6:13b]) and (2) to avoid persecution ("these ones are compelling you to be circumcised only in order that they might not be persecuted because of the cross of Christ" [6:12b]).

c. *Defense of Paul's character and status.* The rebuke section of 1:6–10 also anticipates Paul's upcoming defense (in the body of the letter) of both his character and status. Whereas 1:7–9 focuses on Paul's opponents and their false gospel, which results in the divine judgment of their being accursed, 1:10 focuses on Paul and defends him from attacks by these opponents. As Douglas Moo (2013: 75–76) observes, "Paul concludes the paragraph [of 1:6–10] by contrasting himself, as a true servant of Christ, with these false teachers."

Paul first defends *the integrity of his character* by means of two rhetorical questions: "Am I now trying to win the approval of people, or of God? Or am I seeking to please people?" (1:10a). The contemporary reader should not miss the irritated and defensive tone of these questions, which may be better conveyed in the following paraphrase: "I just finished calling on God to curse anyone who is advocating a different gospel than the one I originally preached to you, and I did so twice! Now do these sound like the words of a people-pleaser to you?!"

Most scholars recognize that Paul is defending himself here, refuting the claims of his opponents that he is a hypocrite who would say and do whatever is necessary to please his audience: sometimes Paul would advocate circumcision, as in the case of Timothy (Acts 16:1–3), but in other situations he would claim that this Jewish rite and other regulations of the law are not necessary. This denial of being a people-pleaser in 1:10a anticipates his later rhetorical question: "But if I, brothers and sisters, am still preaching circumcision, why then am I being persecuted? In that case the scandal of the cross would be removed" (5:11). This verse interrupts, rather abruptly and awkwardly, the logical flow of a paragraph (5:7–12) that deals extensively with Paul's opponents in Galatia. The unexpected appearance of this verse almost certainly stems from Paul's need to respond to a question about the integrity of his character raised by his opponents and spread widely by them among the Galatian readers. Those who prepared the New Living Translation (NLT) are so certain that this is what is going on that they add the words "as some say I do" to Paul's rhetorical question.[17]

Second, Paul defends *the authority of his status* by means of a conditional clause: "If I were seeking to please people, I would not be Christ's slave" (1:10b). The first part of the clause reaffirms the denial he has just made (in the two rhetorical questions): he is not a people-pleaser.[18] The second part of this clause makes a more powerful assertion about the status of Paul than is commonly recognized: "[I am] *Christ's* slave." Above we noticed not only the word order, which stresses the one to whom Paul belongs, but also that this term of self-identification involves authority (see discussion above under "Exhortative Function").

We have not yet highlighted, however, how this emphasis at the end of the thanksgiving section on the authoritative status of Paul anticipates the defense of Paul's apostolic position given at the beginning of the letter body. The material of Gal. 1:11–2:14, which can be formally identified as an "autobiographical report" (for more on this epistolary convention, see chap. 4), involves a defense not just of Paul's gospel but also of his apostleship, both of which were given to him not by any human leader but by divine authority. Paul therefore carefully lays out for his Galatian readers events from his early life, conversion, and commission (1:13–17); his first visit to Jerusalem (1:18–24); his second visit to Jerusalem (2:1–10); and a dramatic episode in Antioch (2:11–14)—all with the purpose of demonstrating the opening claim of the letter body (1:11–12), namely, that he did not, as his opponents imply or openly charge, get his gospel or his authority as an apostle to preach that gospel from any human authority such as Peter, James, or other so-called pillars of the Jerusalem church but received his gospel and apostleship directly from Jesus Christ himself. Paul's description of himself as "*Christ's* slave" in 1:10, therefore, like his expansion of the sender formula in the letter opening (1:1a, "an apostle not from men nor through a man but through Jesus Christ and from God the Father"), anticipates the extended defense of Paul's status given in the beginning of the letter body.

---

17. Notice also The Message, which renders Gal. 5:11: "As for the rumor that I continue to preach the ways of circumcision . . ."

18. This denial is expressed in the "if" clause (the technical term is "protasis") which, in a second-class condition as is found here, assumes the untruth of what is being hypothesized: "If I were [*but I am not*] seeking to please people."

4

The Body

When dealing with the letter body, the method of epistolary analysis differs slightly from the way it approaches the other major parts of the letter. For the opening, thanksgiving, and closing sections of a given Pauline letter, this method mostly involves comparing what Paul writes in one letter with the rest of his correspondence: one observes changes in the form of the various epistolary conventions found in these sections and then considers how these changes are not likely to be accidental but deliberate, thereby revealing more clearly the intention of the apostle. This approach works well in the opening, thanksgiving, and closing sections because these major parts of the letter are formally very consistent—so consistent that any changes in Paul's typical or expected form can be readily identified by the "alert" reader who is aware of the apostle's epistolary practices. This approach, however, cannot be followed in exactly the same way in the letter body for the obvious and important reason that the content of each letter body varies widely as Paul addresses the specific and unique problems faced by his various congregations.

Therefore, when studying the body of a letter, the method of epistolary analysis involves comparing what Paul writes in one letter with the contents of other extant letters of his day rather than with the rest of his own correspondence. The goal of such comparative formal analysis is to identify the ways in which the apostle employs epistolary conventions or stereotyped formulas commonly used in ancient letters. The modern reader understandably fails to recognize these borrowed formulas in Paul's letters because they are no longer used as they were in the letters of the apostle's era. Nevertheless, as important as it is to identify the *form* of these borrowed formulas in Paul's letters, it is more important to understand what *function* these formulas have, since it is the latter that often provides the payoff for exegesis. For example, one might be able to impress family and friends by identifying the words of 1 Cor. 1:10 ("I appeal to you, brothers and sisters, by the name of our Lord Jesus Christ, that . . .") as an appeal formula, but that knowledge alone will not help in understanding the text any better. What is needed in addition is the knowledge of what *function* an appeal formula has and how Paul might be using this epistolary convention to strengthen the persuasive force of his argument or exhortation. Consequently, in this chapter my analysis of the various epistolary conventions and other liturgical and literary forms often found in the body of Paul's letters will emphasize the function of these formal elements and the ways in which this knowledge can help the modern reader to understand better both what the apostle literally says and the fuller meaning or intention of his words.

Transitional Formulas

Determining the proper boundaries of the passage in question is an important first step in any form of exegesis. It ensures that our interpretation begins and ends at the correct place and that the interpretation of individual verses takes place within the parameters of the larger unit to which the verses belong. Modern translations signal the boundaries of the text and transitions in Paul's letters by means of chapter divisions, paragraph breaks, indented lines, and even the addition of headings that indicate the subject matter of the following verses. None of these transitional markers, however, are given in the original Greek text and thus should not be viewed as either inspired or authoritative. Paul provides his readers with different kinds of clues to mark the boundaries of his discussions and his transitions to new subject matter or a new stage in his argumentation. These clues consist in the apostle's strategic use of epistolary conventions or letter-writing formulas.

Appeal Formula

FORM

The appeal formula, which was widely used in the ancient world, occurs in both private letters and official correspondence where the author requests that the readers take some course of action (see esp. Mullins 1962; Bjerkelund 1967). This formula typically consists of four elements (Bjerkelund 1967: 43–50):

1. The verb of appeal, "I appeal/urge/exhort" (*parakaleō*) or its synonym, "I ask" (*erōtaō*), from which this epistolary convention derives its name, in the first person and present tense.
2. The recipients of the appeal.
3. A prepositional phrase indicating the source of authority by which the letter sender issues the appeal (this element normally occurs only in official correspondence and not in private letters).
4. The content of the appeal, typically introduced by a "that" clause (either the conjunction *hina* or an infinitive).

The same four elements can be found in Paul's use of the appeal formula. For example, the words of Rom. 12:1–2 can be readily understood as following this fourfold structure:

1. *The verb of appeal*	I appeal
2. *The recipients of the appeal*	to you, brothers and sisters,
3. *A prepositional phrase*	by the mercies of God
4. *The content of the appeal*	that you present your bodies. . . .

The high number of occurrences of the appeal formula in Paul's letters reveals the important role that this epistolary convention plays in his correspondence: Rom. 12:1–2; 15:30–32; 16:17; 1 Cor. 1:10; 4:16; 16:15–16; 2 Cor. 10:1–2; Phil. 4:2 (2×); 1 Thess. 4:1, 10b–12; 5:12, 14; 2 Thess. 2:1–2; 1 Tim. 2:1; Philem. 9–10 (2×); see also Heb. 13:19, 22; 1 Pet. 2:11.

FUNCTION

The primary function of the appeal formula is to signal a major transition in the text, either from the end of the thanksgiving section to the beginning of the letter body (1 Cor. 1:10; Philem. 9–10; see also 1 Tim. 2:1) or, as more typically happens, a transition within the body of the letter (Rom. 15:30–32; 16:17; 1 Cor. 4:16; 16:15–16; 2 Cor. 10:1–2; Phil. 4:2 [2×]; 1 Thess. 4:1; 4:10b–12; 5:12, 14; 2 Thess. 2:1–2).

In addition to this primary function of marking transition, however, the appeal formula also has a secondary function. This additional function stems from the presence of the third formal element—the prepositional phrase indicating the source of authority by which the author issues the appeal. Paul's use of this element corresponds closely to the pattern established in official letters of the period, where rulers write to those under their authority. This is significant because, in official correspondence, the appeal formula signals a friendlier, less heavy-handed approach than the use of more conventional commands. If a provincial ruler or government official had a good relationship with his letter recipients and was optimistic that they would obey his appeal to do something, he would not aggressively "command" them and so unnecessarily risk causing offense but instead would more diplomatically "appeal" to them. Paul deliberately uses the appeal formula in this nuanced manner: in situations where his authority is not questioned and he is confident that his exhortation will be obeyed, he chooses not to "command" his readers in a heavy-handed manner but instead to "appeal" to them in a more friendly way.

INTERPRETATIVE SIGNIFICANCE

Paul's awareness of the softer sense expressed by the appeal formula is clear from its twofold occurrence in his Letter to Philemon, where the apostle explicitly contrasts commanding the slave owner with appealing to him: "Although in Christ I could be bold and *command* you to do what you ought to do, more because of love I *appeal*—I, Paul, an old man and now also a prisoner of Christ Jesus—I *appeal* to you concerning my child, to whom I gave birth in prison, Onesimus . . ." (Philem. 8–10). The friendly, less heavy-handed tone of the appeal formula can also be seen by comparing Paul's responses to the problem of idleness in 1 and 2 Thessalonians. In the first letter, the apostle twice "appeals" to his readers about church members who are taking advantage of the hospitality and generosity of fellow Christ-followers and who are refusing to engage in self-sufficient work: he "appeals" to the whole church "to work with your hands . . . in order that you may have need of no one" (1 Thess. 4:10b–12); later he "appeals" to the whole church "to admonish the rebellious idlers" within their congregation (5:14). In the second letter, however, the problem of idleness has worsened rather than improved, forcing Paul not only to treat the matter at much greater length (2 Thess. 3:6–15) but also to "command" his readers on this matter rather than appeal to them (3:6; see also 3:12). The softer sense expressed by the appeal formula also explains why this epistolary convention does not occur anywhere in Galatians, which is hardly accidental or surprising given the apostle's strained, if not broken, relationship with these churches.

Disclosure Formula

FORM

The disclosure formula occurs with greater frequency in Greco-Roman letters than even the widely attested appeal formula, and so it is hardly surprising that this epistolary convention also often appears in Paul's letters. The formula appears in a variety of forms, but its one essential feature is the presence of a verb of knowing. Five Greek verbs belong to the semantic domain of "to know" (*oida*, *ginōskō* and its compound form *epiginōskō*, *gnōrizō* ["make known"], and the negative *agnoeō* ["not know"]), and all five occur in the different forms of the disclosure formula found in both Greco-Roman and NT letters. It is this key verb of knowing that caused Terence Mullins, in his early study of this formula, to label such expressions as "disclosure" (1964: 46: "I call this form the Disclosure"), reflecting his belief that this epistolary convention disclosed or shared information that the sender of the letter wanted to make known to his recipients.

The disclosure formula occurs in at least six distinct forms (see White 1971: 93; 1972: 11; 1986: 204–8; Reed 1997: 211–12):

Table 4.1: Six Possible Patterns of the Disclosure Formula

1. *Full formula, stated positively*	I/we want you to know that . . .
2. *Full formula, stated negatively*	I/we do not want you not to know that . . .
3. *Abbreviated formula*	We/you know that . . .
4. *Abbreviated formula*	I/We make known to you that . . .
5. *Imperatival formula*	Know that . . .
6. *Motivation for writing formula*	I/we have written so that you may know that . . .

The different forms of the disclosure formula lead Porter and Pitts (2013: 427) to define this epistolary convention as follows: "The disclosure formula expresses the author's desire for the audience to know something, commands the audience to know something, or informs the audience of something in support of a statement or argument."

FUNCTION

The primary function of the disclosure formula is transitional: to signal a major (or less often a minor) shift either in the subject matter or in a stage of Paul's argumentation. As John White (1972: 11) observes, this epistolary convention is "employed generally for transitional purposes." Paul uses the disclosure formula, along with another transitional marker—the vocative form of address "brothers and sisters" (see the fuller discussion of the vocative form of address below)—to indicate the major shift away from the thanksgiving section to the beginning of the letter body in five of his letters:

Rom. 1:13	I do not want you not to know, brothers and sisters, that . . .
2 Cor. 1:8	For we do not want you not to know, brothers and sisters, concerning . . .
Gal. 1:11	For I make known to you, brothers and sisters, the . . .
Phil. 1:12	I want you to know, brothers and sisters, that . . .
1 Thess. 2:1	For you yourselves know, brothers and sisters, the . . .

The disclosure formula, however, also indicates major transitions *within* the body of the letter. A particularly clear example of this is found in 1 Cor. 12:1–3, where the shift from the preceding discussion of divisions over the Lord's Supper celebrations (11:17–34) to the lengthy, three-chapter discussion of spiritual gifts (12:1–14:40) is signaled by no less than three different forms of the disclosure formula, along with two other transitional markers—the "now about" formula (see the fuller discussion of this transitional marker below) and the vocative "brothers and sisters":

"Now about" formula	[1]Now about spiritual gifts,
Vocative form of address	brothers and sisters,
Full disclosure formula (negative)	I do not want you not to know.
Abbreviated disclosure formula	[2]You know that when you were pagans, you were enticed and led astray to idols that could not speak.
Abbreviated disclosure formula	[3]Therefore, I make known to you that no one speaking by the Spirit of God ever says "Let Jesus be cursed!" and no one can say "Jesus is Lord" except by the Holy Spirit.

The end of this lengthy three-chapter discussion of spiritual gifts (12:1–14:40) and the beginning of a chapter-long discussion of the resurrection (15:1–58) is similarly signaled by the presence of the disclosure formula and the vocative form of address: "I make known to you, brothers and sisters, . . ." (15:1).

Interpretative Significance

In addition to its primary function of marking transition, the disclosure formula also serves to indicate degrees of either Paul's pleasure or displeasure with his readers. For example, Paul uses a particular form of the disclosure formula in 1 Corinthians, asking his readers there no less than ten times the following rhetorical question: "You know, don't you, that . . . ?" (3:16; 5:6; 6:2, 3, 9, 15, 16, 19; 9:13, 24). These are not real questions in the sense that Paul genuinely inquires whether the Corinthians know something. They are all introduced in Greek with the special negative *ouk*, indicating that these are rhetorical questions in which Paul is not asking something but asserting something; he clearly expects the answer in every case to be: "Yes, we do know this." In other words, this rhetorical question is designed to highlight information that his readers already know (so virtually all commentators; see, however, Edsall 2013). Consequently, the presence of the disclosure formula in the form of these rhetorical questions indicates Paul's clear displeasure with his Corinthian readers: they do, in fact, know these things, and thus the apostle is disappointed and even angry that they seem to need reminding. The situation is similar to a teacher asking the students ten times in one class period, "You know this point, don't you?!" After only a couple of these rhetorical questions, the students in the class may start sinking lower and lower in their seats because they would rightly perceive that their teacher is frustrated at having to remind them of what they already know and is actually rebuking them by repeatedly asking these questions.

The tenfold occurrence of this form of the disclosure formula in 1 Corinthians, then, is yet additional clear evidence of the growing tension that exists between Paul and the Corinthian church. In the repeated use of this form of the disclosure formula, Ciampa and Rosner (2010: 160) rightly see "Paul's growing impatience with the Corinthians' failing to act on what he had taught them only earlier" and that Paul's words have "moved from a polite admonishment to a full reprimand." The Corinthians have a false pride based on their own wisdom and knowledge, making the implied rebuke even more pointed: "Can it be that you who boast in your own knowledge don't know this?!" (Fee 1987: 146n3).

Another example of how the disclosure formula, along with its primary function of marking the transition to a new topic, also signals degrees of Paul's pleasure or displeasure with his readers can be seen in three sequential passages from 1 Thessalonians. The first passage, 4:1–12, deals with encouraging behaviors that please God; the second, 4:13–18, deals with comfort concerning deceased believers at Christ's return; and the third, 5:1–11, deals with comfort concerning believers still alive at Christ's return. The primary transitional function of the disclosure formula can be observed in all three passages:

- 4:1 opens with a volley of transitional markers (the double appeal formula "we ask and appeal" and the vocative form of address "brothers and sisters"); 4:2 further marks this transition with the abbreviated form of the disclosure formula: "You know what commands we gave you through the Lord Jesus."
- 4:13 opens with the full form of the disclosure formula stated negatively and the vocative form of address: "We do not want you not to know,

brothers and sisters, about those who are asleep in order that you may not grieve like the rest who have no hope."

- 5:1 opens with still more transitional markers (the "now about" formula and the vocative form of address "brothers and sisters"); 5:2 further confirms this transition with the abbreviated form of the disclosure formula: "For you yourselves accurately know that the day of the Lord comes like a thief in the night."

The additional function of the disclosure formula—to indicate degrees of either Paul's pleasure or displeasure with his readers—can also be observed in the subtle but significant shift from the abbreviated form of this epistolary convention in 4:2 to its full form stated negatively in 4:13 and then back to its abbreviated form in 5:2.

The first of the three paragraphs (4:1–12) clearly deals with topics that Paul has previously shared with his Thessalonian readers. No less than four times in this paragraph, Paul asserts that he is not presenting them with new exhortations but rather is repeating and clarifying matters already dealt with during his mission-founding visit: "as you received from us how you must walk and so please God" (4:1); "for you know what commands we gave you" (4:2); "just as we indeed told you before and solemnly warned" (4:6); "just as we commanded you" (4:11).

This contrasts sharply with the second of the three paragraphs (4:13–18), which deals with a new topic that Paul has never addressed with the Thessalonian believers: the fate of believers who die before Jesus's glorious return. Whereas the preceding paragraph and the rest of the letter frequently refer to the readers' existing knowledge with the abbreviated disclosure formula "you know" (1:5; 2:1, 2, 5, 11; 3:3, 4; 4:2; 5:2) and expressions like "you remember" (2:9), such language is strikingly absent in 4:13–18. Paul accordingly signals the shift from the previously shared material of 4:1–12 to the never-taught-before material of 4:13–18 by introducing this second paragraph with the full form of the disclosure formula stated negatively: "We do not want you not to know . . ." (4:13).[1]

The apostle, however, had taught the Thessalonians already about the subject matter of the third paragraph—the day of the Lord—and so he signals

---

1. This explains why another transitional device in 1 Thess. 4:13, the "now about" formula, was moved from its normal and expected position at the head of the sentence (as it is both in the preceding paragraph in 4:9 ["Now about brotherly and sisterly love . . ."] and the following paragraph in 5:1 ["Now about the times and seasons . . ."]) to the middle ("Now . . . about those who are asleep"). Paul's need to insert a specific form of the disclosure formula that would signal the introduction of material he has not taught them earlier required that the "now about" formula be moved to a later position in the sentence.

the transition back to previously shared material by introducing the next paragraph with the abbreviated disclosure formula, "You yourselves accurately know that the day of the Lord comes like a thief in the night" (5:2). Paul has already signaled the return to previously shared material in the opening verse by stating that "you have no need to be written to" (5:1b) about the day of the Lord, since as the following verse spells out, "you yourselves accurately know" about that specific subject.

The shift in the different forms of the disclosure formula, therefore, reveals different degrees of Paul's pleasure or displeasure with his Thessalonian readers, as well as other information that is key to interpreting the text properly. The matters covered in the first paragraph (4:1–12)—the call to lead lives of holiness in their sexual conduct (4:3–8) and to demonstrate brotherly and sisterly love (4:9–12)—are already known to the Thessalonian believers. Hence Paul is justifiably disappointed with his converts in Thessalonica, a disappointment reflected in his cool tone, serious warning statements, and strong language (e.g., 4:6b, "the Lord is an avenger . . . as we solemnly warned"; 4:8, "rejects not a human being but God"; 4:11b, "just as we commanded you").

On the matter covered in the second paragraph (4:13–18), however, Paul is not displeased with his readers: he cannot fault them for not knowing what he has not yet taught them! Consequently, his tone is softer, and he is very pastoral in his response. Although he has taught the Thessalonians about the bodily resurrection of believers at Christ's return, he has not provided them with sufficient details about the way the resurrection of deceased believers coordinates with Christ's return so that they need not grieve excessively over "those who are asleep." He thus presents never-taught-before material in 4:13–18 with the pastoral goal that his readers be comforted, as is clear from the paragraph's pastoral closing in 4:18: "Therefore comfort one another with these words."

On the matter covered in the third paragraph (5:1–11), Paul signals twice that he is returning to previously shared material: the Thessalonians' existing knowledge about the fate of living believers on the day of the Lord is both implied in the expression "you have no need to be written to" (5:1b) and stated explicitly in the abbreviated disclosure formula "you know" (5:2). This double reference emphasizes the knowledge that the Thessalonians already have on this subject—an emphasis further stressed by the addition of both a personal pronoun and an adverb to the disclosure formula: "you *yourselves* know this *accurately*." This heavy emphasis on the Thessalonians' previous knowledge might be seen as a justification for Paul to be that much more indignant about their fear of the day of the Lord and that much more justified in his rebuke of them. The context, however, makes it clear that Paul's heavy emphasis on the Thessalonians' previous knowledge is instead intended to comfort his readers. In sharp contrast to the rest of humanity who are ignorant about the day of the Lord, the believers in Thessalonica are sufficiently informed about that eschatological event such that they will not be surprised by it or fear its coming. In this case Paul's emphasis on what his readers already know, therefore, is intended not to rebuke them but to comfort them, as is clear once again from the paragraph's pastoral closing in 5:11: "Therefore comfort one another and build each other up."

"Now About" Formula

FORM

Another epistolary convention widely used in Greco-Roman letters is the "now about" formula. This convention, roughly equivalent to the abbreviation "re:" ("regarding") used in modern correspondence, has a simple and fixed two-part form in Greek: it consists of the preposition "about, concerning" (*peri*), which normally takes its object in the genitive case, and the adversative particle "now, but" (*de*). This two-part formula in Greek (*peri de*) is rendered in various ways in Bible translations: "now about," "now concerning," or "but concerning." The "now about" formula is placed at the head of the sentence in a position of emphasis rather than after the main verb, where prepositional phrases like this are typically located.

FUNCTION

The first specific study of the "now about" formula was conducted by Chalmer Faw (1952), whose analysis of this epistolary convention in the Pauline letters and four other NT texts led him to conclude that it "is a formula of reply to specific questions or problems" and that "in Pauline usage it is confined to the answering of specific questions or problems brought up in letters from the churches to which he is writing" (1952: 221). A subsequent and much more comprehensive study by Margaret Mitchell (1989) of the "now about" formula in ancient Greek literary texts and both literary and private letters demonstrated that Faw's conclusions overstated the function of this epistolary convention and that its use needed to be more carefully nuanced. Mitchell's analysis convincingly showed four things:

1. The "now about" formula should not be identified narrowly as a "formula of reply" or "answering formula." Although it *can* be used to respond

to specific questions, it is not restricted to this use but can also be used by the author to introduce a new topic that the author chooses to raise.

2. The "now about" formula does not require the existence of a previous letter sent to the author. The formula can also be used to respond to a question given orally or, as the first point above highlights, no question at all but a new topic that the author chooses to raise.

3. When the "now about" formula occurs multiple times in the same document or letter, it does not provide information about the order in which questions were originally posed to the author. The author can arrange the sequence of responses to follow his own strategic purposes.

4. When the "now about" formula occurs, there is no reason to assume that this is the only way an author could introduce a new topic in the rest of the letter. There are several topic-changing formulas that an author could use within the same document, regardless of how the topic has come to be known.

These observations lead Mitchell to the following definition of the "now about" formula: it "is simply a topic marker, a shorthand way of introducing the next subject of discussion. . . . By the formula *peri de* an author introduces a new topic the only requirement of which is that it is readily known to both author and reader" (1989: 234).

Interpretive Significance

The "now about" formula, which occurs seven times in 1 Corinthians (7:1, 25; 8:1, 4; 12:1; 16:1, 12), provides key epistolary evidence for both the composition and internal structure of this letter. Paul composes the letter during his lengthy stay in Ephesus in response to two different pieces of information that he received about the Corinthian church. First, he received an *oral report* from members of the household of Chloe, likely a wealthy businesswoman in Ephesus, whose employees had just returned from Corinth, where they learned about several embarrassing problems in the local church (1:11, "For it has been reported to me by Chloe's people that . . ."; see also 5:1, "It is actually reported that . . ."). Second, he also received a *letter* sent to him from the Corinthian church (7:1, "Now about the matters of which you wrote . . ."). The letter body of 1 Corinthians, therefore, falls into two major halves: chapters 1–6, where Paul responds to the oral report, and chapters 7–16, where he responds to their written letter.

For the most part the structure for the second half of the letter body is in turn signaled by the multiple occurrences of the "now about" formula as

Paul takes up the various topics and questions raised in the letter that the Corinthians have just sent him. As noted above, the mere presence of the "now about" formula does not require the existence of a previous letter sent to Paul by the Corinthians, since letter writers of the ancient world used this formula to respond also to oral reports or to introduce new topics that the author chose to raise. Nevertheless, since Paul explicitly refers to a previous letter he received from the Corinthian church (1 Cor. 7:1), it is reasonable to conclude that the apostle's use of the "now about" formula does respond to a series of questions that they raised:

Table 4.2: The "Now About" Formula in 1 Corinthians

7:1	*"Now about the matters which you wrote"*: formula introduces the unit of 7:1–24, which covers a variety of topics closely connected and under the broad theme of marriage.
7:25	*"Now about virgins"*: formula introduces the unit of 7:25–40, which covers additional matters related to the broad theme of marriage.
8:1	*"Now about meat sacrificed to idols"*: formula introduces the unit of 8:1–11:1, on whether Christians are permitted to participate in cultic meals.
12:1	*"Now about spiritual gifts"*: formula introduces the unit of 12:1–14:40, dealing with the Corinthians' misuse of speaking in tongues, which only builds up the individual tongues speaker, rather than practicing various spiritual gifts according to the principle of love, which builds up all members of the church.
16:1	*"Now about the collection for the saints"*: formula introduces the unit of 16:1–11, giving specific instructions on how the Corinthians can contribute financially to the relief offering that Paul is collecting for needy Jewish Christians in Jerusalem.
16:12	*"Now about Apollos"*: formula introduces a brief comment about the travel plans of Apollos, who played an important role in the history of the Corinthian congregation.

Although the "now about" formula provides the necessary key for discerning the internal structure of the second half of 1 Corinthians, two sections are not introduced by this epistolary convention: 11:2–34, which deals with two issues related to Corinthian worship gatherings: the role of women (vv. 2–16) and divisions in their Lord's Supper celebrations (vv. 17–34); and 15:1–58, which deals with the bodily resurrection of believers. The absence of this formula in introducing these two passages should not be seen as evidence against the literary integrity of 1 Corinthians. There is no support for partition theories that assume that all the sections in the letter introduced with the "now about" formula belong to a single letter and that sections introduced without this formula come from a separate correspondence and were incorporated later into the existing document (for the various partition theories of 1 Corinthians, see Merklein 1984; Hurd 1983: 43–47; Thiselton

2000: 36–39). The survey of the "now about" formula by Mitchell (1989) demonstrates that an author could choose from among several topic-changing formulas within the same document, regardless of how the topic has come to be known. Thus it is not problematic for the unity of 1 Corinthians that Paul introduces his discussion of the resurrection with a different transitional formula, namely, the disclosure formula (15:1, "I make known to you, brothers and sisters, . . ."). And though not a widely used epistolary convention, Paul does have an introductory formula to signal the beginning of both his discussion of women and worship (11:2, "I praise you because . . . ," followed by the disclosure formula in 11:3, "I want you to know that . . .") and of the Lord's Supper and worship (11:17, "I do not praise you because . . .").

The "now about" formula also occurs three times in 1 Thessalonians to introduce three paragraphs that all follow immediately after each other:

Table 4.3: The "Now About" Formula in 1 Thessalonians

4:9	*"Now about brotherly and sisterly love"*: formula introduces the unit of 4:9–12, which affirms the mutual love already occurring in the Thessalonian church but also exhorts certain idle members not to take advantage of this mutual love by not working and relying on the hospitality of fellow congregational members.
4:13	*"Now . . . about those who are asleep"*: formula introduces the unit of 4:13–18, which comforts the Thessalonian church about the fate of deceased members at Christ's return (the "now about" formula here does not occur at the head of the sentence, as it normally does, but has been moved to a later position due to the addition of the disclosure formula).
5:1	*"Now about the times and the seasons"*: formula introduces the unit of 5:1–11, which comforts the Thessalonian church about the fate of living members at Christ's return.

These three incidences of the "now about" formula in 1 Thessalonians, like its multiple occurrences in 1 Corinthians, illustrate again its function in marking a transition from one major unit or main topic to another. This formula introduces Paul's response to a letter sent to him from the Corinthians (1 Cor. 7:1), which has led several commentators to conclude that the apostle here is similarly responding to a letter sent to him from the Thessalonians, who asked him specific questions about the practice of mutual love (1 Thess. 4:9), the fate of deceased believers at Christ's return (4:13), and the fate of living believers at "the times and the seasons" (5:1) connected with the final judgment (so Milligan 1908: 126; Frame 1912: 140, 157; Faw 1952; Masson 1957: 51–52; Malherbe 2000: 217, 243, 255; Green 2002: 202). We have already seen, however, that the use of the "now about" formula need not necessarily imply the existence of a previous letter. Since there is no explicit reference to a letter from the Thessalonians as there was for the Corinthians (1 Cor. 7:1), it is better to conclude that each occurrence of the "now about" formula introduces a new subject that Paul raises in response to the oral report brought to him from Thessalonica by Timothy (1 Thess. 3:6, "But Timothy has now come to us from you and has brought good news about your faith and love . . .").

Vocative Form of Address

FORM

The most common marker of transition by far in Paul's letters is his use of the vocative form of address. The specific word chosen by the apostle to address his readers is the plural "brothers," which is increasingly translated in Bibles as "brothers and sisters" to signal to the modern reader that the apostle does not have only male believers in view as his target audience. In a few rare cases, Paul will vary his vocative form of address, either adding the exclamatory particle "O" beforehand and an adjective or substituting the expected "brothers and sisters" with a different noun: "O foolish Galatians" (Gal. 3:1); "O man" (Rom. 2:1, 3; 9:20); "O Corinthians" (2 Cor. 6:11); "O Philippians" (Phil. 4:15); "O man of God" (1 Tim. 6:11); "O Timothy" (1 Tim. 6:20). The vocative is unique in the Greek language because it has no syntactical relationship to the main clause. Consequently, it is marked off from the rest of the sentence in English translations with a comma, both before and after the form of address (except when the form of address is located at the head of the sentence), and in this way can be easily recognized even by the nonspecialist in the Greek language, as with "I appeal to you, brothers and sisters, by the name of our Lord Jesus Christ, that . . ." (1 Cor. 1:10); "For consider your call, brothers and sisters, that . . ." (1:26); "When I came to you, brothers and sisters, I did not come . . ." (2:1); "But I, brothers and sisters, could not speak to you as . . ." (3:1).

FUNCTION

In addition to its grammatical function as a form of address, the vocative also has a literary function: as a transition marker indicating either a major or minor shift in Paul's argument. This transitional function has already been amply demonstrated in the examples cited above involving the appeal formula and disclosure formula, where the vocative form of address is often added to strengthen the impact of these epistolary conventions. Additional examples can be easily seen in any of Paul's letters.

The vocative form of address also signals to Paul's readers the nature of the apostle's relationship with them and whether he is pleased or displeased with them. If the apostle simply used the vocative form of address as a literary device by which to mark important transitions in his letter, he could have accomplished this with a neutral title that was either based on his readers' location (such as "Corinthians" in 2 Cor. 6:11 or "Philippians" in Phil. 4:15) or more generic (such as "O men and women," a natural extension of "O man" in Rom. 2:1, 3; 9:20). That Paul almost always chose not to use neutral or generic titles such as these, then, is significant and revelatory.

His emotive exclamation "O foolish Galatians" (Gal. 3:1), for example, does two important things. First, by identifying the readers as "Galatians," Paul "effectively refocuses their attention explicitly on their own situation in Galatia—a very apt place to do so, as he has just recounted what happened in Antioch and has made it transparent for the Galatian situation" (Tolmie 2005: 103). Second, by identifying the readers also as "foolish," Paul powerfully rebukes them and conveys how seriously he views their spiritual condition. As Richard Longenecker (1990: 99) notes, the vocative "O foolish Galatians" is "biting and aggressive in tone. Yet more than just a reprimand, it expresses Paul's deep concern, exasperation, and perplexity." Paul's predominant choice of address, "brothers and sisters," is likewise significant. It should be read not merely as a generic reference to Christians (as is typically done by modern readers, probably due its high frequency in Paul's letters) but as giving his original readers a clear signal of his fondness and familial love for them.

INTERPRETIVE SIGNIFICANCE

Despite its relatively brief three-chapter length, 2 Thessalonians has seven occurrences of the vocative form of address "brothers and sisters," all of them signaling not only important shifts (both major and minor) in his treatment of key topics in the letter but also his deep affection for his Thessalonian readers.

The major transition from the letter opening (1:1–2) to the thanksgiving (1:3–12) is marked by the first occurrence of the vocative form of address: "We ought to give thanks to God always concerning you, brothers and sisters, as it is fitting, because . . ." (1:3). That this vocative address is not typically part of the thanksgiving section but occurs only in the thanksgivings of the Thessalonian correspondence is significant and stresses the affectionate relationship that Paul enjoys with this congregation. This vocative address was used heavily in 1 Thessalonians to characterize the relationship between the apostle and his readers (1:4; 2:1, 9, 14, 17; 3:7; 4:1, 10b, 13; 5:1, 4, 12, 14, 25), as were intimate family metaphors such as "infants" (2:7b), "nursing mother (2:7c), "father" (2:11), and "orphaned" (2:17). The use of the vocative "brothers and sisters" here in 2 Thess. 1:3 in a letter written to the same audience only a short time later, therefore, continues this use of kinship language and, along with the emphatic "we ourselves" in the following verse, stresses the affectionate nature of the relationship that exists between Paul and his converts in Thessalonica. There is no justification, therefore, for the claim made by some scholars that the apostle's language here is decidedly distant and cool compared to the intimacy and warmth of his other thanksgivings, and that Paul's authorship of the letter is consequently in doubt (so, e.g., Dibelius 1937: 33; Bailey 1978–79: 137; Trilling 1980: 43–44; Furnish 2007: 132). This interpretation fails to recognize not only Paul's strategic and unique addition of the vocative "brothers and sisters" to the thanksgiving but also his exuberant commendation that the Thessalonians' faith is "growing *abundantly*" (the prefix *hyper* before the verb *auxanō* adds emphasis) so that he proudly boasts about them to other churches (2 Thess. 1:3).

The next major transition from the thanksgiving (2 Thess. 1:3–12) to the body of the letter (2:1–3:15) is similarly signaled by the vocative form of address, which is added to two other epistolary conventions that typically mark a key shift in the letter: the appeal formula (here with the synonym "ask" instead of "appeal") and the "now about" formula:[2] "Now we ask you, brothers and sisters, about the coming of our Lord Jesus Christ and our gathering to him, that . . ." (2:1). The first of the two key topics taken up in the body of the letter deals with comforting the Thessalonians concerning a false claim about the day of the Lord (2:1–17). Two minor shifts in Paul's treatment of this topic are signaled by the third and fourth occurrences of the vocative form of address: the comfort in knowing that God ensures the salvation of the Thessalonian believers (vv. 13–14) and the command to stand firm by holding fast to Paul's teachings (v. 15).

The only other key topic taken up in the body of the letter deals with the problem of idle members within the Thessalonian church (3:1–15). The major shift to this new subject is signaled by two more occurrences of the vocative form of address (the fifth and sixth occurrences in the letter): one to introduce the general exhortations (vv. 1–5) that set the stage for this sensitive topic (v. 1: "Finally, brothers and sisters, . . .") and the other to introduce the specific exhortations (vv. 6–15) that deal with disciplining the rebellious idlers (v. 6, "But we command you, brothers and sisters, in the name of our Lord Jesus Christ that you keep away from every believer who continues to walk in a rebelliously idle manner"). The presence of these two occurrences of the vocative "brothers and sisters" also serves to stress the intimate bond that

---

2. The Greek prepositional phrase *hyper de* used here is likely a synonym for the epistolary formula *peri de*.

Paul enjoys with his Thessalonian readers and so makes them more disposed to obey the exhortations, both general (vv. 1–5) and specific (vv. 6–15), that he is about to give.

The seventh and final occurrence of the vocative form of address in verse 13, along with the emphatic personal pronoun "you," signals a minor shift within 3:1–15; Paul leaves behind his words of application directed narrowly to the idle members within the Thessalonian congregation (vv. 11–12) and issues closing commands that are more broadly aimed at the church as a whole (vv. 13–15). Paul's choice to introduce this final unit with the vocative "brothers and sisters" may be linked to his climactic exhortation within this same unit that the Thessalonian church as a whole should not consider the disciplined person "as an enemy" but rather admonish him or her "as a brother or sister" (v. 15). The apostle who consistently and repeatedly identifies his Thessalonian readers as "brothers and sisters" now calls on them to treat idle members in the same loving and familial way.

Autobiographical Section

Form

The body of Paul's letters often contain a section that belongs to the genre of autobiography or autobiographical report—a section of the letter in which the apostle provides a self-description of his past activities.[3] Although these autobiographical sections do not possess any recognizable structure or other formal elements, they nevertheless can be identified and distinguished from their surrounding material by a common subject matter: Paul's life and the gospel he preaches. Another common feature of these autobiographical sections is their location: they are positioned at the beginning of the letter body, immediately following the thanksgiving section (Rom. 1:11–16a; 2 Cor. 1:8–2:17, continued in 7:5–16 and 10:7–12:13; Gal. 1:11–2:21; Phil. 1:12–26; 3:2–14; 1 Thess. 2:1–16).

Function

Traditionally these autobiographical reports have been understood to function not merely as sources of information about Paul's life but as vindication and reaffirmation of his authority over the letter recipients. Paul is not so vain and narcissistic that he simply wants his readers to be knowledgeable about the

---

3. The fullest treatment of the autobiographical statements in Paul's letters is the monograph of Lyons 1985; see also Roetzel 1982: 34–35; Gaventa 1986; Aune 1987: 189–90.

various activities of his past life. Instead he knows that a message is intricately connected with its messenger, and that questions about his character and authority naturally lead to questions about the trustworthiness and truthfulness of his gospel. The apostle, therefore, uses the autobiographical sections to answer questions and even criticisms about his role as a gospel messenger in order to bolster his readers' confidence in his gospel message. David Aune (1987: 189–90) explains the traditional understanding of Paul's autobiographical sections: "Such statements . . . are often understood as attempts by Paul to defend himself and his gospel from the accusation of opponents."

This apologetic or defensive function explains why these autobiographical sections are located at the beginning of the letter body. If Paul wants to ensure that the contents of his letter will be accepted and obeyed, it is necessary for him to respond at the outset to any criticisms that may be directed against him and so win back the trust and confidence of his readers. As Hendrikus Boers (1975–76: 153) observes: "In most of Paul's letters, after the thanksgiving, characteristically follows as a discrete section the apostolic apology in which the apostle speaks of himself and the gospel he proclaims, evidently to establish or reaffirm himself and his proclamation with his readers."

The apologetic function of the autobiographical reports, however, is strongly rejected by George Lyons (1985) in his extensive study of this epistolary section in two of Paul's letters: Gal. 1:11–2:21 and 1 Thess. 2:1–16. Lyons argues that the apostle's self-descriptions are intended to provide his readers with a concrete illustration of someone who exemplifies the gospel. The autobiographical reports, therefore, have an implicit paraenetic, or exhortative, function:

> Succinctly and simply put, Paul's autobiographical remarks function not to distinguish him from his converts nor to defend his person or authority but to establish his *ethos* as an "incarnation" of the gospel of Jesus Christ. He highlights his "autobiography" in the interests of this gospel and his readers. He is concerned that, by imitating him, they too should incarnate the gospel. . . . His autobiographical remarks rarely supplement the major concern of a letter, but rather support it by means of a flesh-and-blood illustration. (Lyons 1985: 226–27)

Although the majority of scholars have not found Lyons's argument convincing for the autobiographical statements in Gal. 1:11–2:21, there has been a rather wide acceptance of his analysis of Paul's self-description in 1 Thess. 2:1–16. This endorsement is largely due to a significant shift that had already taken place in scholarship regarding the perceived function of this specific passage. Thus I leave this general discussion of Paul's autobiographical statements and turn to the more narrow issue of the function of 1 Thess. 2:1–16.

Interpretative Significance

There is widespread agreement that 1 Thess. 2:1–16 should be formally identified as an autobiographical section. The key verses of this passage read as follows:

[1]For you yourselves know, brothers and sisters, about our visit to you, namely, that it was not insincere, [2]but though we had suffered beforehand and had been shamefully mistreated in Philippi, as you know, we had courage in our God to speak to you the gospel of God in spite of great opposition. [3]For our appeal was not from deception, nor from an impure motive, nor made with deceit, [4]but as we have been examined by God to be entrusted with the gospel, so we speak, not as those who please people but those who please God, the one who examines our hearts. [5]For we never came with a word of flattery (as you know), nor with a motive of greed (God is our witness!), [6]nor were we demanding honor from people, neither from you nor from others [7](even though we could have insisted on our importance as apostles of Christ), but we became infants among you. As a nursing mother cherishes her own children, [8]so we, because we cared so much for you, were pleased to share with you not only the gospel of God but also our own selves, because you became beloved to us. [9]For you remember, brothers and sisters, our labor and toil; while working night and day in order not to burden any of you, we preached to you the gospel of God. [10]You are witnesses, and God also, how holy and righteous and blameless we were to you believers, [11]just as you know how we dealt with each one of you like a father with his children, [12]appealing and encouraging and imploring you in order that you may lead a life worthy of God, the one who is calling you into his own kingdom and glory.

But while there exists a consensus that this passage belongs to the epistolary category of autobiography, there is sharp disagreement over its function: Is Paul recounting his past actions during his mission-founding visit in Thessalonica in order to defend himself from real or potential accusations (the traditional apologetic function) or to present himself as a model for his readers to imitate (the challenging exhortative function)?

Until relatively recent times there had been widespread agreement that Paul in 1 Thess. 2:1–16 was in some real sense defending himself. Although some claimed that Paul was under attack from *inside* the church,[4] the vast majority, under the influence of Acts 17:1–9, saw the charges as coming from *outside* the church, namely, from unbelieving Jews in Thessalonica.[5] But while scholars

---

4. From either Judaizers (Hendriksen 1955: 11; Neil 1957: xv–xvi, 33–47), gnostics (Schmithals 1972: 128–218; Harnisch 1973), spiritual enthusiasts (Lütgert 1909; Jewett 1972), or millenarians (Meeks 1983; Jewett 1986: 102–4, 159–78).

5. E.g., Milligan 1908: xxxi–xxxii; Lake 1911: 76; Frame 1912: 9–10, 90; Plummer 1918: xvii–xviii, 17–18; Morris 1959: 22; Unger 1962: 40–41; Holtz 1986: 65–66.

debated the exact identity of Paul's opponents in Thessalonica, they did agree that Paul in 1 Thess. 2:1–16 was defending himself from actual accusations and that the function of this autobiographical section was apologetic. Thus in the late 1960s Walter Schmithals (1972: 151) could say with justification: "On this point the exegetes from the time of the Fathers down to the last century have never been in doubt."

The situation dramatically changed, however, with the publication of Abraham Malherbe's 1970 article that highlighted the striking parallels in language and thought between Paul in this passage and the orator-turned-Cynic-philosopher Dio Chrysostom (AD 40–120) in his Alexandrian oration (*Oration* 32).[6] In this speech, Dio raises a several problems with the actions and motives of certain Cynic philosophers and contrasts this with the character-istics found in a true philosopher. Since Dio in this speech is not responding to any specific accusations made against him personally, Malherbe assumed that Paul in 2:1–16 was also not defending himself against actual accusations. Instead, the antithetical statements ("not *x* but *y*") of this passage should be viewed as a traditional theme and common vocabulary of the philosopher depicting himself. Malherbe concluded, therefore, that the function of 2:1–16 is not defensive but exhortative: Paul is presenting the behavior of himself and his fellow missionaries as a model for the Thessalonian believers to follow. Malherbe's article, along with the later study of Pauline autobiography by Lyons (1985), caused a paradigmatic shift to take place in biblical scholar-ship concerning the function of 2:1–16. The widespread agreement among interpreters today is that the autobiographical statements of this passage have an exclusively exemplary or paraenetic function and that the traditional defensive function is no longer a realistic option.[7]

Despite this new consensus, there are compelling grounds for viewing the primary function of 2:1–16 as defensive or apologetic (Weima 1997a; 2014: 121–25).

1. There is the evidence of the unexpected reference to the mission-founding activity of Paul and his coworkers in 1:5 as part of the thanksgiving (1:2–10). The significance of this verse becomes clear through a comparison of this thanksgiving with the thanksgivings of Paul's other letters. Whereas in his other thanksgivings Paul focuses on *his readers* and his thanksgiving to God for *them*, here in 1:5 Paul focuses on *himself* and the righteous

---

6. Malherbe (1970) developed the earlier claims of Martin Dibelius (1937: 7–11).

7. So, e.g., Stegemann 1985; Wanamaker 1990: 91, 101; Schoon-Janssen 1991: 39–65; Richard 1995: 88–89; Walton 1995; Gaventa 1998: 5–6; Holmes 1998: 60; Malherbe 2000: 79–81, 134; Shogren 2012: 81–83.

character of *his* activity among them. The picture is of Pastor Paul starting off as he normally does in the thanksgiving section, first pointing his finger straight up to heaven as he directs his thanksgiving to God ("We give thanks to God . . .") and then pointing his finger at the Thessalonian readers for what God is doing in and through their lives ("because we constantly remember your work of faith and labor of love and steadfastness of hope . . ."). What comes next, however, is not typical, as Paul unexpectedly points his finger back to himself as he defends how he conducted himself during his mission-founding visit in Thessalonica ("our gospel was not among you in word alone but also in power—both in the Holy Spirit and much conviction, as you know what kind of men we were among you because of you"). One is struck, however, not just by the mere presence of this unparalleled statement in a thanksgiving section but also by the prominent location (before the additional causes of thanksgiving in 1:6–10), the length, and the defensive tone of this verse. Because the thanksgiving section typically functions to foreshadow the central issues of the letter as a whole, it appears that Paul in 1 Thessalonians is very much concerned about defending his character and already here in the thanksgiving anticipates the lengthy defense that he will present in 2:1–16.

2. A defensive function for 2:1–16 is supported by the apostolic parousia—a section of the letter in which Paul seeks to make his parousia, or "presence," more powerfully felt among his readers—found in the immediately following passage of 2:17–3:10 (a fuller discussion of this epistolary convention is given later in this chapter). Paul uses this epistolary convention in 1 Thessalonians to reassure the believers of his continued love and care for them. The need for Paul to reassure the Thessalonians of this was due to his sudden separation from them (2:17–20) and the following persecution (3:1–5) that they had to endure—events that apparently left Paul feeling vulnerable to criticism for his failure thus far to return to them. Thus there exists a parallel between the function of the apostolic parousia of 2:17–3:10 and the autobiographical section of 2:1–16. Just as 2:17–3:10 is a defense of Paul's *present* absence from the Thessalonians, so also 2:1–16 is a defense of Paul's *past* ministry among them.

3. A variety of unique features of the antithetical statements ("not *x* but *y*") in 2:1–16 provide still further evidence that Paul is very much concerned with defending the integrity of his character and actions during his mission-founding work among them. One such unique feature is Paul's double appeal to God as a "witness" (2:5, 10). The apostle rarely invokes God as a witness in his letters (elsewhere only in Rom. 1:9; 2 Cor. 1:23;

Phil. 1:8), and our passage is the only place where he does it twice. Another notable feature is Paul's twofold claim in 2:4 that God has "examined" him and his coworkers ("we have been examined by God to be entrusted with the gospel . . . God, the one who examines our hearts"). Elsewhere Paul always uses the verb "examine" (*dokimazō*) in the active voice with a human person or group of persons as its subject, but only here does he use it in the passive voice with God as its subject. This striking twofold reference in 2:4 to God's activity of "examining" the missionaries adds significant weight to the legal-like language of 2:5 and 2:10, where the apostle appeals to God and the Thessalonians as witnesses and so further supports a polemical context.

4. Perhaps the most important feature about the antithetical statements in 2:1–16 is their frequency. Eight such statements can be found elsewhere in 1 Thessalonians (1:5, 8; 2:17; 4:7, 8; 5:6, 9, 15). These antithetical statements, however, are scattered throughout the letter, whereas five occurrences can be found in just the first eight verses of 2:1–16 (vv. 1–2, 3–4, 4b, 5–7a, 8b; see also 2:13). Furthermore, in contrast to the other antithetical statements in the letter, all five instances in 2:1–8 are autobiographical: they refer to Paul and his coworkers. Finally, some of these five autobiographical antithetical statements are clearly being emphasized with the repeated use of the negative: there is a threefold occurrence of the negative in the antithetical statement of 2:3–4 and a fivefold occurrence of the negative in the antithetical statement of 2:5–7a. Therefore, although the mere presence of antithetical statements does not necessarily prove the existence of a polemical context, the several unique features of the antithetical statements in 2:1–16 strongly suggest that Paul here is not merely presenting himself as a model to be imitated but rather is countering accusations of some kind. When it is further recognized that Paul explicitly identifies opponents who are persecuting the church (2:14, "your own fellow citizens"), this creates an even greater presumption that the antithetical statements of 2:1–16, even if they have a rhetorical flair, correspond to a historical reality.

5. The traditional defensive function of 2:1–16 gains still further support when we consider Paul's repeated appeals to the Thessalonians' firsthand experience of his character and conduct during his original ministry among them. The disclosure formula in the abbreviated form "you know" occurs eight times in the letter as a whole, with fully half of these occurrences in our relatively brief passage (2:1, 2, 5, 11; see also 1:5; 3:3–4; 4:2; 5:2). There is yet another appeal to the Thessalonians' personal experience

of Paul in 2:9, in the introductory expression "For you remember, brothers and sisters." His appeal to God as a witness in 2:10 ("You and God are witnesses") also includes the Thessalonian believers themselves (note the emphatic position of "you") as those who observed the "holy, righteous, and blameless" conduct of the missionaries with their own eyes. Thus Paul makes no less than six explicit appeals in 2:1–16 to the firsthand experience that the readers had with him during his original ministry among them. These repeated appeals are not, as elsewhere in the letter, focused on the teaching and commands that the apostle has previously shared with them (so 3:3; 4:2; 5:2) but on the moral conduct and behavior of Paul during his original ministry among them.

The evidence surveyed above indicates that modern interpreters have too quickly abandoned the long-held view that Paul in 1 Thess. 2:1–16 is in some real sense defending himself (so also Still 1999: 137–49; Holtz 2000; S. Kim 2005; Fee 2009: 52–53). Although not all the factors discussed above are equally significant, they have the cumulative effect of legitimizing the claim that the primary function of this passage is defensive or apologetic. Non-Christians in Thessalonica—the "fellow citizens" (2:14) of the believers in that city—not only oppressed and harassed the church but also raised questions about the integrity of its founder, Paul, and his coworkers. Although the Thessalonian believers did not buy into these charges, in the context of a young church separated from its leader and under heavy social pressure to resume their former pagan practices, Paul feels the need to answer these accusations. He effectively accomplishes this goal by beginning the letter body with an autobiographical reminder of his original ministry among them, which in a pointed fashion defends his integrity and that of his fellow missionaries and so reestablishes the trust and confidence of his readers. Renewed trust in the apostle (and so also in his message) would not only encourage the Thessalonian believers to stand firm in the midst of heavy social pressures (esp. 3:1–10) but also ensure that they would obey the instructions that he will give them in the second half of the letter (4:1–5:22).

Apostolic Parousia

Another epistolary convention often used by Paul in his letters is the "apostolic parousia."[8] The Greek word *parousia* has not only the sense of "coming,

8. See the discussion of this epistolary convention in Funk 1967; White 1972: 98–109; Boers 1975–76: esp. 146–49, 153; Aune 1987: 190–91; Schnider and Stenger 1987: 92–107; Jervis 1991: 110–31; Trebilco 1993; Johnson 2006; Luckensmeyer 2009: 60–61.

arrival" (this term in the NT often refers to the second coming of Jesus) but also "presence." The term "apostolic parousia," therefore, refers to a section of the letter where Paul is particularly concerned to make his "presence" felt by his readers. The apostle, of course, is already present in some sense to the recipients through the reading of the letter, which is a substitute for his actual presence. Yet his letters often contain a distinct section where Paul tries to make his presence more fully felt by the recipients. The most effective way he accomplishes this is by referring to a future visit that he plans to make to his readers. When such a visit is not possible, however, Paul makes his presence more powerfully experienced through two alternate means: he refers either to the sending of one of his emissaries for a visit or to the act of writing the letter itself.[9] Some have wrongly focused only on references to visits that Paul himself hoped to make and thus identify such passages as a "travelogue" (so, e.g., Doty 1973: 43; Mullins 1973). There is, however, an important distinction between the terms "travelogue" and "apostolic parousia": travelogue refers in a limited sense to future visits or travels of Paul; apostolic parousia refers more comprehensively to the presence of Paul, whether this is experienced by means of a future visit from the apostle, the arrival of his emissary, or the letter itself (see Funk 1967: 249).

Form

The apostolic parousia as an epistolary convention was first identified and formally analyzed by Robert Funk (1967). Using Rom. 15:14–33 as his model, Funk proposed that the apostolic parousia consists of five major units. Funk's conclusions were later modified by Ann Jervis (1991: 112–14), who uses the three means by which Paul emphasizes his presence to suggest that the apostolic parousia consists instead of three functional units: (1) the Letter Writing Unit, which includes the manner in which Paul is writing, the apostolic authority he has to write, and an appeal for the readers to obey his teaching; (2) the Sending of Emissary Unit, which includes a reference to Paul's dispatch of his emissary, the credentials of this representative, and what Paul expects his envoy to do; and (3) the Apostolic Visit Unit, which includes Paul's stated intention or desire to visit, his submission to God's will regarding this visit, the reason(s) for his past inability to visit, and the reason for the projected visit.

The difficulty with both of these formal analyses is that the parallels between the various apostolic parousias are not great enough to warrant the identification of specific units and subunits. It is better, therefore, to speak

---

9. But see Mitchell (1992), who argues that sometimes it was more effective for Paul not to make a personal visit but to send one of his envoys instead.

of the apostolic parousia as a distinct epistolary convention that exhibits a rather loose form or structure in which certain key words and expressions are frequently found.[10] This means that, in contrast to a comparative analysis of the more formally consistent sections of Paul's letters (i.e., the opening, thanksgiving, and closing), less significance ought to be attached to any variations in form between the various apostolic parousias.

Function

Paul does not inform his readers about his future travel plans and those of his emissaries merely to satisfy their curiosity or to provide details about himself and others for their general interest. Instead, the apostolic parousia is a literary device that Paul uses to exert his authority over his readers. As Funk (1967: 249) observes: "All of these [i.e., references to either Paul's impending visit, the sending of his emissary, or his writing of the letter] are media by which Paul makes his apostolic authority effective in his churches. The underlying theme is therefore the apostolic parousia—the presence of apostolic authority and power." This authoritative function of the apostolic parousia should not be interpreted as a power-hungry ego trip by the apostle but instead as a useful literary means of placing his readers under his authority such that they will obey the contents of the letter. As John White (1984: 1745) asks and answers in a rhetorical fashion: "How does he [Paul] purpose to rectify, if inadequate, or to reinforce, if right-minded, his recipients' present status? By referring to one or another aspect of his apostolic authority and power."

Interpretative Significance

PHILEMON 22

The authoritative function of the apostolic parousia can be most easily seen in Paul's brief letter to Philemon where the apostle announces his impending visit: "At the same time, prepare a guest room for me, for I am hoping through your prayers to be granted to you" (Philem. 22). This is hardly an innocent remark about Paul's travel plans that is tacked on to the end of the letter for Philemon's general interest, nor does it stem simply from the apostle's optimism about being released soon from house arrest in Rome. The statement about Paul's future arrival functions instead as an indirect warning to Philemon: the apostle promises to come to the city of Colossae and check personally

---

10. David Aune 1987: 190: "The absence of a consistent structure [in the apostolic parousia] suggests that we are dealing with a *topos* or theme with a number of subordinate motifs." So also Lyons 1985: 209; Mitchell 1992: 641n3; Luckensmeyer 2009: 60–61.

whether his petition on behalf of the slave Onesimus has been obeyed by the runaway's owner, Philemon. The situation is similar to my telling one of my recently graduated students that I will be attending their local church in a couple of weeks and that I look forward to hearing them preach. No matter how confident my former students may be in their preaching skills, none is ever completely happy to hear me say such words. Although students may outwardly say how nice it will be to see me, inwardly they are apprehensive and anxious, since they know that I will be personally present and able to see firsthand whether they are doing the things I have taught them. Paul uses the apostolic parousia in his letter to Philemon to place added pressure on the slave owner to comply with his appeal.

1 Corinthians 4:14–21

The authoritative function of the apostolic parousia can also be readily seen in 1 Cor. 4:14–21. This passage contains all three of the means by which Paul often emphasizes his presence: a reference to his act of writing the letter (vv. 14–16), his sending to the Corinthian believers one of his representatives (v. 17), and the promise (threat?) of a personal visit to Corinth (vv. 18–21).

First Paul draws his Corinthian readers' attention to the writing of the letter itself: "I am not writing this to shame you but to admonish you as my beloved children" (v. 14). The explicit reference to the act of writing evokes an image of Paul taking up parchment and quill and writing them this letter, with the result that he is more present in the minds and the midst of his Corinthian readers than he was just a few moments earlier when this same letter was merely being read to them by the letter carrier. The image thus evoked is not that of a nanny hired to watch over someone else's children but an authoritative father who is worthy of imitation: "For you might have thousands of child-care workers in Christ, but you do not have many fathers. For I fathered you in Christ Jesus through the gospel. Therefore, I appeal to you, become imitators of me" (vv. 15–16). In the patriarchal society of the Roman world, a father was an imposing figure with unlimited power over his children, and here we see Paul attempting to invoke this authority over the Corinthian readers (Lassen 1991). But not only does Paul present himself as their father; his hyperbolic comparison of himself with thousands of child-care workers stresses that he is their *only* father. As Gordon Fee (1987: 185) observes, "His unique relationship to them was that of 'father,' and that gave him a special authority over and responsibility toward them. With this language, therefore, he is both reasserting his authority and appealing to their loyalty, which had obviously eroded in this church."

The second means by which Paul emphasizes his presence among the Corinthian readers is his reference to sending them one of his most important representatives: "Because of this I am sending to you Timothy, who is my beloved and faithful child in the Lord, who will remind you of my ways, which are in Christ Jesus, just as I teach everywhere in every church" (v. 17). This verse unmistakably implies that Timothy is going as Paul's representative and that Timothy's presence in the Corinthian church should be treated by them as if Paul himself were present in their midst. This sense is conveyed both by the fact that Paul is the one who is sending Timothy to them ("I am sending to you Timothy") and that the purpose of Timothy's mission is to remind the Corinthians of Paul's teachings ("my ways"). Also significant is Paul's description of Timothy as "my beloved and faithful child." Such language is not intended to introduce the Corinthians to someone they do not know (Timothy was with Paul for some, if not much, of his eighteen-month stay in Corinth) but to showcase the credentials of Paul's representative. The apostle is not sending to the Corinthians a mere messenger boy but a beloved child who is amply qualified to represent the teachings of one who is both his and the Corinthians' spiritual father. Paul's presence in the Corinthian congregation, therefore, is enhanced by virtue of his dearly loved and trusted representative, Timothy.

The third way that Paul in this passage stresses his presence lies in his repeated references to a visit that he himself will make to Corinth:

> [18]Some have become arrogant as if I were not coming to you. [19]I will come to you soon, if the Lord wills, and then I will know not the talk of these arrogant people but their power. [20]For the kingdom of God is not a matter of talk but of power. [21]What do you want? Shall I come to you with a rod, or with love in a spirit of gentleness?

Paul's failure to return to Corinth for some years after his eighteen-month, church-founding visit to the city apparently emboldened some members to act in an arrogant manner toward the apostle and assume that he was never coming back. Paul seeks to reassert his authority over such members and those under their influence by referring, no less than three times in these verses, to the reality of a future visit that he will make to Corinth. Paul's third and final reference to his future visit (v. 21) is especially authoritative. His mention of coming "with a rod" refers to the "rod of correction" mentioned extensively in the OT (Exod. 21:20; 2 Sam. 7:14; Prov. 10:13; 13:24; 22:15; 23:13–14; 29:15; Lam. 3:1; Sir. 30:12), recalling the father metaphor from the beginning of the passage. In essence, Paul is asking the Corinthian church: "Do I have to come to you as a father who needs to discipline his wayward children with the rod? Or will my presence among you—in this letter, in my sending Timothy to you, and in my own future visit—cause you to change your attitude and conduct to such a degree that I can come in the way that I prefer to come, namely, with love in a spirit of gentleness?"

1 Thessalonians 2:17–3:10

In the two examples from Philemon and 1 Corinthians, Paul uses the apostolic parousia to exert his authority over his readers and thereby place added pressure on them to obey his exhortations. The apostle, however, can also use this literary device to accomplish different purposes. In 1 Thess. 2:17–3:10, the apostolic parousia fulfills a secondary function. The passage makes extensive use of two of the means by which Paul typically makes his presence more powerfully felt: he mentions his repeated attempts to revisit the Thessalonian converts in person (2:17–20) and his initiative in sending Timothy to them as his representative in order to strengthen their faith despite persecution (3:1–5). The intended function of this apostolic parousia, however, differs from that found elsewhere in Paul's letters. Here the apostle makes his presence more strongly felt among the Thessalonian believers not so much to exert his authority as to reassure them of his continued love and care for them. As Ann Jervis (1991: 116) concludes in her comparative analysis of this epistolary convention: "Thus the dominant function of the apostolic parousia of 1 Thessalonians is to express Paul's love for his Thessalonian converts and to encourage them in their faith."

There was little need for the apostle to emphasize his authority over the Christians in Thessalonica, since he enjoyed a good relationship with them in which his apostolic status and power were not in doubt (note, e.g., the omission of the expected title "apostle" in the letter opening of 1:1). There was a need, however, for Paul to emphasize his ongoing love and concern for the Thessalonian believers, since his sudden separation from them (2:17–20) and the subsequent persecution that they had to endure (3:1–5) apparently left the apostle feeling vulnerable to criticism about his failure to return. The apostolic parousia, therefore, functions as an effective literary device by which Paul emphasizes his presence among the Christians in Thessalonica in such a powerful way that they are reassured of his continued love for them, and any lingering uncertainty over his inability to return is removed. This reassurance of the apostle's love in turn encourages the Thessalonian believers to remain steadfast in their faith despite the persecution that they are currently experiencing.

Paul's emphasis on his apostolic presence in 2:17–3:10, however, also has a larger function in the letter as whole. As with the autobiographical or apostolic defense in 2:1–16, so also the apostolic parousia here in 2:17–3:10 serves to reestablish the trust and confidence of Paul's readers such that they will submit to the exhortative material (paraenesis) that follows in the second half of the letter (4:1–5:22).

Confidence Formula

Another epistolary device in Paul's repertoire of persuasive techniques is an expression of confidence in his readers. Five clear examples of this are found in his existing letters:

Rom. 15:14	And I myself have confidence about you, my brothers and sisters, that you yourselves are full of goodness, filled with all knowledge, and able to instruct one another.
2 Cor. 2:3	being confident about you all that my joy is the joy of you all
Gal. 5:10	I have confidence in the Lord that you will take no other view than mine.
2 Thess. 3:4	And we have confidence in the Lord about you that what things we are commanding, you are indeed doing and will continue to do.
Philem. 21	Confident of your obedience, I write to you, knowing that you will do even more than I say.

Other expressions of confidence can be found in the apostle's correspondence, but these do not express Paul's confidence *in his addressees* and so should be distinguished from the examples cited above. Thus, for example, Paul's statement in Phil. 2:24 ("And I have confidence in the Lord that I myself will come quickly also"), despite having the key verb "to have confidence" expressed in the first person, does not refer to the Philippian readers and so does not provide another instance of this literary device (so also Rom. 8:38; Phil. 1:6, 25).

Form

The identification of a "confidence formula" was first made by John White in his study of the letter body in both nonliterary papyri and Paul's letters (1972: 104–6). On the basis of three Pauline texts (Rom. 15:14; Gal. 5:10; Philem. 21), White discerned a "formula" consisting of four standard elements: (1) the emphatic use of the first-person pronoun "I"; (2) the perfect form of the verb expressing confidence (*pepoitha*); (3) the reason why the speaker is confident; and (4) the content about which the speaker is confident (introduced by the conjunction "that" [*hoti*]). Since White could not find exact parallels of the confidence formula in secular letters of the ancient world, he further proposed that this epistolary device was a Pauline invention.

These observations about both the form and the uniqueness of the confidence formula were subsequently challenged by Stanley Olson (1984; 1985). Instead of a relatively fixed "formula," Olson looked more broadly for "expressions" of confidence that ancient letter writers, including Paul, had in their addressees. Thus, for example, a businessman's statement in a letter to a friend who was helping him in some commercial matter that "I know that you will do everything well" (P.Oxy. 745) and Paul's statement to the Corinthians that "I have great pride in you" (2 Cor. 7:4) qualify for Olson as expressions of confidence, even though the specific verb "to be confident" is lacking. But though Olson consequently concludes that "it is not accurate to speak of *formulas* of confidence," he nevertheless concedes that "in some instances the language is stereotyped and approaches the formulaic" (1985: 295).

Function

The formula or expression of confidence should not be seen as a naïve or innocent remark about how optimistic Paul is that his recipients will do something; rather, it is a persuasive technique used by the apostle to influence the recipients of his letters to act in such a way that they are worthy of the confidence that he has in them. Just as in the exhortative function of the thanksgiving section, where there is an implicit challenge for Paul's readers to live up to the thanksgiving that the apostle brings to God about them (persuasion through praise), so also in the confidence formula there is an implicit challenge for Paul's readers to live up to the confidence that the apostle has in them (persuasion through confidence). As Olson (1985: 289) correctly observes: "The evidence of a variety of parallels suggests that such expressions [of confidence] are usually included to serve the persuasive purpose. Whatever the emotion behind the expression [i.e., whether the expression of confidence is genuine or not], the function is to undergird the letter's requests and admonitions by creating a sense of obligation through praise."

In a similar way, after raising a specific issue with their child, a parent might continue: "You are old enough to make up your own mind on this matter and not to have me as your parent tell you what you ought to do. But I am confident that you will do the right thing." Although such a statement of confidence sounds initially flattering to the recipient, it nonetheless involves the application of pressure. Most children do not like to hear such words, since they feel the sense of obligation not to do what they might really want to do but instead what their parent confidently expects them to do. So also Paul employs the confidence formula to create a sense of obligation among his readers to honor their spiritual father's confidence in them and thus do the things that he wants them to do.

Interpretative Significance

The second and final major topic of 2 Thessalonians deals with the problem of the "rebellious idlers" (*ataktoi*, 1 Thess. 5:14a)—those in the Thessalonian church who refuse to obey Paul's repeated instructions about the need for self-sufficient work and who instead continue to live a lazy lifestyle, taking advantage of the charity of fellow congregational members. The apostle first addressed this problem during his initial visit to Thessalonica (a visit alluded to in 1 Thess. 4:11b; 2 Thess. 3:7–10) and dealt with it again, albeit briefly, in his first letter (1 Thess. 4:11b–12; 5:14a). But instead of getting better, the problem grew worse. And so, for yet a third time and at much greater length, Paul takes up the issue in 2 Thess. 3:1–15.

Paul's exhortations in this lengthy, third treatment of the problem fall into two major units: verses 1–5 and 6–15. Commentators typically fail to see how these two units are meaningfully connected. They question the logic of Paul's argument, claiming that it is "disjointed" (Wanamaker 1990: 273), lacks "unity and focus" (Richard 1995: 373), and is "not altogether clear" (Marshall 1983: 212). But though verses 1–5 deal with disparate topics, they are joined together by a common function: to prepare the readers in Thessalonica to hear and heed the exhortations that come in verses 6–15. Maarten Menken (1994: 125) correctly observes how Paul's general exhortations in 3:1–5 "make them receptive to his specific injunctions that will follow in 3.6–12." Gordon Fee (2009: 310–11) similarly sees that 3:1–5 involves "an introductory word of praise intended to gain a good hearing from them before addressing this difficult issue [those in the church who are rebelliously idle] once more."

One important "introductory word of praise" in 3:1–5, which also provides a crucial verbal link that connects the two units of verses 1–5 and 6–15, involves the occurrence of a confidence formula in verse 4: "And we have confidence in the Lord about you, that what things we are commanding, you are indeed doing and will continue to do." The persuasive function of the confidence formula here should not be missed. Paul's praise of his Thessalonian readers, as evidenced by his earlier statements in this letter (1:3–4), is indeed genuine but by no means innocent. The apostle deliberately uses this expression of confidence to encourage his Thessalonian readers to live up to his expectations by obeying his upcoming commands in 3:6–15 to discipline the idle members of their congregation and to engage in self-sufficient work.

Here Paul's statement of confidence is clarified by two prepositional phrases: "in the Lord" and "about you." The first phrase, similar to the more common "in Christ," refers to the relationship believers have with the Lord Jesus Christ. The second phrase identifies the recipients toward whom Paul's confidence is directed. The apostle's confidence, therefore, is grounded ultimately not in the Thessalonian Christians themselves but rather "in the Lord," that is, the Lord Jesus Christ, and what he is doing in and through these believers. The confidence formula is a logical consequence of Paul's just-stated assertion (v. 3) that the Lord is faithful and will strengthen the Christians in Thessalonica and guard them from the evil one. This also explains why, in the immediately following verse (v. 5), Paul's intercessory prayer for the Thessalonian church is directed to "the Lord," since he is the ultimate power behind the changed lives of these believers.

The substance of Paul's confidence in the Thessalonian congregation is introduced, as it is in the other confidence formulas (Rom. 14:14; 2 Cor. 2:3; Gal. 5:10; Philem. 21), with the conjunction "that" (*hoti*, 2 Thess. 3:4): "that what things we are commanding, you are indeed doing and will continue to do." The apostle draws attention to the relative clause "what things we are commanding" by moving it from its expected position at the end of the main clause to the beginning.

Expected word order	You are indeed doing and will continue to do *what things we are commanding*.
Word order here	*What things we are commanding*, you are indeed doing and will continue to do.

This highlighting of Paul's action of "commanding" foreshadows the key role that this verb will play in verses 6–15, where "command" is emphasized in two ways. It opens the paragraph (v. 6, "But we command you . . ."), and it is repeated twice within the paragraph (v. 10, "For when we were with you, we also were repeatedly commanding this to you . . ."; v. 12, "To such people we command . . ."). There can be little doubt, therefore, that the referent of the action "we are commanding" is found not by looking *back* to the call for the Thessalonians to remember Paul in prayer in verse 1 (so wrongly Light-foot 1904: 127; Marshall 1983: 217) but by looking *ahead* to the commands in verses 6–15 concerning self-sufficient work and how to deal with church members who are rebelliously idle.

The confidence formula of 2 Thess. 3:4, therefore, functions in two important ways within the larger unit of 3:1–15: it provides a crucial verbal link, joining the general exhortations of verses 1–5 to the specific exhortations of verses 6–15, and it places pressure on the Thessalonian readers to live up to Paul's confidence in them by obeying his commands concerning the disciplining of idle members and the need for self-sufficient work that he is about to give them in verses 6–15.

Paraenesis

A significant percentage of material found in the body of Paul's letters falls into a category known to scholars as "paraenesis."[11] This term (sometimes spelled "parenesis") is a transliteration of a Greek noun meaning "exhortation, advice, urging"[12] and refers to traditional moral and religious exhortation dealing with practical issues of living. The ancient epistolary theorist Libanius lists the paraenetic letter as the first of his many types or "styles" of letters, defining such correspondence as "that in which we exhort someone by urging him to pursue something or to avoid something" (Malherbe 1988: 68–71). This is what Paul often does in his letters: exhorting his readers either to follow or to forsake specific behaviors.

In letters from the Greco-Roman world, paraenesis covers a wide range of moral matters such as the handling of finances, labor, slavery, marriage, the upbringing of children, patriotism, sexual conduct, and one's relationships with others, especially friends (the specific subject of "brotherly love" is widely discussed, although this refers to sibling relationships). Paraenesis often involves traditional moral material, reflecting the conventional wisdom that is widely adopted in society; it is general in nature and thus easily applied to many situations; it is so familiar and widely held that it is frequently presented as a reminder to the audience of what they already know and believe; it is commonly illustrated by individuals who serve as models of virtues to be imitated; and it is typically given by those in authority or those who consider themselves to be morally superior to those whom they exhort (Aune 1987: 191; Thompson 1993: 922).

Form

The paraenetic material in Paul's letters does not exhibit a single, identifiable form. Instead, it appears in a variety of expressions, all with the common

11. On this formal category generally, see Bradley 1953; Doty 1973: 37–39; Roetzel 1982: 35–36; Malherbe 1986: 124–29; Stowers 1986: 91–106; Aune 1987: 191, 194–97; Popkes 1996; Thompson 1993.
12. Only the verbal form occurs in the NT (Acts 27:9, 22).

function of instructing Christians on moral matters and how they ought to live. One frequent and simple form of paraenesis involves the use of commands (the imperative mood in Greek). Paul, as a divinely called apostle (in many cases the founder of the church to which he is writing) occupies a position of authority over his readers, giving him the right to command them how to live. Sometimes these commands occur in isolation within a larger discussion. For example, in his reflections on how Christians ought to relate to secular rulers (Rom. 13:1–7), Paul opens with a single command—"Let every person be submissive to the governing authorities" (13:1)—that is then explained and expanded in the following verses. At other times, however, these commands can be clustered together with little elaboration, as is the case in Rom. 12:9–21:

> ⁹Let love be genuine; hate what is evil, hold fast to what is good; ¹⁰love one another with mutual affection; outdo one another in showing honor. ¹¹Do not lag in zeal, be ardent in spirit, serve the Lord. ¹²Rejoice in hope, be patient in suffering, persevere in prayer. ¹³Contribute to the needs of the saints; extend hospitality to strangers. ¹⁴Bless those who persecute you; bless and do not curse them. ¹⁵Rejoice with those who rejoice, weep with those who weep. ¹⁶Live in harmony with one another; do not be haughty, but associate with the lowly; do not claim to be wiser than you are. ¹⁷Do not repay anyone evil for evil, but take thought for what is noble in the sight of all. ¹⁸If it is possible, so far as it depends on you, live peaceably with all. ¹⁹Beloved, never avenge yourselves, but leave room for the wrath of God; for it is written, "Vengeance is mine, I will repay, says the Lord." ²⁰No, "if your enemies are hungry, feed them; if they are thirsty, give them something to drink; for by doing this you will heap burning coals on their heads." ²¹Do not be overcome by evil, but overcome evil with good.

Instead of using commands, Paul also at times expresses his paraenesis in the friendlier, less heavy-handed form of an appeal formula as he urges his readers to live a particular way. The apostle, for example, begins the final major unit of the letter body in Romans (12:1–15:32) by stating: "Therefore, I appeal to you, brothers and sisters, by the mercies of God, to present your bodies as a living sacrifice, holy and acceptable to God, which is your spiritual worship" (12:1).

Paraenesis can be expressed via the confidence formula. As Abraham Malherbe (2000: 446) observes: "Paul on occasion expresses confidence about his readers as a hortatory or paraenetic device, urging upon them precisely what he says he is confident about." This can be seen in the confidence formula directed by Paul to his Roman readers: "And I myself have confidence about you, my brothers and sisters, that you yourselves are full of goodness, filled with all knowledge, and able to instruct one another" (Rom. 15:14). Such a statement places pressure on the believers in Rome to live up to the confidence that Paul has in them to conduct themselves in the manner that he prescribes.

Paul's prayers for his readers also involve paraenesis. By sharing with his readers the specific content of his prayer to God for them, the apostle not so subtly also prompts them to live up to his hopes and expectations for their lives. Paul, for example, deliberately lets his Roman readers hear these specific words of his prayer to God for them: "But may the God of steadfastness and encouragement grant you to think the same thing among one another, in accordance with Christ Jesus, so that you may with one accord, with one mouth, glorify the God and Father of our Lord Jesus Christ" (Rom. 15:5–6). The moral exhortation in the prayer is impossible for the Romans to miss: Paul is urging the house churches in Rome, divided between the "weak" and the "strong," to pursue like-mindedness and unity.

Paul's teaching or didactic material also implicitly involves paraenesis. The apostle never teaches merely for the sake of increasing his readers' level of correct *knowledge*. Instead, his teaching has the goal of increasing the level of correct *conduct*, which ought to be the natural consequence of correct knowledge. This intimate link between Paul's teaching and his paraenesis is made explicit in commands that are introduced with the particle "therefore" (the so-called paraenetic *oun*: Nauck 1958), which frequently connects Paul's exhortations with the instructions that precede them. Consider this brief paragraph from Rom. 13:11–14:

> [11]And do this, knowing the time: it is already the hour for you to wake from sleep. For our salvation is nearer now than when we became believers; [12]the night is far gone, the day is near. *Therefore*, let us put off the works of darkness and put on the armor of light; [13]let us live honorably as in the day, not in reveling and drunkenness, not in debauchery and licentiousness, not in quarreling and jealousy. [14]Instead, put on the Lord Jesus Christ, and make no provision for the flesh, to gratify its desires.

The teaching of verses 11–12a leads logically ("therefore") to the commands of verses 12b–14. Paul first teaches (or, since they already know this, he more accurately reminds) his Roman readers what time it is: the "night" of the present evil age is "far gone," and the "day"—that is, the day of Christ's return, when the future new age finally arrives in its fullness—is "near." For both the Roman readers and the apostle, "our salvation," that is, their final deliverance from sin and death, is closer now than ever before. And it is in light of the impending day of the Lord that Paul "therefore" commands the Roman readers to "put off" the vices associated with the old age (revelry, drunkenness, debauchery, licentiousness, quarreling, and jealousy) and "put on the Lord Jesus Christ," that is, the virtues exemplified in Christ's life and characteristic of his followers.

It is significant that all these examples of different forms of paraenesis come from Rom. 12:1–15:32. This demonstrates the inherent flexibility of paraenesis not only within the same letter but, even more narrowly, within the same major unit of a letter. Paraenesis does not exhibit any single, identifiable form but can be expressed in a variety of ways: with a sole imperative, a cluster of imperatives, an appeal formula, a confidence formula, a prayer, and even teaching. All these diverse forms serve the common function of instructing readers on moral matters and how they ought to live as followers of Jesus Christ.

Nevertheless, there are two distinct literary types of paraenesis that ought to be highlighted. The first distinct type is the *vice and virtue list*. This form of paraenesis involves the cataloging of various vices that are to be avoided (Rom. 1:29–31; 13:13; 1 Cor. 5:10–11; 6:9b–10; 2 Cor. 12:20; Eph. 5:3–5; Col. 3:5, 8; 1 Tim. 1:9–10; 6:4–5; 2 Tim. 3:2–4), virtues that are to be adopted (2 Cor. 6:6–7; Gal. 5:22–23; Eph. 4:2–3), or mixed vice and virtue lists (Gal. 5:19–23; Eph. 4:31–32; Titus 1:7–10). The various vices or virtues are listed without any explanation or applicatory comment and typically without any connective words such as "and," "nor," or "or." These characteristics are illustrated in the fifteen items included in the vice list from Gal. 5:19–21a:

> [19]Now the works of the flesh are plain: sexual immorality, impurity, promiscuity, [20]idolatry, sorcery, enmities, strife, jealousy, anger, selfishness, dissensions, factions, [21]envy, drunkenness, carousing, and these kind of things.

Whereas the vast majority of the vice and virtue lists present their respective items in an impersonal manner as a sinful *thing* to be avoided or a virtue to be embraced, a few of the vice lists refer instead to sinful *people* to be avoided. These lists ought to be more accurately identified as "offender lists," as is the case for the fourteen types of people listed in 1 Tim. 1:9–10:

> [9]knowing this: that the law is not laid down for the just but for the lawless and the disobedient, the ungodly and the sinners, the unholy and the profane, father-killers and mother-killers, murderers, [10]the sexually immoral, those practicing homosexuality, slave traders, liars, perjurers, and whatever else is contrary to sound teaching.

The second distinct literary type of paraenesis is the *household code*.[13] What marks these moral exhortations out as a distinct type is their focus on the reciprocal responsibilities of the various members of the household in the ancient world: wives and husbands, children and parents, slaves and masters. One full expression of the household code is found in Col. 3:18–4:1:

> [18]Wives, be subject to your husbands, as is fitting in the Lord. [19]Husbands, love your wives and never treat them harshly. [20]Children, obey your parents in everything, for this is your acceptable duty in the Lord. [21]Fathers, do not provoke your children, or they will become discouraged. [22]Slaves, obey your earthly masters in everything, not only while being watched and in order to please them, but wholeheartedly, fearing the Lord. [23]Whatever your task, put yourselves into it, as done for the Lord and not for your masters, [24]since you know that from the Lord you will receive the inheritance as your reward; you serve the Lord Christ. [25]For the wrongdoer will be paid back for whatever wrong has been done, and there is no partiality. [4:1]Masters, treat your slaves justly and fairly, for you know that you also have a Master in heaven.

The only other full expression of the household code in Paul's letters occurs in Eph. 5:21–6:9. Yet there are other paraenetic passages in the apostle's correspondence that are very similar in content and tone, and these should be seen as abbreviated expressions of the household code (1 Tim. 2:1–15; 5:1–8; 6:1–2; Titus 2:1–10). Similar household codes also appear not only elsewhere in the NT (1 Pet. 2:11–3:7) but in other early Christian writings (*Didache* 4.9–11; *Barnabas* 19.5–7; *1 Clement* 21.6–9; Ignatius, *To Polycarp* 4.1–5.2; Polycarp, *To the Philippians* 4.2–3).

The topic of "household management" (Greek *oikonomia*) was common in the secular writing of the ancient world, dating back some four hundred years before the time of Paul. Aristotle, for example, argued that the household was the basic building block of the state, and this consequently required a careful discussion of the three main relationships that make up the household: "The primary parts of the household are master and slave, husband and wife, father and children; we ought therefore to examine the proper constitution and character of each of these three relationships" (*Politics* 1.1235b.1–14). The "household codes" are discussed by various Greco-Roman writers and also by Hellenistic Jewish authors. "This form of teaching, then, was 'in the air,' and it is not surprising that New Testament writers utilize it to instruct early Christians in their household responsibilities" (Moo 2008: 294).

13. Scholars often refer to this material with the German word *Haustafeln*, meaning "house-tables."

The content of the household codes in Paul, however, reveal that the apostle is not merely "cutting" a paraenetical form out of existing documents of his day and then "pasting" it into his own letters. Rather, the apostle's exhortations are unique in the way they not only place obligations on the male head of the household in his dealings with others under his roof but also presume a level of worth and dignity for those under his authority. As N. T. Wright (1986: 147) observes: "Paul has thoroughly Christianized the code, not just by adding 'in the Lord' at certain points, but by balancing carefully the duties and responsibilities of the various family members so that the stronger parties have duties as well as rights, and those who are in a position of submission are treated as responsible human beings, with rights as well as duties." In our modern egalitarian age, Paul's household codes sound jarring because of how much power they hand to husbands, fathers, and masters and the submission required from others. In the patriarchal culture of the apostle's day, however, where the male head of the household had absolute power over his wife, children, and slaves, Paul's household codes would have sounded jarring in the way he limits rather than licenses this cultural norm. As Ben Witherington (2007: 187) points out:

> What most distinguishes this household code [in Col. 3:18–4:1] from those of the pagan or Jewish world in general is that Paul is giving strong limiting exhortations to the superordinate person in the family, the husband/father/master. Non-Christian household codes almost always direct exhortations only to the subordinate members of the household. What is new about the code here then is the Christian limitations placed on the head of the household. This is what would stand out to an ancient person hearing Paul's discourse for the first time.

Function

Although paraenesis in Paul's letters does not exhibit a single, identifiable form but is expressed in a variety of ways, all these diverse forms of paraenesis share in common the general function of instructing Christians on moral matters and how they ought to live. The form may vary, but the function remains the same: paraenesis seeks to influence the behavior of readers in the ethical issues of everyday life.

The traditional nature of paraenesis and its easy application to a variety of situations has caused some to argue that the exhortations of NT writers have little, if any, connection with the specific situation of their audience. The thesis of Martin Dibelius (1936), for example, is that the paraenetic sections of the NT are made up of stock ethical maxims, or *topoi* (topics), drawn from the moralistic teachings of the Greco-Roman world and used in only a general fashion without any direct application to matters being discussed. Commentators have often followed this thesis in claiming that many of Paul's exhortations are of only a general nature and do not reflect the actual problems in the churches to which he writes.

This assumption that the apostle simply repeats traditional ethical instruction that has no direct connection to the specific situations faced by the congregations to whom he is writing is thought to be especially true for one of the two distinct forms of paraenesis: the vice and virtue list. William Doty (1973: 57), for example, states, "In every case the virtues or vices listed are not characteristics of the particular community addressed." To test whether this common claim is true, let us consider the two vice (or, more accurately, offender) lists found back-to-back in 1 Cor. 5:9–11:

> [9]I wrote to you in my letter not to associate with sexually immoral persons—[10]not at all meaning the sexually immoral of this world, or the greedy and swindlers, or idolaters, since you would then need to go out of the world. [11]But now I am writing to you not to associate with anyone who bears the name of brother or sister who is sexually immoral or greedy, or is an idolater, reviler, drunkard, or swindler. Do not even eat with such a one.

There are at least three compelling reasons to believe that Paul has chosen the specific vices listed in 1 Cor. 5:10–11 because they were relevant to the particular situation in the Corinthian church. First, there is the general observation that it is much more plausible that a skilled letter writer like Paul, who gives evidence of adapting and drafting every other part of his correspondence in order to more persuasively deal with specific situations facing his audience, would follow the same pattern in his paraenetical sections. What Leo Perdue (1981: 247) states about James is equally true about Paul: "It is rather odd to suggest that an author who compiles a paraenetic text, even if he uses a good deal of unoriginal material, would not choose admonitions and other traditional materials to address real issues in the life of the community itself." Second, the vice (or offender) list in 1 Cor. 5:10 does not parallel exactly the offender list in the immediately following verse of 5:11: two extra offenders are identified in the second list, and the order in both lists differs slightly. Furthermore, these two lists in 5:10–11 are not at all similar to any of the multiple other occurrences of similar lists in Paul's writings. In fact, there is very little overlap between any of the apostle's vice and virtue lists, which suggests that he did not have a fixed, traditional catalog of ethical items that he simply "cut and pasted" into his various letters (Zaas 1988: 623). Third and most significant, the six sins listed in 1 Cor. 5:10–11 fit very well with the specific problems that Paul addresses in different places in his Corinthian letter (Garland 2003: 189):

- "sexually immoral": The offender at the top of the list is the "sexually immoral," clearly put in this position of importance because of a direct connection to the immediately preceding discussion of a church member's improper sexual relationship with his stepmother (5:1–8). This opening reference to the "sexually immoral" person also anticipates the upcoming discussion of how some Corinthian Christians were engaging the services of prostitutes (6:12–20)—a discussion where the same term occurs no less than four times (6:13, 15, 16, 18; see also 7:2; 10:8).
- "greedy" and "swindlers": The references to the "greedy" and "swindlers" are linked together in the first offender list both by the use of one article for the two nouns and by the conjunction "and" instead of the conjunction "or" used in the rest of the list. The mention of these two linked offenders likely looks ahead to the situation of certain members of the Corinthian congregation who are suing fellow members in the pagan courts for their own financial gain (6:1–11; so Fee 1987: 224). The term "greedy" is also fitting in a more generally applicable way to many members of the Corinthian church who "were obsessed with the ambition to achieve, i.e., to gain more social status, power, or wealth" (Thiselton 2000: 411).
- "idolater": The inclusion in the list of the "idolater" anticipates Paul's lengthy treatment of meat sacrificed to idols (8:1–11:1). Many Corinthian believers, following the common practice of their day, ate meat left over from the sacrifices performed in pagan temples or other buildings devoted to false gods and so became guilty of idolatry. Such religious meals commonly involved not only the sin of idolatry but also the sin of sexual immorality (thereby referring again to the term "sexually immoral" listed first in the offender list), since ancient meals or banquets were often accompanied by sexual entertainment (note how often throughout the NT the sins of "meat sacrificed to idols" and "sexual immorality" are linked together: in addition to 1 Cor. 10:8, see also Acts 15:29; 21:25; Rev. 2:14, 20).
- "reviler": The Greek term used here refers to someone whose speech is highly insulting or abusive, and so may relate in a general way to the Corinthian church's preoccupation with impressive speech (1:10–4:21)—an attitude that led them to revile Paul for the seemingly "foolish" manner in which he presented the gospel.

- "drunkard": Although the problem of drunkenness is not dealt with in an extended way, it is addressed at least twice, suggesting that the Corinthian church also experienced problems in this area. Paul brings the matter up in 10:7 in his citation of Exod. 32:6, "The people sat down to eat and drink and got up to play"—a clear reference to the embarrassing incident when Moses came down from Mount Sinai and found the Israelites engaged in idolatry, sexual immorality, and drunkenness. Paul addresses drunkenness a second time in 11:21, where he rebukes the wealthy members of the Corinthian church in connection with their Lord's Supper celebration: the poorer members of the congregation are hungry, while the rich end up drunk.

It seems clear, therefore, that the vice or offender lists of 1 Cor. 5:10–11 were assembled with the specific situation of the Corinthian church in mind. As David Garland (2003: 188) puts it: "Rather than selecting random excerpts from a canon of sins filed away in his memory, Paul more likely identifies practices that were already destroying the moral fabric of the community or were so prevalent in the surrounding culture that they threatened to encroach on the life of the church." The conclusion of Peter Zaas (1988: 629), who examines not only the offender lists of 1 Cor. 5:10–11 but also that of 1 Cor. 6:9–10, is even stronger: "The vice catalogues of 1 Cor. 5 and 6 are *intricately* connected to the epistolary situation of the letter" (emphasis added).

But although there are some texts where exegetical value is lost by failing to recognize how adaptation of conventional vice and virtue lists reflect the specific situation of Paul's readers, there are other texts where it is unjustified to conclude that each individual item in the list is either being emphasized or is an accurate description of what was actually happening in a given church. In Rom. 1:29–31 no less than twenty-one vices are listed:

[29]They were filled with all unrighteousness, evil, greediness, malice—full of jealousy, murder, rivalry, deceit, craftiness—gossipers, [30]slanderers, God-haters, insolent, arrogant, braggarts, inventors of evil, disobedient to parents, [31]foolish, faithless, heartless, ruthless.

Paul is not trying to highlight vices that are worse than all other vices (note the absence of sexual sins, addressed in the preceding verses). Nor is his goal to distinguish each of these vices from the others, since some are virtually synonymous and involve a high degree of overlap in meaning. And it is not his intention to connect all twenty-one vices with the specific situation faced by the Roman house churches, even though the positioning of "unrighteousness" at the head of the list is almost certainly a deliberate attempt to recall in his readers' minds the double reference to "unrighteousness" at the beginning of the letter body, in 1:18 (Dunn 1988a: 67–68). Paul's purpose is instead revealed in the length of the vice list, which, as the longest of its kind in the NT, enhances its rhetorical effect: in a comprehensive way, the vice list conveys the depth and weight of human sin and so justifies God's wrath (1:18) and the triple reference to God's action of "handing over" such people to their depravity (1:24, 26, 28).

Another debatable matter concerns the function of the second of the two distinct types of paraenesis: the household codes. The issue centers on whether the exhortations dealing with the three-pair pattern of wives-husbands, children-fathers, and slaves-masters have an additional function beyond the general one common to all forms of paraenesis, namely, to instruct Christians on how they ought to live. A widely held view maintains that the household codes possess an apologetic or defensive function.[14] According to this understanding, the commands concerning various members of the ancient household are intended to refute charges that the Christian faith was socially and politically subversive and threatened the "peace and security" of the Roman Empire. Thus, for example, John Muddiman (2001: 278) asserts that "the adoption and adaptation of the household code offered reassurance that the Christian movement posed no immediate threat to the *status quo*."

An apologetic function does seem to be at work in the household code in 1 Peter, where this paraenetic section (2:11–3:7) opens with the following command: "Maintain good conduct among the gentiles, so that in case they speak against you as wrongdoers, they may see your good deeds and glorify God on the day of visitation" (2:12). It is also significant that only a few verses after the household code, Peter exhorts his readers, "Always be prepared to make a defense to anyone who calls you to account for the hope that is in you" (3:15).

Paul is similarly concerned that Christians present a positive image to their pagan neighbors, as is clear from his appeal to the Thessalonians "to make it your ambition to live a quiet life, and to mind your business, and to work with your hands, just as we commanded you, in order that you may walk appropriately before outsiders" (1 Thess. 4:11–12). Nevertheless, this concern likely does not account for the inclusion of the household codes in his letters. In contrast to 1 Peter, there is nothing in the surrounding context of the household codes in either Colossians or Ephesians to suggest that Paul intended this material to function apologetically.

---

14. So, e.g., Balch 1981; 1988; Verner 1983; Aune 1987: 196; MacDonald 2000: 159–69; Osiek and MacDonald 2006: 118–43.

Some have claimed that the household codes in Paul's letters are designed to counteract problematic attitudes among his readers with respect to the emancipation of women and slaves (Crouch 1972). Some early Christians wrongly interpreted remarks like the famous statement of Gal. 3:28, "There is neither Jew nor Greek, neither slave nor free, neither male nor female; for you are all one in Christ Jesus" (see also Col. 3:11), and the reference to a "new creation" in Gal. 6:15 in a universal sense, eradicating all social distinctions. Thus Douglas Moo (2008: 296) states:

> The household codes may be responses to such excesses, reminding Christians that certain institutions continued to exist in the new age and that believers needed to relate appropriately to one another within these institutions. The new family of God gave believers their fundamental identity, but the spiritual family did not eliminate the continuing significance of the physical family and relations appropriate to its smooth functioning.

But if this were Paul's purpose in including the household code in his letters, it does not explain why he includes exhortations to children and parents, since there is no possibility that children would reject their current status. This proposed function of the household code is further undermined by Paul's failure to be more explicit in calling women and slaves to maintain their current status and even more by Paul's exhortation to slaves that "if you are able to gain your freedom, make use of that opportunity" (1 Cor. 7:21b).

There does not appear to be, then, a single function for the use of the household codes. Rather, Peter uses this paraenetic material in one way (apologetic function), while Paul uses it in different ways in different letters, shaping his exhortations so that they better fit the specific context of his readers. For example, the household code in Colossians differs from its occurrence in Ephesians in devoting proportionally greater space to the slave-master relationship (Moo 2008: 298). The Colossian version deals with this relationship in over half of the household code (five out of nine verses), whereas the Ephesian version does so in only a quarter of this material (five out of twenty-two verses). It is likely that the exhortations dealing with the slave-master relationship are expanded in Colossians because this letter is written to the same church that Paul targets in the contemporary Letter to Philemon. It may be that Paul adapts the household code in Colossians so that it better relates to issues connected with the specific problem of the runaway slave, Onesimus. Paul's warning to slaves that "the *wrongdoer* will be paid back for the wrong he has done" (Col. 3:25) seems to have in view the action of Onesimus (note the verbal parallel with Philem. 18: "If he has *wronged* you or owes you anything . . ."), as the apostle reminds other slaves that they should not expect any wrongdoing on their part to be excused because of their new status as Christ-followers (Knox 1959: 32–33; Witherington 2007: 194; Moo 2008: 315).

Paul similarly expands the husband-wife relationship in the household code in Ephesians. He devotes twelve verses to the mutual responsibilities of husbands and wives in Ephesians (5:22–33), whereas in Colossians the household code covers this same subject in just two verses (Col. 3:18–19). The expanded material in Ephesians repeatedly—six times—draws on the Christ-church relationship as a model for the husband-wife relationship, thereby picking up the close relationship between Christ and the church that is a major theme in the earlier chapters in this letter. As Frank Thielman (2010: 368) points out, "The ideas that Christ is the head of the church, that the church is Christ's body—all these were important in [Eph.] 1:3–4:16. Paul now weaves these themes back into his moral instruction, and carries them further, by means of the household code."

Interpretative Significance

The discussion above on both the form and the function of paraenesis has already involved looking at multiple texts in which the interpretive significance of such material has been amply illustrated.

Liturgical Forms

The body sections of Paul's letters also contain various liturgical forms. These forms are not unique to letters but originated in the worship of the early church. Thus, in distinction from the forms examined thus far in this chapter, these cannot be narrowly identified as *epistolary* conventions. Nevertheless, Paul incorporated these liturgical forms into his letters and used them as part of his strategy to persuade his readers; thus a knowledge of their form and function also plays an important part in the interpretive method of epistolary analysis.

Prayers

FORM

Prayers, or as they are more often identified, "benedictions" (Champion 1934: 29–30; Jewett 1969; Mullins 1977; Weima 1994a: 101–4) or "wish-prayers" (Wiles 1974: 45–71), occur with some frequency in Paul's letters, and commentators typically group these passages into the same formal category. Yet three distinct types of prayers can be identified (Weima 1994a: 78–104): (1) the grace benediction, (2) the peace benediction, and (3) the "body" benediction.

The first two types belong to the letter closing and possess a consistent form or structure; the third type is found in the letter body and exhibits greater formal variation. Nevertheless, these benedictions or prayers located in the letter body still have a common structure consisting of five basic elements (see table 4.4: Prayers): (1) the adversative particle "but" (*de*), which sets the prayer apart from the preceding material; (2) the divine source of the prayer, either God and/or the Lord, along with a noun or participial clause that provides a further description of these persons; (3) the wish or content of the prayer expressed in the main verb;[15] (4) the recipient of the prayer, involving (in every instance except one) some form of the personal pronoun "you"; and (5) the purpose of the prayer, expressed by either a *hina* or *eis* clause ("so that . . .").

Table 4.4: Prayers

Letter	Divine Source	Wish	Recipient	Purpose
Rom. 15:5–6	But may the God of endurance and comfort	give	to you	
		the same attitude of mind toward each other that Christ Jesus had		so that together you may with one voice glorify the God and Father of our Lord Jesus Christ.
Rom. 15:13	But may the God of hope	fill	you	
		with all joy and peace in believing		so that you may abound in hope by the power of the Holy Spirit.
1 Thess. 3:11	But may our God and Father himself and our Lord Jesus	clear the way for us to come	to you.	
1 Thess. 3:12–13	But as for you, may the Lord	cause	you	
		to abound and increase in love for one another and for all, just as we also [abound and increase in love] for you,		in order to strengthen your hearts as blameless in holiness before our God and Father at the coming of our Lord Jesus with all his holy ones.

(cont.)

15. The verb is normally expressed in the optative mood—a mood that occurs only rarely in NT Greek. The optative is used to express a wish or an ideal, and so is a fitting mood to use in prayers where one expresses to God what one would ideally like to happen.

Letter	Divine Source	Wish	Recipient	Purpose
2 Thess. 2:16–17	But may our Lord Jesus Christ himself, and God our Father, who loved us and gave us eternal comfort and good hope through grace,	comfort and establish	your hearts	in every good work and word.
2 Thess. 3:5	But may the Lord	direct	your hearts	to the love of God and to the steadfastness of Christ.

This third type of benediction or prayer appears six times in the body sections of Paul's letters: Rom. 15:5–6, 13; 1 Thess. 3:11, 12–13; 2 Thess. 2:16–17; 3:5 (see also Heb. 13:20–21). These benedictions or prayers are also formally distinct from and thus should not be confused with (1) the reference to prayer commonly found in the second part of the opening thanksgiving—the manner of giving thanks (Rom. 1:9; Eph. 1:16; Phil. 1:4; Col. 1:3; 1 Thess. 1:2; Philem. 4); (2) the prayer reports that sometime conclude the opening thanksgiving (Phil. 1:9–11; Col. 1:9–14; 2 Thess. 1:11–12; see Rom. 1:10); and (3) the other prayer reports occasionally found in the body of the letter (1 Thess. 3:10; Eph. 3:14–19).

FUNCTION

These prayers possess a summarizing function: Paul adapts the conventional elements of the prayers such that they recapitulate and place the spotlight on the letter's major concerns and themes (Jewett 1969: 24; Wiles 1974: 68; Weima 1994a). Yet, as noted above in our survey of the different forms of paraenesis, these prayers also have an implicit exhortative function. By sharing with his readers the specific content of his prayer to God for them, Paul not so subtly also lets them know what he hopes and even expects them to do in their lives.

INTERPRETATIVE SIGNIFICANCE

The summarizing function of the prayers found in the letter body can be seen in the two incidences of this liturgical form that occur back-to-back in 1 Thess. 3:11–13:

[11]But may our God and Father himself and our Lord Jesus clear the way for us to come to you. [12]But as for you, may the Lord cause you to abound and increase in love for one another and for all, just as we also [abound and increase in love]

for you, [13]in order to strengthen your hearts as blameless in holiness before our God and Father at the coming of our Lord Jesus with all his holy ones. Amen.

The material of 1 Thess. 2:17–3:10, which immediately precedes this prayer, deals with two closely connected concerns: first, Paul's inability to return to Thessalonica, which his opponents use to raise further doubts about the genuineness of the apostle's care and concern for his new converts (2:17–20); and second, the persecution that threatens the faith of the Thessalonian church (3:1–5). These two concerns are not only skillfully combined and answered in 3:6–10, which deals with Timothy's return and report, but they are also cleverly summarized in the two prayers of 3:11–13.

In 3:11 the wish of the first prayer—that God and the Lord Jesus "clear the way for us to come to you"—echoes the repeatedly stated (four times) desire of Paul in the preceding passage to revisit the Thessalonians (2:17, "to see you face-to-face"; 2:18, "to come to you"; 3:6, "just as we also long to see you"; 3:10, "to see you face-to-face"). In this first prayer the specific wish that God and Jesus "*clear the way* [lit., "road"] for us to come to you" also looks back to the military metaphor of 2:18b, where Paul excuses his failure to return to Thessalonica by explaining that Satan "*blocked our way*"—a reference to the military practice of making cuts in the road to prevent an enemy army from advancing.

In 3:12–13 the second prayer also addresses the two main concerns of the preceding passage. The elliptical phrase "just as we also [abound and increase in love] for you" (v. 12b) echoes virtually verbatim the elliptical phrase "just as we also [long to see] you" in 3:6 and so recalls in a general way Paul's concern throughout 2:17–3:10 to reassure the Thessalonians of his continued love for them despite his absence. The wish of the second prayer—that the Lord increase their love "in order to *strengthen* your hearts" (3:12–13)— provides a verbal link with 3:2, where Paul's purpose in sending Timothy to the persecuted Thessalonian church is "in order to *strengthen* you." The two prayers, therefore, accurately summarize Paul's two primary concerns in the preceding passage, namely his absence from the Thessalonians (2:17–20) and the persecution endured by the Thessalonians (3:1–5).

The second prayer (3:12–13), however, not only recaps the two major concerns of the preceding material but also foreshadows three key themes that will be developed in the second half of the letter (4:1–5:22): love for others, holiness, and the second coming of the Lord Jesus. First, the wish of the prayer that the Lord cause the Thessalonians "to abound and increase in love for one another and for all" anticipates the discussion of brotherly and sisterly love in 4:9–12 and the implications of loving one another in 5:12–22. Second, the purpose of the prayer, namely that the Thessalonians be "blameless in holiness," and also the final prepositional phrase "with all his holy ones" (i.e., "saints") look ahead to the discussion of holiness in sexual conduct in 4:3–8, where the word "holiness/holy" in various forms plays a key role, occurring no less than four times (4:3, 4, 7, 8 ["his Spirit who is holy"]). Third, the closing temporal reference in the prayer to "the coming of our Lord Jesus," along with the "all" in the final phrase "with all his holy ones," have in view Paul's lengthy discussion of the return of Christ in 4:13–18 and 5:1–11. These two paragraphs comfort readers with the fact that *all* believers—not only the living Christians in Thessalonica but also "those who have fallen asleep," over whom the church is grieving—will be present and reunited at Christ's return.

The two prayers of 1 Thess. 3:11–13, therefore, are not merely *concluding* prayers (the title used by some commentators: Oepke 1963: 166; Gaventa 1998: 45; Reinmuth 1998: 135; Malherbe 2000: 211) but *transitional* prayers (so also Witherington 2006: 101, but from a rhetorical perspective; and Boring 2015: 123). The emphasis in these prayers is less on the apologetic concerns found in the first half of the letter than on the paraenetic, or exhortative, concerns in the second half, where Paul will fulfill the desire he states in 3:10 to "complete the things that are lacking in your faith" (see Frame 1912: 136). The benedictions or prayers in Paul's letters generally have both summarizing and paraenetic functions: "By mentioning the needs of the readers in prayers which they themselves will read together during worship, the apostle is encouraging them before God to strive still harder" (Wiles 1974: 69) to do that which he prays for them. As the opening thanksgiving (1:2–10) implicitly exhorts the Thessalonians to live up to the praise that they receive from Paul, so the two prayers of 3:11–13 implicitly challenge the believers in Thessalonica to make the divine petitions of the apostle a reality in their daily lives.

Doxologies

FORM

Another liturgical form that originated first in Jewish and then in early Christian worship and that Paul, along with other NT writers, incorporated into his letters is the doxology. A doxology is a typically short expression of praise to God. Whereas a benediction, like the grace and peace benedictions often found in Paul's letter closings, or a prayer, like those often found in the letter body, is an invocation to God to bestow a blessing on some person(s) or congregation, the doxology is an expression of praise directed to God. Benedictions possess more of an anthropocentric focus, while doxologies have a theocentric perspective.

Doxologies occur eight times in the letters of Paul and another eight times in the remaining NT letters. This liturgical form occurs not only in the body of NT letters but also in all three main sections: the opening (Gal. 1:5; Rev. 1:5b–6), the body (Rom. 11:36b; Eph. 3:20–21; 1 Tim. 1:17; 1 Pet. 4:11b; 5:11; Rev. 5:13b; 7:12), and the closing (Rom. 16:25–27; Phil. 4:20; 1 Tim. 6:16b; 2 Tim. 4:18b; Heb. 13:21b; 2 Pet. 3:18b; Jude 24–25). If all the NT occurrences of a doxology are included for the sake of comparative analysis (see table 4.5: Doxologies), it becomes clear that the doxology exhibits a fixed pattern consisting of four basic elements (O'Brien 1993: 69; Aune 1997: 44): (1) the object of praise, (2) the element of praise, (3) the indication of time, and (4) the affirmatory response.

Table 4.5: Doxologies

Letter	Object of Praise	Element of Praise	Indication of Time	Affirmatory Response
Rom. 11:36b	To him	be the glory	forever.	Amen.
Rom. 16:25–27	To him who is able . . . to the only wise God	be the glory	forever.	Amen.
Gal. 1:5	To him	be the glory	forever and ever.	Amen.
Phil. 4:20	To our God and Father	be the glory	forever and ever.	Amen.
Eph. 3:20–21	To him who has power . . . to him	be glory in the church and in Christ Jesus	for all the generations of the age of the ages.	Amen.
1 Tim. 1:17	To the King of the ages, immortal, invisible, the only God,	be honor and glory	forever and ever.	Amen.
1 Tim. 6:16b	To him	be honor and dominion	forever.	Amen.
2 Tim. 4:18b	To him	be the glory	forever and ever.	Amen.
Heb. 13:21b	To him	be the glory	forever and ever.	Amen.
1 Pet. 4:11b	To him	belongs the glory and dominion	forever and ever.	Amen.
1 Pet. 5:11	To him	be the dominion	forever and ever.	Amen.
2 Pet. 3:18b	To him	be the glory	both now and to the day of eternity.	Amen.
Jude 24–25	To him who is able . . .	be glory, majesty, dominion, and authority,	before all time and now and forever.	Amen.
Rev. 1:5b–6	To him who loves us . . . to him	be the glory and dominion	forever and ever.	Amen.

(cont.)

Letter	Object of Praise	Element of Praise	Indication of Time	Affirmatory Response
Rev. 5:13b	To him who sits on the throne and to the Lamb	be blessing and honor and glory and might	forever and ever.	The four living creatures say "Amen!" (Rev. 5:14)
Rev. 7:12	To our God	be blessing and glory and wisdom and thanksgiving and honor and power and might	forever and ever.	Amen.

1. *The object of praise.* The first formal element in a doxology is the object of praise: the one to whom glory is given is identified typically by either the relative pronoun "to whom" or the personal pronoun "to him." The precise identity of the one being praised must be determined from the antecedent of these pronouns, which is God in all but four of the fifteen occurrences (see 2 Tim. 4:18; 2 Pet. 3:18; Rev. 1:5–6; and 5:13b, where glory is directed instead to Christ).

Of the four basic elements of a NT doxology, the object of praise is the part where letter writers apparently felt the greatest freedom to depart from the norm. These expanded descriptions of God (since God is the most common object of praise) are found not only within the doxology itself, however, but even more commonly in preceding statements that provide the antecedent for the pronouns "to whom" or "to him." The expansion is sometimes short and may seem to be insignificant, as in Phil. 4:20: "To our God and Father." Yet even here it is striking that Paul has highlighted his close personal relationship to God in the immediately preceding verse by using the intensely personal expression "*my* God." When combined with the adapted praise formula in the doxology, Paul's use of this rare expression serves to reassure his Philippian readers that he has firsthand experience of how the God who met all his needs would also meet "all *your* needs" (4:19). The shift in the doxology itself to the plural "*our* God *and Father*" also looks intentional as "Paul unites himself with his converts in this ascription of praise" (O'Brien 1991: 550; see also Hawthorne 1983: 209).

In other instances, however, the expansion of the object of praise can be much more extensive, as, for example, in Jude 24–25: "To him who is able to keep you from falling and to present you without blemish before the presence of his glory with rejoicing, to the only God, our Savior through Jesus Christ our Lord. . . ." Both types of expansions, brief and extensive, can be found in the doxologies used in Paul's letters.

2. *The element of praise.* The second formal element in a doxology describes the kind of praise that is being ascribed to God. In almost every occurrence of the doxology in NT letters, the element of praise is "glory," which in Greek is *doxa*—hence the title of this liturgical form. The term "glory," however, does not have the secular Greek meaning of "fame, recognition, renown, honor, prestige" (BDAG 257) but the religious OT sense of a glorious quality belonging to God. In addition to "glory," some doxologies ascribe to God other elements of praise such as "power," "honor," "authority," "blessing," and so on. The act of attributing to God such glory or one of these additional elements of praise does not imply that any of these things is not currently present, but rather acknowledges an existing divine attribute. The doxology, therefore, is not merely a pious wish ("To whom *may there be* glory") but a declarative statement ("To whom *is* glory").

3. *The indication of time.* The third formal element in a doxology indicates the intended duration of the praise ascribed in the preceding section. The prepositional phrase "unto the ages of the ages"—an idiom meaning "forever and ever"—occurs in every doxology, with only slight variations and elaborations.

4. *The affirmatory response.* The fourth and final formal element in a doxology is the affirmatory response. In every case where there is an affirmatory response, the response is "amen" (*amēn*). This term is a Greek transliteration of a Semitic word whose root has the sense of truthfulness. In the OT, "amen" functions as a formula of affirmation, either in the acceptance of an oath or curse (Num. 5:22; Deut. 27:15–26; Jer. 11:5; Neh. 5:13) or in the confirmation of praise to God, as in the doxologies that close the first four books of the Psalms (Pss. 41:13; 72:19; 89:52; 106:48; see also 1 Chron. 16:36). The affirmatory sense of "amen" is also evident in the Septuagint (LXX), which translates this Semitic word as "May it be so!" (*genoito*) or, less frequently, "Truly!" (*alēthōs*). In the Jewish synagogue the worshipers responded with an "amen" to each of the three sections of the Aaronic blessing, as well as to any prayer or praise uttered by another, thereby voicing their public agreement with what was just spoken. In the worship services of early Christians, the "amen" similarly expressed the congregation's agreement with what their leader or others were saying (1 Cor. 14:16; Rev. 5:13–14).

In light of its consistent use in both Judaism and early Christianity, the presence of "amen" at the end of a doxology in Paul's letters has been typically understood as an anticipation of the affirmatory response *of his readers.* In other words, Paul knows that his letter will be read aloud in the presence of the whole house church and, when the part of his letter containing the doxology is read, he anticipates that his hearers will naturally respond with "Amen!" and so includes *their* affirmatory response in the actual text of the letter. But while his readers likely would have responded this way, the presence of the "amen" also reflects the affirmatory response *of Paul*: the apostle himself publicly testifies that what he has just stated about God in the first element of the doxology—the object of praise—and the glory that is ascribed forever and ever to this God are indeed not merely pious platitudes but something for him that in a very personal way is "true" (see Thielman 2010: 245).

FUNCTION

A survey of the various NT contexts in which doxologies occur reveals that this liturgical form has a consistent literary function: it brings the preceding discussion in a letter to a climactic close. This concluding function of the doxology is most evident in letters where this liturgical form occurs in the closing, either as part of the closing or as the last literary convention within this final section (Rom. 16:25–27; Phil. 4:20; 2 Tim. 4:18; Heb. 13:21b; 1 Pet. 5:11; 2 Pet. 3:18; Jude 24–25). But even in those instances where the doxology occurs within the body of the letter, it always concludes previous material and so marks the end of one section or unit and the beginning of another (Rom. 11:36; Eph. 3:20–21; 1 Tim. 1:17; 6:16; 1 Pet. 4:11; Rev. 5:13b; 7:12). In the one instance where the doxology occurs within the opening of the letter, it similarly brings this section to a close (Gal. 1:5; see also Rev. 1:5b–6). The concluding function of the doxology in NT letters probably stems from its similar function in the liturgy of worship, both Jewish and Christian.

INTERPRETATIVE SIGNIFICANCE

I have already discussed the interpretative significance of the doxology that occurs in Gal. 1:5 as part of Paul's significant expansion of the sender formula in that letter. Here I examine two other doxologies that have been carefully elaborated by the apostle so that they not only fulfill their main function of bringing the previous discussion in the letter to a definitive close but also recall key themes or ideas presented earlier in the letter.

Ephesians 3:20–21. The first of two additional doxologies to be studied more closely comes from Eph. 3:20–21:

> [20]To him who has power to do far more abundantly than all we ask or think, according to the power that is working in us, [21]to him be glory in the church and in Christ Jesus for all the generations of the age of the ages. Amen.

This doxology illustrates well the concluding function of this liturgical form. Ephesians 3:14–21 marks the end of one section and the beginning of another. In fact, this doxology occurs at what is widely recognized as a major hinge point in the letter, where Paul turns away from the more "theological" material of the first half of the correspondence (1:3–3:21) to the more overtly paraenetic, or exhortative, material of the second half (4:1–6:20). This major shift is further signaled by the presence in 4:1 of both the appeal formula ("I appeal to you . . ."), a key transitional formula in Paul's letters, and the so-called paraenetic *oun* ("therefore").

This doxology, however, also illustrates well Paul's skill in adapting the form of the doxology so that it recalls for the readers major points already raised in the letter. The apostle significantly expands the first element of the doxology, the object of praise, from the simple "To him" to "To him who has power [*dynamenō*] to do far more abundantly than all we ask or think, according to the power that is working in us." Two other doxologies similarly open with the description of God as "To him who has power to . . ." (Rom. 16:25–27; Jude 24–25), but "it would be a major mistake to conclude from this that it is merely a formal or traditional feature that Paul unthinkingly takes over at this point" (Thielman 2010: 241). In this doxology Paul emphasizes the power of God by adding a prepositional phrase that locates this divine power within believers: "according to the power [*dynamis*] that is working [*energoumenēn*] in us." This emphasis on the twice-mentioned power of God that is "working" in believers is noteworthy, since the apostle has similarly emphasized God's power that is available to both Paul and the Ephesian believers throughout the first half of the letter and leading up to this concluding doxology:

- In the prayer report (1:15–22) Paul tells his readers that this power of God lies at the heart of his constant remembrance of them: he is asking God to enlighten their hearts that they may know "the immeasurable greatness of his power [*dynamis*] in us who believe, according to the working [*energeia*] of his great might" (1:19).
- In 1:20–23 this same power of God is confessed to have been at work in the resurrection of Christ from the dead, to make alive those who were dead in their sin but who now are capable of doing good works (2:1–10), and to unite Jews and gentiles into one new body, thereby creating peace (2:11–22).
- In 3:1–13 this power of God is revealed to stand behind the effectiveness of Paul's ministry to the gentiles. Despite his being the least of all

the saints, "Of this gospel I was made minister according to the gift of God's grace that was given me by the working [*energeia*] of his power [*dynamis*]" (3:7).

• And in 3:14–19, finally, Paul's passionate prayer on behalf of his Ephesian readers indicates that this power of God is available to all believers: "that God may grant you to be strengthened with power (*dynamis*) through his Spirit in the inner human being" (3:16).

Therefore the expansions evident in the doxology of Eph. 3:20–21, including its double reference to God's "power" and description of that divine power "working within us," ought not to be seen as accidental and thus insignificant. This doxology rather provides yet another example of the literary skill of the apostle, who has shaped this ascription of glory to God in such a way as to remind the reader of a key theme developed in the first half of the letter.

This conclusion strengthens the likelihood that another expansion of this doxology is similarly deliberate and thus significant. The second formal element of the doxology, the element of praise, locates the glory "in the church and in Christ Jesus." Among Paul's eight doxologies, this is the only instance where he expands the element of praise. His reference to God being glorified first "in the church" refers to how the mere existence of the Ephesian congregation as a united body of gentile and Jewish believers reveals the reconciling work of God and thus brings him glory (as O'Brien [1999: 258] puts it: "the church is the masterpiece of God's grace"). Earlier in the letter (Eph. 2:11–22), Paul has highlighted how these two distinct groups have now become "one" in Christ, with the result that the church is "a dwelling place of God in the Spirit" (2:22). More explicit is Paul's claim that it is "through the church the manifold wisdom of God might now be made known" (3:10). The apostle's reference to God being glorified also "in Christ Jesus" refers to another key idea found in the letter, namely, the intimate relationship between the church and Christ. As Frank Thielman (2010: 244) explains, "Here the emphasis lies on the unity of Christ and the church, something Paul also emphasizes in Ephesians (1:23; 5:30–31). The plan of God for the unification of the universe revolves around the church and Christ and their close relationship with each other. It is fitting, then, for Paul to say that God is glorified in both."

Romans 16:25–27. A second example of a skillfully adapted doxology is found in Rom. 16:25–27:[16]

---

16. Although many conclude that these verses are a secondary addition to the letter, compelling arguments can be cited to defend the authenticity of this passage (see Hurtado 1981; Stuhlmacher 1994; Weima 1994a: 218–19; Moo 1996: 936–37; Schreiner 1998: 8–10, 816–17; Marshall 1999).

[25]To him who is able to strengthen you according to my gospel and the preaching of Jesus Christ, according to the revelation of the mystery that has been kept secret for long ages past [26]but is now revealed and has been made known by the prophetic writings according to the commandment of the eternal God, to bring about the obedience of faith for all the gentiles; [27]to the only wise God, through Jesus Christ, be the glory forever. Amen.

This doxology provides yet another illustration of two important characteristics about Paul's use of this liturgical form. First, Rom. 16:25–27 clearly demonstrates the concluding function of the doxology, since these verses mark the end not merely of a paragraph, or even that of a major unit within the letter, but of the letter as a whole. Second, it also demonstrates Paul's ability to skillfully adapt this liturgical form so that it echoes earlier material in the letter:

- The identification of God as one "who is able to strengthen you" (16:25a) reflects previous references to the power of God and the strength he gives to believers (1:11, 16; 9:17; 15:13, 19).
- The expression "according to *my* gospel" (16:25a), not found in Paul's other letters, is paralleled exactly in 2:16 and, even more important, echoes the apostle's concern in the letter opening (1:1–7), thanksgiving (1:8–15), and apostolic parousia (15:14–32) to share *his* gospel with the Roman believers (for a fuller development of this point, see Weima 2003: 17–33).
- The notion of the gospel as a "mystery that has been kept secret for long ages past but is now revealed" (16:25b–26a) parallels the thought of 1:17 and 3:21, which also are key statements in the overall theme of the letter.
- This mystery "has been made known by the prophetic writings according to the commandment of the eternal God" (16:26), as Paul has clearly demonstrated through the letter by means of repeated OT quotations and allusions.[17] More specifically, the phrase "by the prophetic writings" (16:26) is a deliberate allusion to the letter opening, where the phrase "by his prophets in the Holy Scriptures" (1:2) is intended to stress the continuity between Paul's gospel and that of the OT: in the Letter to the Romans, Paul is not presenting a new gospel but one that is in full agreement with the writings of the OT prophets.
- The goal of making the mystery of the gospel known is "to bring about the obedience of faith for all the gentiles" (16:26)—the same goal as

17. Paul quotes the OT at least fifty-three times in Romans, almost twice as often as in all his other letters combined.

stated both in the letter opening (1:5, "to bring about the obedience of faith for all the gentiles") and in the apostolic parousia (15:18, "to bring about the obedience of faith"). It also reflects Paul's concern throughout the letter to show that the gospel extends equally to gentiles as well as to Jews, so that both are now one in Christ (the word "gentile" is an important word in Romans, occurring thirty times).

These links between the doxology and the rest of the letter have not gone unnoticed. Over a century ago William Sanday and Arthur Headlam (1897: 436) observed that "the doxology sums up all the great ideas of the epistle." More recently James Dunn (1988b: 913), though viewing it as a post-Pauline addition, recognizes that "the doxology succeeds quite well in summing up the central themes of the letter." Thomas Schreiner (1998: 811) similarly states: "What we have here [Rom. 16:25–27] is a carefully formulated and syntactically complicated conclusion that is redolent of the central themes of Romans. In particular, the topics that received emphasis in 1:1–7 are summoned to the reader's attention again. Romans 1:1–7 and 16:25–27 therefore function as an *inclusio* for the contents of the letter." The recapitulating character of this doxology has an important implication for the debate over its Pauline authorship. I will demonstrate in the next chapter that Paul typically adapts and shapes his inherited closing conventions so that they better reflect the key issues discussed earlier in the letter. In light of this, it would not be beyond Paul's ability or practice to take a conventional doxology and expand it in such a manner as to echo the central purpose(s) of his Romans letter.

Confessions and Hymns

Other liturgical forms that originated in the worship of the early church and were incorporated into letters by Paul and other NT authors include confessions and hymns—formulaic statements on the essential beliefs of the earliest Christ-followers, which they either recited or sung together as part of their worship.[18] The existence of confessions and hymns in Paul's letters is strongly implied by references in his writings to teaching that he originally "received" and then "passed on" to his readers (1 Cor. 11:23; 15:3), "the tradition(s)" that he taught (1 Cor. 11:2; 2 Thess. 2:15; 3:6), "the rule of teaching" to which the Roman Christians were committed (Rom. 6:17), and "the good confession" made by Timothy (1 Tim. 6:12). The existence of such material in Paul's letters is further suggested by his explicit reference to the singing of hymns

---

18. Scholars also refer to this material with such terms as "creeds," "traditions," "formulas of faith," "kerygma," "homologies," and "liturgical formulations."

in corporate worship (1 Cor. 14:26, "When you come together, each one has a hymn . . .") and his exhortations to "address one another in psalms and hymns and spiritual songs, singing and making melody to the Lord with all your heart" (Eph. 5:19; so also Col. 3:16–17). That Paul's letters contain both confessions and hymns is widely attested by biblical scholars.

Nonspecialist readers of Paul's letters, by contrast, sometimes balk at the thought that the apostle has incorporated confessions and hymns into his correspondence. The hesitation stems from the belief that a gifted writer like Paul would not need to borrow any material since he was more than capable of creating his own content. There may also be the idea that any borrowed material is less important than, and not as authoritative as, material written by the apostle himself, who was uniquely inspired by the Holy Spirit. Yet just as there are good reasons why even today an accomplished preacher might quote a well-known confession of the church or a beloved hymn in a sermon, so also there are good reasons why a skilled author like Paul similarly incorporated both confessions and hymns in his letters.

Form

The form of confessions and hymns embedded in Paul's letters varies greatly, ranging from brief, single-statement affirmations of faith to extended, complex compositions. Over the past century a consensus has emerged about the criteria for identifying such liturgical material (Longenecker 1999: 10–11, 15–16, 21):

1. The presence of words and phrases not used elsewhere in an author's writings (hapax legomena = "things having been spoken one time"), or not with the meaning or in the manner found in his other writings. Such phenomena suggest that the text in question was likely composed by someone else.

2. The noun "confession" (*homolia*) or the verb "confess" (*homologeō*) to signal the presence of a formulaic statement of faith.

3. The verbs "preach" (*euangelizō*, *kēryssō*, or *katangellō*), "believe" (*pisteuō*), "teach" (*didaskō*), or "testify" (*martyreō* or *martyromai*), typically followed by the conjunction "that" (*hoti*) to introduce a direct or indirect quotation.

4. The presence of parallel structures that reflect Jewish or Hellenistic poetic conventions.

5. The frequent use of the relative pronoun "who" (*hos*) to begin passages, which is not a normal or expected way to open a new section.

6. A preference for participles over finite verbs, suggesting an original oral background.
7. A contextual dislocation, such as the presence of poetic material in a prose section or the presence of doctrinal material in an ethical section.
8. The affirmation of a basic Christian conviction, usually concerning the work or person of Jesus Christ.

Of course, not all or even most of these criteria are present in every occurrence of a confession or hymn. Nevertheless, these are the formal (items 1–6) and content (items 7 and 8) characteristics that strongly point to Paul's incorporation of confessions and hymns into his various letters.

FUNCTION

There does not appear to be a single function for the embedding of confessions and hymns in Paul's letters; rather, the apostle employs these formulaic statements of faith in a variety of ways. As Richard Longenecker (1999: 48) observes:

> Sometimes they [Paul and other NT writers] used confessional materials to establish rapport with their readers. At other times they used them to summarize the essence of their presentations, thereby capping off and showing the validity of their arguments. More often, however, they used confessional materials as the basis of their arguments, working from what was commonly accepted to what yet needed to be said.

The common feature in these varying functions is that Paul never merely *cites* confessions and hymns but always *contextualizes* liturgical materials: the apostle adapts and connects such formulaic statements of faith to the specific epistolary situation so that it supports his strategy of persuasion. Thus, for example, we have already observed in the letter opening of Romans how Paul strategically includes the following confession about his gospel: "concerning his Son, who was from the seed of David according to the flesh, who was appointed Son of God in power according to the Spirit of holiness, from the resurrection of the dead, our Lord Jesus Christ" (Rom. 1:3–4). The context is one where Paul is in the unusual position of writing to a church that he had neither founded nor even visited before, and even worse, to a church where some were raising questions about his orthodoxy (Rom. 3:8; see also 6:1). He deliberately expands the letter opening to reassure his Roman readers about both the legitimacy of his apostleship and the trustworthiness of his gospel. By quoting a confession that the Christians in Rome knew and perhaps themselves recited in worship, Paul effectively demonstrates that he shares with them a common gospel. In this particular example, the apostle uses a confession to, as Longenecker (1999: 48) puts it, "establish rapport" with his readers.

INTERPRETATIVE SIGNIFICANCE

In this section I will present three texts that are widely recognized as either a confession or a hymn, each one of differing length: first, a single-statement confession (1 Thess. 4:14); second, a multiple-line confession (1 Cor. 15:3b–5); and third, a lengthy hymn (Phil. 2:6–11).

1 Thessalonians 4:14. In the context of comforting the Thessalonian Christians who are grieving over fellow believers who have died prior to Christ's return, Paul states: "For since we believe that Jesus died and rose, so also, through Jesus, God will bring with him those who have fallen asleep" (1 Thess. 4:14). In the first half of this verse, Paul is not reminding the Thessalonians of his own preaching on the death and resurrection of Christ but instead quoting for them a confession of the broader church about this belief. Several factors strongly suggest that the words "Jesus died and rose" are a creedal formula that the apostle here cites in part:

- The introductory phrase "we believe that" is used elsewhere to introduce a confession (Rom. 10:9) and assumes that what follows is already well known to the Thessalonians.

- The use of "Jesus" alone is rare for Paul: he normally employs the fuller designations "Jesus Christ," "Christ Jesus," or "the (our) Lord Jesus Christ." The meager sixteen occurrences of "Jesus" alone—seven of which occur in a single passage (2 Cor. 4:5–14)—among the hundreds of Pauline references to Christ cause Werner Foerster (*TDNT* 3:289) to state, "It is still astonishing that the simple 'Jesus' is so rare in the NT epistles."

- Even more striking is the presence of the verb *anistēmi* ("to rise"), which Paul uses only here and in verse 16 (perhaps under the influence of v. 14) and in quotations from the OT (Rom. 15:12; 1 Cor. 10:7) and other sources (Eph. 5:14). Paul's preferred verb by far when referring to the resurrection is *egeirō*, which occurs no less than thirty-seven times in his letters. The apostle's favored term is made even more unique when contrasted with other NT authors who do employ *anistēmi* to speak of the resurrection (Mark 8:31; 9:9, 10, 31; 10:34; 12:25; 16:9; Luke 18:33; 24:7, 46; John 6:39, 40, 44, 54; 11:23, 24, 25 [cognate noun]; 20:9; Acts 2:24, 32; 13:33 [participle], 34; 17:3, 31).

- Elsewhere Paul always refers to *God*'s activity in raising Jesus (or the dead) rather than, as here, to Jesus rising (Rom. 4:24, 25; 6:4, 9; 7:4; 8:11, 34; 10:9; 1 Cor. 6:14; 15:4, 12, 13, 15, 16, 17, 20, 29, 32, 35, 42, 43, 44; 2 Cor. 1:9; 4:14; 5:15; Gal. 1:1; Eph. 1:20; Col. 2:12; 1 Thess. 1:10; 2 Tim. 2:8). The presence of a confession would account for not only this change but also the break in the expected parallelism between the first half of the verse, where Jesus is the subject, and the second half, where God is the subject.
- Finally, as Beverly Gaventa (1998: 64) states, "The sheer economy of words ('Jesus died and rose') is consistent with the notion of traditional language that has been pared down to the essentials."

If, then, the sentence "Jesus died and rose" is almost certainly a single-statement confession of the early church, how does this citation function in the larger unit of 4:13–18? How does Paul contextualize this confession so that it enhances his primary purpose in this passage of comforting his Thessalonian readers? The apostle's citation of this confession has the rhetorical effect of increasing the authority of his words: the death and resurrection of Jesus are not merely a private belief of Paul or even of just the Thessalonian congregation but are something affirmed by the entire early church. And by reminding his readers of this confession, a weighty and trustworthy word of the church, Paul makes his argument in verse 14 that much more powerful: since the entire early church believes that "Jesus died and rose," the Thessalonian believers can be sure that Christ's resurrection guarantees their loved ones' resurrection such that these deceased believers will be alive and able to participate fully in the glory of Christ's return.[19]

1 Corinthians 15:3b–5. Near the beginning of his lengthy treatment of the resurrection of believers in 1 Cor. 15:1–58, Paul cites what is almost universally recognized as a multiple-line confession of the early church about the death and resurrection of Christ (the words in square brackets are not part of the original confession but added by the apostle):

> [That] Christ died for our sins according to the Scriptures;
> [and that] he was buried;
> [and that] he was raised on the third day according to the Scriptures;
> [and that] he appeared to Cephas and then to the Twelve. (1 Cor. 15:3b–5)

19. For a fuller treatment of Paul's argument in 1 Thess. 4:14, which assumes and therefore omits a key step in the logical connection between the first half of the verse and the second half, see Weima 2014: 316–20.

The reasons for concluding that these words were not written by Paul himself but that he is reciting a very early creedal formulation include the following:

- Paul introduces 15:3b–5 with the words, "For I delivered to you as of first importance what I also received" (15:3a). The two main verbs, "I delivered" (from *paradidōmi*) and "I received" (from *paralambanō*), which also occur earlier in the letter in 11:23 in connection with the quotation of words from the Lord's Supper tradition, are technical terms from Paul's Jewish background for the receiving and subsequent passing on of traditional religious instruction. The apostle did not pen the immediately following words about Christ's death and resurrection himself: he originally "received" them in the form of a confession of the church sometime after his conversion to Christ, and he later "delivered" them to the Corinthian church early on, during his eighteen-month ministry in Corinth.

- The majority of words and expressions in 15:3b–5 are not typical of Paul's vocabulary in his writings. The phrases "according to the Scriptures" (found twice in these verses), "he was buried," "on the third day," and the noun "the Twelve" occur nowhere else in the apostle's letters (thus are hapax legomena). Although the phrase "Christ died" occurs three more times (Rom. 14:9, 15; 1 Cor. 8:11) and there is one reference elsewhere to how Christ gave himself "for our sins" (Gal. 1:4, which quite likely also cites a confession), the full expression "Christ died for our sins" found here also does not appear anywhere else in Paul's writings. The form of the verb "he was raised" (perfect passive) appears only here and in the subsequent argument of chapter 15, where its first occurrence (15:4) is part of the confession, and its following occurrences (15:12, 13, 14, 16, 17, 20) involve Paul alluding to its earlier citation as part of the confession. Similarly, the Greek passive translated "he appeared" occurs only here (15:5), in the immediately following verses (15:6–8), and in 1 Tim. 3:16, which most scholars also consider to be a quotation of confessional material. Such a high concentration of non-Pauline words and expressions within the space of just a few verses is striking and strongly suggestive of quoted material.

- The four lines of 15:3b–5 possess a highly stylized structure that is presented in two carefully balanced units: one dealing with Christ's death (vv. 3b–4a) and the other dealing with his resurrection (vv. 4b–5). The first line ("Christ died") and third line ("he was raised") are emphasized by virtue of each being modified by a prepositional phrase of the same length (four words in Greek: "on behalf of our sins" and "on the third day") and by another prepositional phrase with exactly the same wording ("according to the Scriptures"). The second line ("he was buried") and fourth line ("he appeared") each reinforce the preceding line: Christ's burial confirms that he truly died, and his appearance confirms that he truly was raised.

- The content of 15:3b–5 is introduced by the striking fourfold use of the conjunction "that" (*hoti*) to mark out the words in each of the four lines as a quotation (the so-called *hoti recitativum*) as well as the conjunction "and" (*kai*) for emphasis (Murphy-O'Connor 1981: 583–84; Thiselton 2000: 1189). The presence of a separate conjunction "that" as the equivalent of quotation marks before each of the four lines is emphatic: grammatically, it would have been sufficient to include this conjunction only before the first line of the citation.

- There is evidence of contextual dislocation: the material of 15:3b–5 places equal emphasis on both the death of Christ (first two lines) and the resurrection of Christ (second two lines), whereas the larger context of 15:1–58 emphasizes only the resurrection of Christ (Kloppenborg 1978: 351).

What function does this confession about the death and resurrection of Christ have in its larger context? The key to answering this question is recognizing that the central problem addressed in 1 Cor. 15:1–58 does not involve the Corinthians' denial of *Christ's resurrection* but of their *own resurrection*. As Paul puts it: "How can some of you say that there is no resurrection of the dead?" (15:12; note also his statement "if the dead are not raised" repeated throughout the chapter: vv. 16, 29, 32). More specifically, the problem concerns the Corinthians' denial of a *bodily* resurrection: the hyperspiritual Christians in Corinth were improperly influenced by contemporary Greek religion and philosophy, which had no place for the physical body in the afterlife, and so these believers "found the notion of a resurrection of the *body* crass and embarrassing" (Hays 1997: 253). In correcting their denial, Paul's persuasive strategy is first to remind the Corinthians of what they already correctly believe concerning the resurrection of Christ (15:1–11), and then to use this commonly held belief about Christ's resurrection as the basis on which to argue for believers' bodily resurrection (15:12–58). As Gordon Fee observes, "Paul is not here [15:1–11] setting out to *prove* the resurrection of Jesus. Rather, he is reasserting the commonly held ground *from which* he will argue against their assertion that there is no resurrection of the dead" (1987: 718, emphasis original).

That this is Paul's tactic can be seen in how he frames the introductory section (15:1–11) of his chapter-long discussion: he opens (15:1–2) and closes (15:11) his introduction by reminding the Corinthians twice that they already believe his preaching about the resurrection. This tactic also explains why Paul cites a confession of the early church about the death and resurrection of Christ in 15:3b–5: Paul not so subtly reminds them that his preaching about the resurrection, which they do indeed believe, is also in complete agreement with what the entire early church believes. The confession adds weight to the foundational belief in Christ's resurrection that Paul is establishing and will build upon in the remainder of the chapter, as he argues for believers' resurrection. Anthony Thiselton (2000: 1188) articulates this function of the confession as follows: "Most writers agree that the commonality of the pre-Pauline tradition which Paul cites and endorses does indeed constitute what [Anders] Eriksson calls a shared presupposition or an agreed basis for further argument." Longenecker (1999: 52–53) similarly observes how Paul uses the confession in 15:3b–5 as the commonly held grounds for his exhortations in the remainder of the chapter:

> Throughout all of 1 Corinthians 15, Paul bases his arguments on the confessional statement about Christ's resurrection in verse 4 (cf. also v. 12). He does this explicitly in declaring the fact of a future and personal resurrection of believers (vv. 12–34), by analogy to argue for the corporeal nature of their resurrection (vv. 35–49), and by implication to assert the necessity of their resurrection if they are ever to be clothed with immortality (vv. 50–58). . . . [Paul] contextualizes confessional materials by focusing on the formulaic confession of 15:3b–5, which informs all that he writes in chapter 15.

Philippians 2:6–11. Among the obvious early Christian hymns in praise of Christ found in NT letters (Col. 1:15–20; 1 Tim. 3:16b; 1 Pet. 2:22–23), the one that has drawn the greatest attention and discussion by biblical scholars is Phil. 2:6–11, which most translations present in a format that highlights its poetic character:

> 6Who, being in very nature God,
> did not consider equality with God something to be used to his own
>   advantage;
> 7rather, he made himself nothing
> by taking the very nature of a servant,
> being made in human likeness.
> 8And being found in appearance as a man,
> he humbled himself
> by becoming obedient to death—
> even death on a cross!

[9]Therefore God exalted him to the highest place
and gave him the name that is above every name,
[10]that at the name of Jesus every knee should bow,
in heaven and on earth and under the earth,
[11]and every tongue acknowledge that Jesus Christ is Lord,
to the glory of God the Father. (NIV)

Although this passage is commonly referred to as a "hymn," this term should not be taken in the way it is commonly understood today, as a religious song where the last word of one line typically rhymes with the last word of the line that immediately follows it and where each line has a perfectly matched number of syllables. The term "hymn" instead refers to the same kind of material that I have (above) called confessions—formulaic statements on the essential beliefs of the earliest Christ-followers, which they either recited or sang together in their worship gatherings. The word "hymn" was applied very early on to the cited material of Phil. 2:6–11, and the term has become rather fixed in references to this passage ever since.

The number of scholarly studies on this passage is both impressive and intimidating.[20] Yet despite all this attention, little consensus has emerged concerning this passage's origin and authorship (Is it entirely pre-Pauline, pre-Pauline with later additions by the apostle, or Pauline?), its form and structure (Is it really a hymn? If so, what is its internal structure?), its original background (Does its contents draw from the OT, gnosticism, Hellenism, wisdom, or something else?), and the precise meaning of several of its key words and phrases. My purpose here is not to examine all these debatable issues but is much more modest and narrowly focused: first, to summarize the reasons why there is widespread (though by no means universal) agreement that Phil. 2:6–11 comprises an early hymn in honor of Christ; and second, to show how the hymn functions in the letter, demonstrating again that Paul never simply cites liturgical forms but always contextualizes his quoted material so that it supports his larger purposes in the letter as a whole.

First, the key reasons why the majority of biblical scholars view Phil. 2:6–11 as an early Christian hymn—composed independently of and prior to the writing of Philippians and then later incorporated into the apostle's letter—involve the following:

- The passage exhibits a strongly poetic, rhythmic character that distinguishes it quite clearly from normal prose. As Moisés Silva (2005: 93) comments: "Although one can hardly prove that verses 6–11 in whole

---

20. The bibliography of O'Brien (1991: 186–88) lists nearly one hundred works on Phil. 2:6–11.

or in part constitute a formal poem or hymn, it would be foolhardy to deny the strong poetic qualities of the passage. Even the label 'elevated prose' does not do justice to the rhythm, parallelisms, lexical links, and other features that characterize these verses."

- The passage as a whole exhibits a carefully balanced structure. Although there are disagreements about the number and relationship of its constituent parts, the passage, on both grammatical and content grounds, falls naturally into two sections: verses 6–8, with its two finite verbs describing Christ's humiliation, and verses 9–11, with its two finite verbs describing God's exaltation of Christ. Furthermore, there is a logical link between these two balanced sections that is highlighted by the connecting "therefore also"[21] that opens verse 9: the humiliation or self-sacrificial actions of Christ (vv. 6–8) are the reasons *why* God exalted Christ (vv. 9–11: "Therefore also God . . .").

- The passage begins with the relative pronoun "who" (*hos*), which, despite being an abrupt and awkward introduction, is exactly how four widely recognized Christ-hymns begin (Col. 1:15–20; 1 Tim. 3:16b; Heb. 1:3; 1 Pet. 2:22–23).

- The passage contains a high percentage of words that either do not appear elsewhere in Paul's letters (thus are hapax legomena) or are used with a different meaning (see R. Martin 1983: 16–21; O'Brien 1991: 199–200).

- The passage exhibits contextual dislocation: the content of the passage is highly doctrinal, revealing important theological truths about Christ's humiliation and exaltation, but the context of the passage is ethical, functioning to reinforce proper Christian conduct.

- The passage omits themes typically found in Paul's Christology and soteriology. Although there are dangers with such an "argument from silence" (i.e., making a conclusion based on what someone does *not* say), it is nevertheless striking that such an extended section on Christ as 2:6–11 lacks foundational Pauline ideas such as redemption through the cross (there is no mention of Christ's death as being "on behalf of us"), the resurrection of Christ, and the place of the church (R. Martin 1983: 49–50).

Second, the hymn possesses a strategic role in both its immediate and wider contexts: it functions to ground Paul's exhortations on proper moral conduct. Although the hymn, on the basis of its content, may have originally

21. The Greek text includes the word "also" (*kai*), which the NIV omits from its translation.

been composed for christological or soteriological reasons, this is not how the apostle uses it in the immediate context of 1:27–2:18 or in the wider context of the letter as a whole. As Gerald Hawthorne (1983: 79) observes, "Paul's motive in using it [the Christ-hymn] here is not theological but ethical. His object is not to give instruction in doctrine, but to reinforce instruction in Christian living." Furthermore, as witnessed above with the confessional material of 1 Thess. 4:14 and 1 Cor. 15:3b–5, here too the quoting of an early Christian hymn adds weight or authority to Paul's ethical argument. As Ralph Martin (1983: xxxiv–xxxv) puts it,

> But it [the hymn] also is cited because it represents a shared possession with his readers, and Paul could confidently assume that by quoting it he would command their assent to its chief thrust, namely, that Christian existence is most tellingly understood and lived under the lordship of Christ whose mandate— "encouragement in Christ" (v. 1)—is brought to bear on the troubles afflicting the Philippian community.

The concern for proper moral conduct emerges in the letter body first in 1:27–2:4, which opens, "Only let your manner of life be worthy of the gospel of Christ so that whether I come and see you or am absent, I may hear that you stand firm in one spirit, with one mind striving side by side for the faith of the gospel" (1:27). The same concern for proper moral conduct also lies at the heart of 2:12–18, where Paul similarly exhorts the Philippian believers "now not only as in my presence but much more in my absence that you work out your own salvation" (2:12), "do all things without grumbling and questioning" (2:14), and "be blameless and innocent, children of God without blemish in the midst of a crooked and perverse generation, among whom you shine as lights in the world" (2:15). Sandwiched between these two framing paragraphs and providing the grounds for these ethical exhortations is 2:5–11, with its citation of the hymn and its presentation of Christ as the ultimate model for moral conduct (2:5, "Have this mind among yourselves, which is yours in Christ Jesus"). The commands of 2:1–4 to demonstrate humility and concern for others over one's own interests are powerfully illustrated in the self-effacement of Christ and his self-sacrifice in service of others that are celebrated in the first half of the hymn (2:6–9). And the exaltation of Christ—he is declared "Lord"—in the second half (2:9–11) also challenges the Philippians to live in such a blameless way that their conduct acknowledges the rule of Jesus. The link between the hymn and the surrounding ethical exhortations is made explicit in the immediately following verse of 2:12, where the Philippians are called on to "obey" the one who was "obedient to death, even death on a cross" (2:8b).

The theme of imitation powerfully expressed in the Christ-hymn undergirds the concern for proper moral conduct not only in the immediate context of 1:27–2:18 but in the rest of the letter as well. It anchors Paul's presentation of the sincere concern of Timothy (2:19–24) and the sacrificial actions of Epaphroditus (2:25–30) as positive examples to be imitated, in contrast to the false leaders in the church who "look after their own interests, not those of Jesus Christ" (2:21). The hymn also anchors Paul's threefold use of himself in the letter as a model for the Philippians to imitate:

- In 1:30 Paul uses his own experience of suffering for the sake of the gospel as an example to encourage his readers who are also experiencing persecution for their faith: "What you have seen in me and now have heard in me."
- In 3:17 Paul holds up his own life and the lives of other faithful Christians as models for them to follow as they seek to live within a pagan world, whose moral values differ radically from those who live as followers of Christ: "Be fellow imitators of me, brothers and sisters, and mark those who thus live according to our example."
- And in 4:9 Paul again commands the Philippians to follow his example: "What you have learned and received and heard and seen in me, do!"

The Christ-hymn functions to anchor all these exhortations for the Philippians to imitate Paul, since in Paul's theology he is imitating Christ, as he explicitly states elsewhere (1 Cor. 11:1, "Be imitators of me, as I am of Christ").

This brief survey of the Letter to the Philippians makes clear the strategic role that the Christ-hymn of 2:6–11 plays not just in the immediate context of 1:27–2:18 but also in the broader context of the letter. The claims that this passage "is the most important section of the letter" (Hawthorne 1983: 76; so also O'Brien 1991: 186) and is "the climax of the argument of the epistle[;] . . . the arguments both preceding and following draw their force from this passage" (Fowl 2005: 89) are thus not guilty of hyperbole but are both justified. Paul uses this hymn of the early Christian church in honor of Jesus Christ to ground in a most powerful way the main exhortations in the letter.

Other Literary Forms

Paul's letters also contain literary forms that ought not to be considered narrowly as epistolary conventions or liturgical forms but as a separate category. These literary forms do not originate in the letter-writing practices of the ancient world or in the worship of the early church but in the OT and other Jewish writings. Paul knows the OT writings so well that he is influenced by and borrows not just their content (theology) and vocabulary but also their literary forms. These are "cross-genre" literary forms—forms that originate in one genre of Scripture (Hebrew poetry and also, on a more conceptual level, Hebrew prose) yet are later incorporated into another genre (letters). Two such forms commonly found in Paul's letters are the *inclusio* and the chiasm. These two literary forms occur not just in the letter body but in all four major sections of the apostle's letters. Nevertheless, the length of the letter body—compared to the opening, thanksgiving, and closing—not surprisingly means that a higher number of occurrences of these inclusios and chiasms are found in the body of Paul's letters.

Inclusio

FORM

An inclusio involves the repetition of a key word, phrase, or sentence at both the beginning and end of a literary unit, thereby marking its boundaries. By analogy, if the text of a literary unit is a picture, then the key word, phrase, or sentence strategically located at the beginning and end of the text is the frame containing that picture.[22]

Hebrew poetry makes extensive use of this literary device, as illustrated in the final five psalms of the Psalter (146–50), which all begin with the exhortation, "Praise the LORD," and all end with the identical exhortation, "Praise the LORD." Psalm 118 is framed by the exhortation, "Give thanks to the LORD, for he is good; his love endures forever," which opens the twenty-nine-line text, and exactly the same exhortation closes the text: "Give thanks to the LORD, for he is good; his love endures forever." Psalm 8 begins and ends with the same affirmation: "LORD, our Lord, how majestic is your name in all the earth!" (Ps. 8:1, 9). Although all these examples involve the repetition of *identical* elements, an inclusio can also be formed with the repetition of *corresponding* elements. As Richard Moulton (1895: 56) explained some time ago, an inclusio consists of a literary unit that is "enclosed between an identical (or equivalent) opening or close." Psalm 29, for example, opens with the command, "Ascribe to the LORD glory and strength," and closes with a similarly worded affirmation that fulfills this command, "The LORD gives strength to his people."

---

22. Other terms used to describe this literary form include "bracketing," "envelope structure" (the text is contained or "enveloped" within the repeated opening and closing), and "ring composition."

FUNCTION

The primary function of an inclusio is clear from the examples cited above: it marks the boundaries of a literary unit. Writing about Hebrew poetry, Tremper Longman states, "The inclusio delimits a poetic unit, providing a strong sense of beginning and close. Thus the term *inclusio* indicates that everything that is found between the two occurrences is 'included' in the unit. . . . By framing the poem or parts therein, the device evokes a sense of coherence to the text" (2008: 323).

INTERPRETATIVE SIGNIFICANCE

An obvious occurrence of an inclusio in Paul's letters is in 1 Thess. 3:1–5; notice the number of terms that are repeated and the close similarity of these repeated terms:

> [1]Therefore, *because we could no longer contain it*, we thought it best to be left behind in Athens alone, [2]and *we sent Timothy*, our brother and coworker of God in the gospel of Christ, *in order to* strengthen you and *comfort you concerning your faith*, [3]so that no one may be shaken by these afflictions. For you yourselves know that we are destined for this. [4]For indeed when we were with you, we kept telling you beforehand: "We are destined to suffer affliction," as indeed it has happened and you know. [5]For this reason, *because I could no longer contain it, I sent [Timothy] in order to learn about your faith*, fearing that in some way the Tempter had tempted you and that our work might have been in vain.

Paul creates an inclusio between his opening words of 3:1–2 and his closing words of 3:5: the plural expression "because we could no longer contain it, . . . we sent Timothy . . . in order to . . . comfort you concerning your faith" (3:1–2) is repeated virtually word for word (but in the singular form) in the expression "because I could no longer contain it, I sent [Timothy] in order to learn about your faith" (3:5). This inclusio functions to mark the boundaries of 3:1–5 as a distinct unit within the larger discussion of 2:17–3:10.

In 2:17–3:10 Paul addresses two closely connected concerns: his absence from the Thessalonians (2:17–20) and the Thessalonians' faith in the face of persecution (3:1–5). In the first unit, 2:17–20, the apostle is concerned that his inability to go back to the Thessalonian church for a return visit might be used by those outside the church—the "fellow citizens" (2:14) who are oppressing the church and questioning the integrity of its founder—to raise further doubts about the genuineness of Paul's care and concern for his new converts. In 2:17–20 Paul responds to this danger over his continued absence by employing the apostolic parousia—an epistolary device that makes his presence more powerfully felt among the Thessalonian readers such that they are reassured of his love and care for them.

The second unit (3:1–5) is set apart from the surrounding material by the inclusio formed between the near-identical words of 3:1–2 and 3:5. In this paragraph Paul is concerned about the persecution that threatens the faith of the Thessalonian church. The same evil, supernatural power who lies behind Paul's inability to return to Thessalonica ("but Satan blocked our way," 2:18) is also at work in the afflictions experienced by the Thessalonian believers ("the Tempter had tempted you," 3:5), threatening to destroy the success of the apostle's missionary work. In 3:1–5 Paul responds to this danger by again making his presence more powerfully felt in the church (by the continued use of the apostolic parousia): he refers to the sending of his emissary Timothy, whose mission is to strengthen the Thessalonian church in their faith. The inclusio allows Paul to refer not once but twice to his sending of Timothy (3:1–2 and 3:5), adding emphasis to his action and so stressing to the Thessalonian readers the depth and genuineness of his personal concern (note the shift in the inclusio from the plural to the singular) over the persecution that they are enduring.

These two concerns of the first and second units are skillfully combined and answered in the third unit (3:6–10), which deals with Timothy's return and report. Paul's first concern—to reassure the Thessalonians of the genuineness of his love for them, despite his ongoing absence (2:17–20)—is answered in Timothy's report about "your love and that you have a good remembrance of us always, longing to see us just as we also long to see you" (3:6b). Paul's second concern about the faith of the persecuted believers in Thessalonica (3:1–5) is answered in Timothy's report about "your faith" (3:6a), a faith that remains strong in the face of affliction.

Chiasm

FORM

A chiasm is a literary device where the various elements of a text are arranged in a balanced order: the elements are first presented in a series (ABC . . .), and then the same elements are repeated *in reverse order* (. . . C′B′A′). Any number of elements may compose a chiasm, forming either a balanced scheme (e.g., ABCC′B′A′) or an uneven scheme with an isolated center (e.g., ABCDC′B′A′), but a minimum of four elements are needed to make the inversion of order possible. In fact, the four-element chiasm (ABB′A′) is the form that occurs most frequently and the form from which the name of this literary device is derived. The term "chiasm" originates from the Greek letter *chi*, which looks like an English X and so reflects the balanced ABB′A′ order:

Simple Chiastic Structure

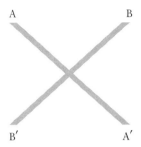

Psalm 145:2, for example, reads: "Every day I will praise you, and I will extol your name forever and ever." In this simple chiasm, the time reference "Every day" (A) and the verbal clause "I will praise you" (B) are repeated in the balancing second line but in reverse order: first comes the similar verbal clause, "I will extol your name" (B′), and then the similar time reference, "forever and ever" (A′).

With regard to Paul's use of this literary device in his letters, it is important to distinguish the simple, four-element chiasm (sometimes called a "micro-chiasm") from the complex, multiple-element chiasm (sometimes called a "macro-chiasm"). Although there is clear and compelling evidence that the apostle employs simple chiasms in his letters, the existence of complex chiasms in his writings is questionable. There have been several attempts to establish unambiguous parameters and reliable controls by which such longer and elaborate chiasms can be confidently identified.[23] Nevertheless, when scholars apply their criteria and propose that a lengthy section of a Pauline letter does, in fact, follow a chiastic structure, the resulting proposal typically reveals more about the clever ingenuity of the modern commentator than about the clear intention of the apostle.

FUNCTION

A chiasm can function in different ways, depending on its own unique circumstances. All chiasms, however, serve to mark the boundaries of a literary unit and give it coherence. This function is more important than modern readers typically

23. See, e.g., Lund 1942: 40–42; D. Clark 1975; Blomberg 1989: 4–8; Porter and Reed 1995: 214–21; Thomson 1995: 13–45.

recognize, since they are helped in this regard by all kinds of signals—chapter divisions, verse divisions, headings, indentation, punctuation, footnotes, and so on—none of which are found in the original text, which follows a *scriptio continua* ("continuous script") format. Thus, as Ian Thomson (1995: 35) observes: "Chiasmus functions in the text as a structuring device that helps to divide one section of material from another. . . . Chiasmus is one of the devices that serves to divide a section of undifferentiated text from that around it."

Simple chiasms—the type employed by Paul in his letters—also function to add emphasis. Since the repeated elements (B′ and A′) do not say anything new but restate with either identical or synonymous terms and expressions in reverse order what has already been stated in the first half (A and B), Paul's argument is not advanced in any significant way. Nevertheless, the repetition of the elements in the chiasm has the rhetorical effect of emphasizing the apostle's words.

Interpretative Significance

In chapter 6 I discuss Philem. 5, an excellent example of how recognizing the occurrence of a simple chiasm in a Pauline letter can solve an exegetical problem. Galatians 1:1–2a (discussed in chap. 2) is another example where recognizing a chiasm can explain two peculiar features of Paul's words in the sender formula. Here I present two additional examples of chiasms in Paul's letters that illustrate the functions of this literary convention.

1. *Inclusio between the letter opening and the letter closing.* The chiasm's function of marking the boundaries of a literary unit explains the presence and order of the opening greeting and the closing grace and peace benedictions. The opening greeting in all Paul's letters, "Grace and peace," is repeated in reverse order in the letter closing, which is typically introduced by the peace benediction and, after the presence of other closing conventions, brought to a definitive end by the grace benediction:

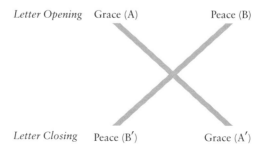

Letter Opening	Grace (A)	Peace (B)
Letter Closing	Peace (B′)	Grace (A′)

The pattern of aligning a closing peace benediction with God ("the God of peace," 1 Thess. 5:23) and a closing grace benediction with Christ ("the grace of our Lord Jesus Christ," 5:28) follows naturally from the opening greeting, where the same two wishes are linked in chiastic fashion with the same two divine figures: "Grace and peace be to you from God our Father and the Lord Jesus Christ" (1:2). The recognition of how Paul uses this chiasm to frame the overall structure of the letter also provides additional evidence for why the peace benediction is not, as some scholars claim,[24] part of the end of the letter body but rather the beginning of the letter closing. Finally, this bracketing of Paul's letters by a chiastic repetition of the grace and peace wish explains why the peace and grace benedictions occupy the first and final spots respectively in the letter closing.

2. *1 Thessalonians 5:5.* The function of a simple chiasm in adding emphasis to the text can be seen in 1 Thess. 5:5: "For you are all children of light and children of day; we are not of night or of darkness." The larger context of 5:1–11 involves the day of the Lord and the Thessalonians' curiosity about the timing of that end-time event, but their primary concern is whether they will avoid the wrath connected with that future day. In the first half of verse 5, Paul responds to his readers' anxiety by asserting that they need not fear the judgment that will take place on the day of the Lord, "for you are all children of light and children of day." The phrase "child/children of" (lit., "son/sons of") is a Jewish expression that denotes one or more persons who share in something. The specific phrases "children of light and children of day," therefore, identify the Thessalonians as those who share in the qualities of light and day—here metaphorical references to their moral status of righteousness and their presence with Jesus on the day of the Lord.

What is stated positively in the first half of verse 5 is now repeated negatively in the second half: "We are not of night or of darkness." Paul deviates from his normal pattern by omitting any connecting particle that would clarify the relationship between the second half of the verse with the first half.[25] The reason for this omission is that the relationship between the two halves of the verse is made clear instead through the chiastic structure that he constructs: the first and the fourth elements (light/darkness) are contrasted with each other, as are the second and third (day/night):

24. Roller 1933: 66–67, 196–97; White 1983: 442; 1988: 97. A number of commentaries on Paul's letters also adopt this position.
25. The technical term for this phenomenon is "asyndeton," omission of conjunctions.

Chiasm of 1 Thessalonians 5:5

A You are all children of light
   B and children of day.
   B′ We are not of night
A′ or of darkness.

Although the second half of verse 5 adds nothing new in terms of content but repeats in reverse order and in a negative fashion the point already made positively in the first half of the chiasm or verse, the reiteration that this literary device makes possible has the rhetorical effect of emphasizing Paul's words of comfort to his Thessalonian readers. They are not only "children of light and children of day" but are also "not of night or of darkness"; thus they can be confident about avoiding God's wrath on the day of the Lord.

5

The Closing

The fourth and final major section of Paul's letters—the closing—is the "Rodney Dangerfield" section of the apostle's correspondence: it doesn't get any respect. Whereas scholars have exerted much effort in analyzing the form and function of Paul's thanksgivings, letter bodies, and, to a lesser degree, letter openings, they typically neglect his letter closings.[1] Biblical commentaries generally treat the final section of the letter in a cursory manner and are at a loss to explain how a particular closing relates to its respective letter as a whole. The method of epistolary analysis, however, recognizes that the letter closing, like the other major sections of Paul's letters, is a carefully and cleverly constructed unit. The apostle shapes and adapts the various epistolary conventions found in the closing so that they echo and reinforce key concerns addressed earlier in the body of the letter—sometimes even summarizing and recapitulating those concerns. This final epistolary unit, therefore, functions much like the thanksgiving section, but in reverse. As the thanksgiving foreshadows and points ahead to the major concerns to be addressed in the body of the letter, so the closing serves to highlight and encapsulate the main points previously taken up in the body. Consequently, the letter closing potentially has great interpretative value, providing important clues for understanding the key issues and themes addressed in the body of the letter, as well as our understanding of the apostle's readers and their historical situation.

1. For the three assumptions, all of them false, that lead scholars to neglect the letter closing, see Weima 2014: 413–14.

Five epistolary conventions consistently occur in Paul's letter closings, and I will treat each one in the order in which it typically appears:

1. The peace benediction
2. The hortatory section
3. The greetings
4. The autograph
5. The grace benediction

The Peace Benediction

The epistolary convention that typically signals the beginning of the letter closing is the peace benediction. The location of this prayer as the first or second item in the closing (in contrast to the grace benediction, which always comes in the last position) stems from the chiasm that Paul creates between the opening greeting ("Grace to you and peace from God the Father and the Lord Jesus Christ") and the closing peace and grace benedictions.

Formal Analysis

The peace benediction occurs seven times in Paul's various letter closings (Rom. 15:33; 16:20a; 2 Cor. 13:11b; Gal. 6:16; Phil. 4:9b; 1 Thess. 5:23; 2 Thess. 3:16), and this epistolary convention exhibits a clear and consistent pattern involving four basic elements (see table 5.1: The Peace Benediction).

Table 5.1: The Peace Benediction

Letter	Introductory Element	Divine Source	Wish	Recipient
Rom. 15:33	But may	the God of peace	be with	you all.
Rom. 16:20a	But	the God of peace	will soon crush Satan under your feet.	[you]
2 Cor. 13:11b	And	the God of love and peace	will be with	you.
Gal. 6:16	And			as many who will follow this rule,
			peace and mercy be upon	them and upon the Israel of God.

Letter	Introductory Element	Divine Source	Wish	Recipient
Phil. 4:9b	And	the God of peace	will be with	you.
1 Thess. 5:23	But may	the God of peace himself	sanctify you completely, and may your whole spirit and soul and body be preserved blamelessly at the coming of our Lord Jesus Christ.	[you]
2 Thess. 3:16	But may	the Lord of peace himself	give you peace at all times in every way.	[you]

First, there is the "introductory element," which varies depending on the location of the peace benediction within the closing. When the peace benediction occupies the first position (Rom. 15:33; 1 Thess. 5:23; 2 Thess. 3:16; see Rom. 16:20a), the introductory element is the adversative particle "but" (*de*), which sets the letter closing apart from the letter body. But when the peace benediction is preceded by other closing conventions (2 Cor. 13:11b; Gal. 6:16; Phil. 4:9b), the introductory element is the conjunction "and" (*kai*).

Second, there is the "divine source" of the wish, which is normally "God" (the only exception is 2 Thess. 3:16; God as the divine source is implied in Gal. 6:16), in contrast to the grace benediction, where the divine source is always "(our) Lord Jesus Christ." This pattern of aligning a peace benediction with God and a grace benediction with Christ follows naturally from the greeting in the letter opening, where the same two wishes are linked in chiastic fashion with the same two divine figures ("Grace and peace to you from God our Father and the Lord Jesus Christ"). Added consistently to the divine source is the qualifying phrase "of peace," from which the peace benediction derives its name. The fuller expression "the God of peace," rare in the literature of Paul's day,[2] describes God as the source and thus also the giver of peace. The meaning of this "peace" that God gives involves not the Greek sense of the absence of conflict but the OT concept of "shalom"—a restoration of the fellowship and harmony that before the fall characterized humankind's relationship with God, with one another, and with the creation (see Rom. 2:10; 8:6; 14:17; Eph. 6:15; W. Foerster, *TDNT* 2:402–8).

Third, the content or "wish" of the peace benediction is complicated by the fact that some of these closing benedictions use the verb "to be," either given or implied, while others have a transitive verb (i.e., a verb that takes a

2. In literature written before the end of the first century CE, the phrase "the God of peace" occurs only twice outside of Paul's closing peace benedictions: *T. Dan* 5.2; Heb. 13:20.

direct object). In the former type, the content of the wish is taken from the qualifying phrase "of peace" so that Paul's prayer "May the God of peace *be* with you" is tantamount to saying "May the God of peace *give* you peace." In fact, the peace benediction of 2 Thess. 3:16 states this wish explicitly: "May the Lord of peace himself give you peace." In the latter type, the content of the wish still includes peace (since the source is similarly "the God of peace") but also includes an additional wish expressed by the transitive verb.

The fourth and final element in a Pauline peace benediction is the "recipient" of the wish: those who receive God's peace. Whenever this element appears, it has (with one important exception) some form of the personal pronoun "you."

The typical or expected form of Paul's peace benediction, therefore, exhibits the following basic form: "But may the God of peace be with you."

Interpretative Significance

1 THESSALONIANS 5:23

An understanding of the typical form of the peace benediction reveals the uniqueness and potential significance of the form of this epistolary convention found in 1 Thess. 5:23. Instead of the simple and relatively fixed formula, "But may the God of peace be with you" (Rom. 15:33; 2 Cor. 13:11; Phil. 4:9b), the peace benediction in the closing of 1 Thessalonians reads: "But may the God of peace himself sanctify you completely, and may your whole spirit and soul and body be preserved blamelessly at the coming of our Lord Jesus Christ." Here Paul has greatly expanded the third element, the wish, to include two additional clauses that echo two major themes addressed earlier in the body of the letter: the call to holy or sanctified living and comfort concerning Christ's return.

1. *Call to holy/sanctified living*. The theme of holiness or sanctification is expressed in the peace benediction by the two main verbs that convey the wish of the prayer: "may he sanctify" and "may it be preserved blamelessly." These two verbs and the two clauses of which they are a part form a chiasm (more obvious in its original Greek order than in English translation):

A verb: "may he sanctify/make holy"
  B recipients: "you"
    C adjective: "completely"
      "and"
    C′ adjective: "whole"
  B′ recipients: "your spirit and soul and body"
A′ verb: "may it be preserved blamelessly"

This chiasm reveals that the second clause is intended not to add a new idea but to reiterate, in reverse order, the idea already expressed in the first clause, thereby adding emphasis to its stated theme of holiness or sanctification. That holiness involves not just selected aspects or activities of a person's life, but one's entire being and conduct is stressed by the two rare and synonymous adjectives, "completely" (*holoteleis*) and "whole" (*holoklēron*), which both refer "to being complete and meeting all expectations" or "a high standard" (BDAG 703–4). The first adjective modifies "you" and so describes Paul's prayer that the God of peace will sanctify the Thessalonians "completely." The second adjective modifies "spirit and soul and body" and so describes Paul's prayer that God preserve blamelessly the Thessalonians' "whole" being. Thus the apostle petitions God (and also implicitly exhorts his Thessalonian readers) for nothing less than their total and complete sanctification.

Although the call to holy or sanctified living comes distinctly to the fore in the second half of the letter (4:1–5:22) and most explicitly in 4:3–8, the same concern can also be found in the thanksgiving (1:2–10) and first half of the letter (2:1–3:13). Paul opens 1 Thessalonians by commending his readers for their "work of faith and labor of love" (1:3), for the outward and visible signs of a holy life that testify to how they have "turned to God from idols in order to serve a living and true God" (1:9). Indeed, their "faith toward God," manifested in their holy lives, has served as a powerful example to all the believers in Macedonia and Achaia (1:7–8). Paul then defends his conduct during the mission-founding visit to Thessalonica by appealing to, among other things, "how holy and righteous and *blameless* [*amemptōs*, the same term used in the peace benediction, 5:23] we were to you believers" (2:10). This holiness exemplified in the lives of Paul and his coworkers becomes in turn the ground on which the apostle challenges the Thessalonians "to lead a life worthy of God" (2:12). The concern for sanctified living also manifests itself in the purpose of the prayer that climaxes the first half of the letter: "in order to strengthen your hearts as *blameless* in *holiness* before our God and Father at the coming of our Lord Jesus with all his *holy* ones" (3:13).

The second half of the letter (4:1–5:22), with its paraenetic or exhortative focus, highlights to an even greater degree the theme of holiness/sanctification. God's will for the Thessalonians is explicitly identified as "your *holiness*" (4:3). Believers must abstain from sexual immorality and learn how to control their bodies "in *holiness* and honor" (4:4). The reason why they should live this way is that "God did not call us for impurity but in *holiness*" (4:7), and so he "gives his Spirit who is *holy* to you" (4:8b). Sanctified lives are further characterized by love for fellow Christians, which involves, among other things, working with one's own hands and thus being dependent on no one (4:9–12). The theme of holiness even occurs in the midst of a lengthy discussion about Christ's return (4:13–5:11), where Paul identifies his readers as "children of light and children of day" in contrast to those "of night or of darkness" (5:5; see also 5:4, 7, 8). These repeated metaphors of light and day versus darkness and night, common to the OT and Jewish literature of Paul's day, are used here, as in his other letters (see esp. Rom. 13:12–13; also Rom. 1:21; 2:19; 1 Cor. 4:5; 2 Cor. 4:6; 6:14; Eph. 4:18; 5:8–11; 6:12; Col. 1:13), to refer to holy living, to the sanctified lives that the Thessalonians are leading. And though the term is not explicitly used, holiness continues to be a concern in the final exhortations about congregational life and worship (5:12–22). For if the Thessalonians want God to "sanctify" them "completely" and to preserve their "whole spirit and soul and body blamelessly," then they need to respect their congregational leaders (vv. 12–13a), be at peace among themselves (v. 13b), admonish the rebellious idlers (v. 14a), encourage the fainthearted (v. 14b), be devoted to the weak (v. 14c), deal patiently with all (v. 14d), pursue what is good (v. 15), and so on.

It is clear, therefore, that the emphasis on holiness expressed in the peace benediction of 5:23 echoes, both in content and in direct verbal links, the statements and exhortations given throughout the rest of 1 Thessalonians. Paul has carefully adapted and expanded this traditional epistolary convention belonging to the letter closing so that it recapitulates one of the key themes of his correspondence to the Thessalonians, driving home one last time to his readers the importance of holy or sanctified living.

2. Comfort concerning Christ's return. A second major theme of the letter, namely comfort concerning Christ's return, is expressed in the peace benediction by means of the added prepositional phrase, "at the coming of our Lord Jesus Christ." This reference to Christ's second coming is all the more striking because it does not occur in any other peace benediction.

Paul has prepared the Thessalonian readers well throughout the thanksgiving and body sections of the letter to be reminded about Christ's return in the closing. He opens his correspondence by giving thanks to God for the Thessalonians' "steadfastness of hope in our Lord Jesus Christ" (1:3), which, in the context of the letter as a whole, refers not merely to a general hope in the person and work of Christ but more narrowly to their abiding confidence in his imminent return from heaven to bring about their deliverance. At the end of the thanksgiving section, this idea is confirmed with the climaxing statement that the Thessalonian readers have turned from idols not only to serve God but also "to wait for his son from the heavens, . . . who rescues us from the coming wrath" (1:10)—an explicit reference both to Christ's return and to the final judgment that will take place at his return. Instead of facing judgment on that day, the Thessalonian believers will be Paul's "crown of boasting . . . before our Lord Jesus Christ at his coming" (2:19). To ensure that result, the apostle closes the first half of the letter by praying that Christ will establish their hearts unblamable in holiness before God "at the coming of our Lord Jesus with his holy ones" (3:13).

The return of Christ is a theme developed much more explicitly in the second half of the letter, where Paul devotes two large sections (4:13–18; 5:1–11) to this very subject, highlighting in this material especially the pastoral concern of providing comfort.[3] The first passage (4:13–18) deals with the comforting message that deceased believers will neither miss nor be at a disadvantage at Christ's return, but that *all* Christians—those who have already "fallen asleep" as well as those who remain alive—will participate equally in the glory and splendor of his coming. The second passage (5:1–11) comforts living believers with the truth that, though the day of the Lord will involve a sudden destruction, from which there will certainly be no escape, believers need not fear this eschatological event: they not only enjoy the status of being "children of light" and "children of day," but they have also been elected by God to obtain salvation and eternal life and not to suffer wrath. Thus the long section of 4:13–5:11 is permeated with references, both explicit and implicit, to the topic of Christ's return.

Such a preoccupation with the second coming of Christ, not only in 4:13–5:11 but in the rest of the letter as well, makes it difficult to believe that the unparalleled reference to "the coming of our Lord Jesus Christ" in the peace benediction of 5:23 is fortuitous. Rather, as with the theme of being called to holy living, Paul has deliberately adapted and expanded his typical closing peace benediction so that it echoes another main theme of this letter.

Galatians 6:16

Another peace benediction that deviates significantly from its typical form is Gal. 6:16. Instead of the expected "But may the God of peace be with you," here we find, "And as many who will follow this rule, peace and mercy be upon them and upon the Israel of God." All four elements of the peace benediction differ from the general formula. The first, the "introductory element," has been changed from the contrastive particle "but" to the conjunction "and" because this peace benediction does not occupy the first spot in the closing section: it is preceded by the autograph formula of 6:11 and the following explanatory statements of 6:12–15. Thus instead of using the contrasting particle "but,"

---

3. Each section concludes with the exhortation "Therefore, comfort one another" (4:18; 5:11).

which would set the peace benediction apart from the preceding material, the conjunction "and" is used to more closely link this epistolary convention to the rebuking words that Paul himself, after taking the quill from his secretary, has just written. The second and third elements of this peace benediction are also changed: the "divine source" is omitted, and the "wish" of peace is supplemented by the wish of "mercy." The most significant modification, however, occurs in the fourth element—the identification of the "recipient." Instead of the expected prepositional phrase "with you," the recipient is identified by means of a relative clause, "as many who will follow this rule," followed by a double prepositional phrase, "upon them and upon the Israel of God."

1. *The conditional character of the peace benediction.* The first remarkable feature about this change is how it turns the peace benediction into a conditional blessing: not everyone in the Galatian churches will receive peace and mercy but rather *only* those who will follow the rule previously laid down by Paul in this letter. What the apostle does here is just as striking as it would be for a contemporary pastor to end a worship service by saying in the closing blessing: "Grace and peace be to all those who obey what I have said in my sermon." Nowhere else does the apostle give to any of his peace benedictions or his grace benedictions such a conditional character. This change is not coincidental but conscious and deliberate, as confirmed by the obviously strained relationship that exists between Paul and his readers in Galatia—a strained relationship manifesting itself already in the letter opening, with its strategic alterations (see discussion in chap. 2 under "Interpretative Significance" for how Paul has adapted all three epistolary conventions in the letter opening); the thanksgiving section, which Paul has replaced with a rebuke section (see discussion in chap. 3 under "Galatians 1:6–10"); plus explicit admonitions in the letter body and so not surprisingly also here in the letter closing. Douglas Moo (2013: 399) comments:

> Just as Paul cannot include his usual thanksgiving for his addressees in the introduction, so he cannot promise peace to his readers. Rather, the entire letter stands between the conditional curse of 1:8–9 and the conditional blessing of 6:16 (Betz 1979: 321; Hays 2000: 345). The situation in Galatia is too dire and the reaction of the Galatians too uncertain to allow for such unqualified promises.

2. *The echoing function of the phrase "the Israel of God."* The second remarkable feature about the altered peace benediction in Galatians is Paul's reference to the receivers of the wish with the unusual phrase "the Israel of God." Who is being described in this phrase? Does it refer to a second group distinct from the "them" on whom Paul pronounces a conditional blessing?

This would require the common *conjunctive* use of the Greek word "and," so that the text reads: "upon them *and* upon the Israel of God." Or does it refer to the same group as "them" but described more fully? This would require the rarer *explanatory* use of the Greek word "and," so that the text reads: "upon them, namely, the Israel of God." In the first, "two-group" view, the "them" refers to the Galatian readers who are predominantly *gentile*, and "the Israel of God" refers to *Jews*, either a non-Judaizing group of Jewish Christians in Galatia, a believing Jewish remnant within the broader Christian church, or an eschatological Israel that will be saved at Christ's return. In the second, "one-group" view, the "them" are the predominantly gentile readers in Galatia, whom Paul more fully identifies as "the Israel of God" in order to emphasize that they too, despite their non-Jewish ethnicity, are fully members of God's covenant people.

Although both views can be defended on the grounds of Greek grammar and the use of "Israel" elsewhere in Paul's writings, only one of them is supported by the context of the Galatians letter. And since "context is king" in interpretation, it is this factor that ought to be decisive. It is difficult, if not impossible, to believe that, in a letter where Paul has been at great pains to break down the distinctions that separate Jewish and gentile Christians and has stressed the equality of both groups, he in the closing would give a peace benediction addressed to believing Jews as a separate group within the church. The situation would be like that of a prosecuting lawyer arguing for weeks in a lengthy murder trial that the accused is guilty of the crime, and then suddenly suggest in the closing argument that another person did it. Thomas Schreiner (2010: 383) states this key point well:

> It would be highly confusing to the Galatians, after arguing for the equality of Jew and Gentile in Christ (3:28) and after emphasizing that believers are Abraham's children, for Paul to argue in the conclusion that only Jews who believe in Jesus belong to the Israel of God. By doing so a wedge would be introduced between Jews and Gentiles at the end of the letter, suggesting that the latter were not part of the true Israel. Such a wedge would play into the hands of the opponents, who would argue that to be part of the true Israel one must be circumcised.

Francois Tolmie (2005: 226) makes the same point more succinctly: "Rhetorically speaking, introducing such a new idea ["the Israel of God" refers to a second group, who are Jews] a few lines before the end of the letter would indeed be disastrous, as one of the last impressions he [Paul] would leave the Galatians would be one that undermines most of what he has tried to achieve in the rest of the letter." The context of the letter, therefore, demands that the phrase "the Israel of God" refers to the same group as "them," namely, those *gentile* Christians in Galatia who are walking according to Paul's rule.[4]

What is most significant for my purposes, however, is that the designation "the Israel of God" echoes an important theme in the body of the letter, namely the claim of Paul (apparently in reaction to the message of the Judaizers) that gentile Christians are legitimate heirs of Abraham and thus share fully in the blessings of God's covenant with Abraham and his descendants, the people of Israel. This issue of who rightfully are children and thus heirs of Abraham manifests itself at a number of points in the letter body:

- In 3:6–9 Paul gives an exposition of Abraham's faith: "So you see it is those who have faith who are the children of Abraham. And the Scripture, foreseeing that God would justify the gentiles by faith, preached the gospel beforehand to Abraham, saying, 'In you [Abraham] shall all the nations be blessed.' So then, those who have faith are blessed with Abraham who had faith."

- In 3:14 Paul explicitly states that the purpose of Christ's death on the cross was to allow gentiles to share fully in the blessing of the Abrahamic covenant: "in order that in Christ Jesus the blessing of Abraham might come to the gentiles."

- In 3:15–18 Paul articulates the true nature of the Abrahamic covenant: the promises of this covenant are not intended just for the ethnic offspring of Abraham, the Jews; rather, the promises of this covenant are for God's offspring, Christ, and, as is made clear (later) in 3:29, also for those who are Christ's own, regardless of their ethnicity.

- In 3:26–29 Paul applies this claim about the Abrahamic covenant to the Galatian situation: "For you all are children of God through faith in Christ Jesus. . . . And if you are Christ's, then you are Abraham's offspring, heirs according to promise."

- And finally in 4:21–31 Paul treats the two wives of Abraham (Hagar and Sarah) and his two sons in an allegorical manner. Here he claims that the gentile Christians of Galatia are the true sons and daughters of Abraham, since they are children of promise and children of the free woman (see esp. 4:31): "So, brothers and sisters, we are not children of the slave but of the free woman."

4. Likewise the majority of Galatians commentators: e.g., Dahl 1950; Fung 1988: 311; Longenecker 1990: 297–98; Martyn 1997: 574–77; Hays 2000: 345–46; Köstenberger 2001; Schreiner 2010: 381–83; Moo 2013: 401–3.

It is clear, therefore, that one of Paul's central concerns in the body section of Galatians is to prove that the gentile Christians are truly children of Abraham and share equally with the people of Israel the blessings of the Abrahamic covenant.

In this context, Paul's adaptation of the peace benediction in Gal. 6:16 becomes highly significant and telling. For by closing the letter with a reference to his gentile readers as "the Israel of God," Paul reasserts the claim articulated in the letter as a whole: the gentile Christians in Galatia, by faith in Christ rather than by submitting to circumcision and observing other Jewish laws, have become the true heirs of Abraham together with all Jews who believe, and so can legitimately be called "the Israel of God." As in 1 Thess. 5:23, here too we see Paul adapting the form of the peace benediction such that this epistolary convention now recalls and reaffirms one of the key themes of the letter. That this echoing function of the peace benediction is not fortuitous but deliberate and thus interpretively significant is confirmed by the remaining epistolary conventions in the closing of Gal. 6:11–18, which have likewise been expanded and adapted by Paul in such a way that they also recapitulate the key themes developed throughout the Galatian letter (see Weima 1993).

The Hortatory Section

Formal Analysis

Most of Paul's closings include what can be called a "hortatory section": final commands and exhortations. A comparative analysis of the hortatory section (see table 5.2: The Hortatory Section) reveals that this material is far less tightly structured than the other four epistolary conventions that make up the closing section of Paul's letters. The hortatory sections appear to be ad hoc creations of the apostle, and so it would be wrong to speak of their "form" in the same sense as that of the many stereotyped formulas found in his letters.

Table 5.2: The Hortatory Section

Letter	Introductory Element	Hortatory Material
Rom. 16:17–18, 19b	Brothers and sisters,	I appeal to you to watch out for those who cause divisions and create obstacles contrary to the doctrine that you have been taught; avoid them. For such persons do not serve our Lord Christ, but their own appetites, and by smooth talk and flattery they deceive the hearts of the naïve. . . but I want you to be wise as to what is good and innocent as to what is evil.

(cont.)

Letter	Introductory Element	Hortatory Material
1 Cor. 16:13–16, 22	Brothers and sisters,	be watchful, stand firm in the faith, act like men, be strong. Let all that you do be done in love. Now I urge you—you know that the household of Stephanas were the first converts in Achaia, and that they have devoted themselves to the service of the saints—be subject to such as these, and to every fellow worker and laborer. . . . If anyone has no love for the Lord, let that person be accursed. Our Lord, come!
2 Cor. 13:11a	Finally, brothers and sisters,	rejoice, be restored, be comforted, be of the same mind, live in peace.
Gal. 6:17	Finally,	let no one cause me trouble, for I bear on my body the marks of Jesus.
Phil. 4:8–9a	Finally, brothers and sisters,	whatever is true, whatever is noble, whatever is right, whatever is pure, whatever is lovely, whatever is admirable, if there is anything excellent and if there is anything praiseworthy, think about these things. What things you have learned and you have received and you have heard and you have seen in me do these things.
1 Thess. 5:25, 27	Brothers and sisters,	pray also for us . . . I cause you to swear an oath in the name of the Lord that this letter be read to all the brothers and sisters.
Philem. 20	Yes, brother,	I want some benefit from you in the Lord. Refresh my heart in Christ.

Nevertheless, there are a few features that are common to many of these hortatory sections. They are frequently introduced with the vocative form of address, "Brothers and sisters" (Rom. 16:17; 2 Cor. 13:11; Phil. 4:8; 1 Thess. 5:25; Philem. 20; see 1 Cor. 16:15)—the most common epistolary means of marking transition in ancient Greek letters, whether those of Paul or of others. Another less common means of introducing the hortatory section is with the word "finally" (2 Cor. 13:11; Gal. 6:17; Phil. 4:8). This section is also characterized by the use of the imperative, which is naturally to be expected in hortatory material. In those few instances where the imperative does not occur, a verb of entreaty ("I appeal," Rom. 16:17; 1 Cor. 16:15) or adjuration ("I cause [you] to swear an oath," 1 Thess. 5:27) expresses the commanding tone of Paul's words.

Interpretative Significance

At first blush the hortatory section in Paul's letter closings might appear to be generic in its content—final exhortations that could be given to any and all churches. For example, the closing command of 1 Thess. 5:25, "Brothers and sisters, pray also for us," does not seem to be related in any unique manner to the Thessalonian church and the material in the letter body that Paul has just written to them. Nevertheless, Paul adds to this hortatory section a second command that clearly does reflect the specific situation of the church in Thessalonica: "I cause you to swear an oath in the name of the Lord that this letter be read to all the brothers" (1 Thess. 5:27). This strong exhortation is aimed at the "rebellious idlers" (5:14; see also 2 Thess. 3:6–15): church members who during Paul's mission-founding visit had already demonstrated an unwillingness to obey his teaching about the need for self-sufficient work rather than taking advantage of the generosity of fellow believers (1 Thess. 4:11c, "to work with your hands *just as we commanded you*"; see also 2 Thess. 3:6, 10), whom the church is called on to admonish (1 Thess. 5:14), and who (the apostle understandably now worries) may continue to defy his teaching to them in this letter. It is not just this final command, however, that has specific and direct links to concerns addressed previously in the letter. The hortatory section in all of Paul's letter closings exhibits the same feature, as the apostle brings his correspondence to an end by issuing final commands that are not generic but either minimally address a specific situation in the church or maximally echo and so reinforce key issues already taken up in the letter body.

Philippians 4:8–9a

A good example of a closing hortatory section that reflects a number of central concerns previously presented in the letter is Phil. 4:8–9a. The highly stylized character of the two commands that make up this hortatory section is apparent from the following presentation of the text:

> [8]Finally, brothers and sisters,
> whatever is true,
> whatever is noble,
> whatever is right,
> whatever is pure,
> whatever is lovely,
> whatever is admirable,
> if there is anything excellent and
> if there is anything praiseworthy,
> think about these things!
> [9]What things
> you have learned and
> you have received and
> you have heard and

you have seen in me,
do these things!

A strong majority of commentators believe that the letter closing of Philippians consists only of the final greetings and grace benediction found in 4:21–23. Consequently, they view the two commands of 4:8–9a as belonging not to the closing of the letter but to its body. However, there is compelling evidence that the letter closing begins much earlier, with the exhortative material of 4:8–9a:

- The two commands of Phil. 4:8–9a open with the word "finally" and the vocative "brothers and sisters," both of which are used either alone or together in Paul's other letters to introduce the closing hortatory section (Rom. 16:17; 1 Cor. 16:13; 2 Cor. 13:11a; Gal. 6:17; 1 Thess. 5:25; Philem. 20).
- The hortatory section of Phil. 4:8–9a is followed in 4:9b by a peace benediction, an epistolary convention that always belongs to the closing in Paul's other letters.
- That this peace benediction (Phil. 4:9b) opens not with the contrastive "but" (*de*) but with the conjunctive "and" (*kai*) is significant: the former pattern is used when the peace benediction is the first item in the closing (Rom. 15:33; 1 Thess. 5:23; 2 Thess. 3:16), whereas the latter pattern occurs when the peace benediction is preceded by another closing convention, as is the case here (see also 2 Cor. 13:11 and Gal. 6:16).
- The following material of Phil 4:10–20 constitutes a greatly expanded "joy formula," which is also an epistolary convention sometimes found in the closings of Paul's other letters (Rom. 16:19a; 1 Cor. 16:17).
- If the hortatory section of 4:8–9a is viewed as belonging to the letter closing, it explains why this brief literary unit does not fit very well either logically or literarily with the immediately preceding material of 4:2–7—something that commentators who locate these two commands in the letter body struggle to account for in a convincing manner.

These facts strongly suggest that the letter closing of Philippians consists of 4:8–23 and that the final section of this letter opens with the hortatory section of 4:8–9a. For my purposes, what is significant is that these two closing exhortations reflect well three interrelated topics taken up earlier in the letter body: proper moral conduct, the theme of imitation, and the reaffirmation of Paul's authoritative status.

1. *Proper moral conduct.* The hortatory section of 4:8–9a recalls in a general way the letter's focus on proper moral conduct. The six "excellent" and "praiseworthy" virtues listed in the first command (4:8) all refer to ethical qualities and so reinforce Paul's opening challenge to the Philippians in the thanksgiving section that they be "pure and blameless" (1:10) and "filled with the fruit of righteousness" (1:11). Similarly, in the body of the letter, Paul exhorts his readers to "let your manner of life be worthy of the gospel of Christ" (1:27a), which in their specific context means that they exhibit unity of spirit and mind (1:27b; 2:1–2; 4:2–3). The apostle's concern that the Philippians live morally upright lives also is reflected in his command that they be "blameless and innocent, children of God without blemish in the midst of a crooked and perverse generation, among whom you shine as lights in the world" (2:15). The six virtues listed in the closing hortatory section stand in sharp contrast to the vices responsible for destroying the unity and fellowship of the Philippian congregation: envy (1:15), rivalry (1:15), selfishness (1:17; 2:3, 21), insincerity (1:17, 18), conceit (2:3), and a preoccupation with earthly things (3:19).

2. *Imitation theme.* In the closing hortatory section, Paul reinforces his emphasis on proper moral conduct by evoking another theme that has also been developed throughout the letter body: imitation. After challenging his readers, in the first closing command, to think about the six listed virtues (4:8), he then exhorts them in the second closing command to imitate him: "What things you have learned and you have received and you have heard and you have seen *in me*, do these things" (4:9a). Here in the letter's closing, as he did earlier in its body, Paul clearly presents himself as a model for the Philippians to imitate.

The theme of imitation or modeling manifests itself first in 1:30, where Paul uses his own experience of suffering for the sake of the gospel as an example to encourage his Philippian readers, who were also experiencing persecution for their faith. In fact, Paul's reference here to "what you have seen in me and now have heard in me" (1:30b) parallels in an almost word-for-word manner the latter part of his closing exhortation ("whatever you have heard and you have seen in me," 4:9). Similarly, in 2:17–18 Paul's ability to rejoice even in the face of intense suffering serves as a model for the Philippians to follow. The theme of imitating Paul also appears in 3:17, where the apostle explicitly commands: "Brothers and sisters, be fellow imitators of me and mark those who thus live according to our example." To encourage his Philippian readers to live a proper moral life, Paul holds up his own life and the lives of other faithful Christians as models for them to follow as they seek to live within a pagan world, whose values differed radically from those who live as followers of Jesus Christ.

The theme of imitation in the closing hortatory section also recalls the important section of 2:1–11, where Paul uses Christ's life as a powerful example for the Philippian church to emulate (2:5). In sharp contrast to the self-seeking and proud attitude that was causing division in the church, there stands the self-sacrificial and humble attitude of Christ, who gave up his right of equal status with God to serve and save others. In the same vein, Paul uses Timothy's sincere concern for the Philippians' welfare (2:19–24) and Epaphroditis's sacrificial actions (2:25–30) as positive examples to be imitated, in contrast to the false leaders in the church who "look after their own interests, not those of Jesus Christ" (2:20–21). Paul, no doubt, had these two coworkers in mind when he later exhorts the Philippians not just to imitate him but also to "mark those who thus live according to our example" (3:17).

3. *Reaffirmation of Paul's authoritative status.* A further noteworthy feature about the closing hortatory section of 4:8–9a is the way Paul uses these two final commands to reaffirm, albeit in a subtle manner, his position of leadership and authority. Even though it is not explicitly stated, the close connection between 4:8 and 4:9 naturally leads to the conclusion that the six excellent and praiseworthy virtues are the very things that the Philippians have learned, received, heard, and seen in Paul's life. In this way, the closing hortatory section reaffirms the authority of Paul and his teachings in contrast to his opponents and their conflicting ideas that he has been addressing throughout the letter (1:15–18, 28; 2:1–4, 21; 3:2–11, 18–19). Just as the virtues in 4:8 (implied as belonging to Paul) ought to be seen in contrast to the vices of those causing trouble and division in the church, so also the example of Paul in 4:9a has in view not only the exemplary moral life of the apostle but also the contrast between himself and his opponents in Philippi. This can be seen, for example, in 3:17–19, which contrasts imitating Paul and other faithful leaders (3:17) with copying certain false teachers or earthly minded leaders (3:18–19). In this context, Paul's challenge to imitate him means, then, not simply "Do the things that I do" but also "Recognize my authority; follow what I say, not what my opponents say; be obedient to me" (W. Michaelis, *TDNT* 4:668; Hawthorne 1983: 161).

It is clear that the closing hortatory section of 4:8–9a in no way consists of two generic commands that would be appropriate for any and all churches. Instead, Paul constructed these final exhortations with the specific situation of the Philippian church in mind. The apostle skillfully wrote the closing hortatory section so that it would recall to the minds of his Philippian readers three interrelated topics that he has been highlighting throughout the letter: the need for proper moral conduct; how this type of a virtuous life can be accomplished by imitating Paul, Christ, Timothy, Epaphroditus, and other

faithful leaders; and the reaffirmation of Paul's authoritative status in contrast
to that of his opponents.

2 Corinthians 13:11

The closing commands of 2 Cor. 13:11 provide another example of a hortatory section that is related to concerns addressed previously in the body of
the letter. Paul brings his last letter to the Corinthians to a close with a series
of five succinct imperatives that are given in a rapid-fire, "staccato" fashion
(without any conjunctions or connecting particles) and preceded by the two
introductory elements that typically occur with a hortatory section: "Finally,
brothers and sisters, rejoice, be restored, be comforted, be of the same mind,
live in peace."

There are a number of significant verbal and content links between these
five closing commands and the preceding material in the letter. The first
exhortation, "Rejoice!," recalls not only Paul's words two verses earlier in
13:9a, where he rejoices at the prospect of the Corinthians being strong in
their faith in answer to his prayers ("For we rejoice when . . . you are strong"),
but also Paul's joy for them expressed throughout the letter (1:24; 2:3; 6:10;
7:4, 7, 9, 13, 16; see also 8:2). The second exhortation, "Be restored!," clearly
also echoes Paul's just-stated words in 13:9b, where he prays for the "restoration" of the Corinthians—that this divided congregation be restored to
a unified community, something that the apostle has longed desired for his
Corinthian readers (1 Cor. 1:10, "I appeal . . . that you all agree and that
there be no divisions among you but that you be *restored* in the same mind
and the same knowledge") and that he has been addressing in this letter,
especially in chapters 10–13. The third exhortation, "Be comforted," "reiter-
ates one of 2 Corinthians' main themes—encouragement. In fact, here we
have a theme that ties the end of 2 Corinthians back to the introduction of
the book" (Guthrie 2015: 650, who cites in support the following passages:
1:3–7; 2:7–8; 5:20; 6:1; 7:4–13; 8:4, 6, 17; 9:5; 10:1; 12:8, 18; 13:11). Finally,
the fourth and fifth exhortations—"Be of the same mind!" and "Live in
peace!"—reflect once again the problem of disunity and disharmony in the
Corinthian church, which Paul has been addressing throughout the letter
but especially in the final four chapters. All five of Paul's closing commands
in 13:11, therefore, relate directly to his concern that among the Corinthian
believers there is "quarreling, jealousy, anger, selfishness, slander, gossip,
conceit, and disorder" (12:20).

A number of commentators have drawn attention to how Paul uses the final
commands of 13:11 to echo and reaffirm his previous appeals in the letter for

unity and peace to exist within the Corinthian congregation. Allan Menzies (1912: 104), for example, notes concerning 13:11: "He [Paul] gathers up the main points of what he has urged on them." Similarly, D. A. Carson (1984: 183) comments: "2 Corinthians 13.11 casts a backward glance at the rest of the epistle." And Francis Fallon (1980: 155), to cite yet another among many, also recognizes that Paul's concluding exhortations in 13:11 "sum up his concerns in the preceding chapters and the needs of the community."

The hortatory section in the closing of 2 Corinthians, therefore, provides another example of how Paul's final exhortations are not generic commands in the apostle's repertoire of moral injunctions that he simply tacks on to the end of the letter in a perfunctory fashion or in an unreflective manner.[5] Quite the opposite, 2 Cor. 13:11 illustrates the truth that the apostle has put these five final imperatives together with the specific situation of the Corinthian church in mind and has chosen his vocabulary so that these commands are more accurately "summarizing" commands—exhortations that, despite their brevity, recapitulate and so reinforce key points developed previously in the letter.

The Greetings

Formal Analysis

The sending of greetings was a standard and expected part of letter closings in the Greco-Roman world. It is not at all surprising, then, that the third epistolary convention found in virtually all the final sections of Paul's letter closings are the greetings. Among the different stereotyped formulas found in the closing of the apostle's letters, the greetings exhibit the closest parallels with the same formula in Hellenistic letters. It is helpful to classify the greetings in the apostle's letters into three types according to the different persons expressed in the verb: first-, second-, or third-person types (see tables 5.3a–c: The Greetings).

Table 5.3a: The Greetings—First-Person Type

Letter	Giver	Greeting Verb	Recipients
Rom. 16:22	I, Tertius, the one who wrote this letter,	greet	you in the Lord.

5. Contra the early position of Murray Harris (2008: 544, originally published in 1975), who claimed that Paul here "issues a final appeal couched in general terms." In his subsequent publication on 2 Corinthians, however, Murray states, "Paul's injunction was particularly relevant in Corinth where quarreling needed to be replaced by reconciliation, factionalism by unity, and arrogance by love" (2005: 936).

First-Person Type

Paul himself never uses the first-person type of greeting, "I greet." The only occurrence of this type of greeting is found in Rom. 16:22, where the apostle's secretary, Tertius, personally greets the readers: "I, Tertius, the one who wrote this letter, greet you in the Lord." The absence of the first-person greeting in Paul's letters agrees with the restricted use of this type of greeting in Hellenistic letters. Since Paul conveys his personal greeting in the opening salutation ("Grace to you and peace"), it would be redundant to repeat this personal greeting in the letter closing.

Although Paul's letters contain no explicit examples of a first-person greeting given by the apostle himself, there is a distinctive formula that belongs to this greeting type: "The greeting [is written] with my own hand" (1 Cor. 16:21; 2 Thess. 3:17; Col. 4:18). As Hans Windisch (*TDNT* 1:502) states, "The greeting in the apostle's own hand . . . is materially identical with 'I greet.'" This particular form of a first-person type of greeting is more accurately an "autograph greeting," since Paul signals to his audience that he has taken over from his secretary and is now writing the greeting in his own hand.[6] Paul's use of this phrase to express a greeting appears to be unparalleled in other letters of his day.

Table 5.3b: The Greetings—Second-Person Type

Letter	Greeting Verb	Recipients
Rom. 16:3–5a	Greet	Prisca and Aquila, my fellow workers in Christ Jesus, who risked their necks for my life, to whom not only I but also all the churches of the gentiles give thanks, and also the church in their house.
Rom. 16:5b	Greet	my beloved Epaenetus, who was the first convert to Christ in Asia.
Rom. 16:6	Greet	Mary, who has worked hard for you.
Rom. 16:7	Greet	Andronicus and Junia, my kinsmen and my fellow prisoners. They are well known to the apostles, and they were in Christ before me.
Rom. 16:8	Greet	Ampliatus, my beloved in the Lord.
Rom. 16:9	Greet	Urbanus, our fellow worker in Christ, and my beloved Stachys.
Rom. 16:10a	Greet	Apelles, who is approved in Christ.
Rom. 16:10b	Greet	those who belong to the family of Aristobulus.

(cont.)

6. The autograph will be treated later in this chapter as a separate epistolary convention used in the letter closing.

Letter	Greeting Verb	Recipients
Rom. 16:11a	Greet	Herodian, my kinsmen.
Rom. 16:11b	Greet	those in the family of Narcissus, who are in the Lord.
Rom. 16:12a	Greet	Tryphaena and Tryphosa, those workers in the Lord.
Rom. 16:12b	Greet	Persis, the beloved, who has worked hard in the Lord.
Rom. 16:13	Greet	Rufus, chosen in the Lord; also his mother and mine.
Rom. 16:14	Greet	Asyncritus, Phlegon, Hermes, Patrobas, Hermas, and the brothers who are with them.
Rom. 16:15	Greet	Philologus, Junia, Nereus and his sister, and Olympas, and all the saints who are with them.
Rom. 16:16a	Greet	one another with a holy kiss.
1 Cor.16:20b	Greet	one another with a holy kiss.
2 Cor. 13:12a NRSV	Greet	one another with a holy kiss.
Phil. 4:21a	Greet	every saint in Christ Jesus.
1 Thess. 5:26	Greet	all the brothers and sisters with a holy kiss.
Col. 4:15	Greet	the brothers and sisters in Laodicea, and Nympha and the church in her house.
2 Tim. 4:19	Greet	Prisca and Aquila, and the household of Onesiphorus.
Titus 3:15b	Greet	those who love us in the faith.
Heb. 13:24a	Greet	all your leaders and all the saints.
1 Pet. 5:14	Greet	one another with the kiss of love.
3 John 15b NRSV	Greet	the friends by name.

SECOND-PERSON TYPE

In the second-person type of greeting, Paul enlists the help of his readers in passing on greetings to specific individuals in their church community: "Greet so-and-so." The use of this type of greeting might suggest that the people being greeted were not part of the congregation to whom the letter was addressed. If this were the case, the use of second-person greetings in Romans, for example, would imply that this letter was written only to one of the several house churches in Rome and that Paul authorizes them to pass on his personal greetings to specific individuals who belong to the remaining house churches in the capital city (so C.-H. Kim 1972: 139–40; Mullins 1968: 425–26).

It is clear, however, that Paul expected his letter to be read in all the churches of Rome (1:7, "all those in Rome"; see also 1 Thess. 5:27; Col. 4:16) and that, as a result, he could greet specific people in those churches directly himself. A second-person greeting, therefore, functions virtually as a surrogate for a first-person greeting. If it is next asked "Why then did Paul not use the more personal first-person greeting?" the answer seems to be that the involvement of the congregation as a whole in passing on his greetings to others expresses a stronger sense of public commendation for the individuals being specifically greeted by the apostle.

Table 5.3c: The Greetings—Third-Person Type

Letter	Giver	Greeting Verb	Recipients
Rom. 16:16b	All the churches of Christ	greet	you.
Rom. 16:21	Timothy, my fellow worker,	greets	you.
Rom. 16:23a	Gaius, who is host to me and the whole church,	greets	you.
Rom. 16:23b	Erastus, the city treasurer, and our brother Quartus	greet	you.
1 Cor. 16:19a	The churches of Asia	greet	you.
1 Cor. 16:19b	Aquila and Prisca, together with the church in their house,	greet	you in the Lord.
1 Cor. 16:20a	All the brothers and sisters	greet	you.
2 Cor. 13:12b NRSV	All the saints	greet	you.
Phil. 4:21b	The brothers and sisters who are with me	greet	you.
Phil. 4:22	All the saints, especially those of Caesar's household,	greet	you.
Philem. 23	Epaphras my fellow prisoner in Christ Jesus	greets	you.
Col. 4:10–11	Aristarchus my fellow prisoner and Mark the cousin of Barnabas (concerning whom you have received instructions—if he comes to you, welcome him), and Jesus who is called Justus. These are the only men of the circumcision among my fellow workers for the kingdom of God, and they have been a comfort to me.	greets	you,
Col. 4:12–13	Epaphras, who is one of you, a servant of Christ Jesus, always struggling on your behalf in his prayers, that you may stand mature and fully assured in all the will of God. For I bear him witness that he has worked hard for you and for those in Laodicea and in Hierapolis.	greets	you,
Col. 4:14	Luke the beloved physician and Demas	greet	you.
2 Tim. 4:21	Eubulus and Pudens and Linus and Claudia and all the brothers and sisters	greet	you.
Titus 3:15a	All who are with me	greet	you.
Heb. 13:24b	Those from Italy	greet	you.
1 Pet. 5:13	She who is at Babylon, who is likewise chosen, and Mark, my son,	greet	you.

(cont.)

Letter	Giver	Greeting Verb	Recipients
2 John 13	The children of your elect sister	greet	you.
3 John 15a NRSV	The friends	greet	you.

THIRD-PERSON TYPE

The third-person type of greeting allows Paul to pass on to the letter's recipients the greetings of others who are with him. The apostle serves as an agent, expressing greetings on behalf of specific individuals (Rom. 16:21, 23; 1 Cor. 16:19b; Philem. 23), of well-defined groups (Phil. 4:22), or of very general groups (1 Cor. 16:20; 2 Cor. 13:12b NRSV; Phil. 4:21b). That Paul believes he can speak on behalf of such large groups as "the church in Asia" (1 Cor. 16:19a) or "all the saints" (2 Cor. 13:12b NRSV)—or even more broadly yet "all the churches of Christ" (Rom. 16:16b)—reveals just how comprehensive he perceived his apostolic and authoritative status to be.

All three types of greetings contain the same three basic elements common to the greetings in Greco-Roman letters: (1) the main verb expressing greetings; (2) the giver of the greeting, either Paul (first-person and second-person greetings) or some other person or group (third-person greeting); and (3) the recipients of the greeting, either the addressee(s) or some other specifically named person or group. At times the apostle expands and elaborates each of these three basic elements. The first element of the greeting formula, the verb, for example, is supplemented in 1 Cor. 16:19b by the adverb "heartily" (lit., "many, very much")—a common addition to greetings in Hellenistic letters in order to give them a warmer and more personal tone: "Aquila and Priscilla greet you *heartily* in the Lord." The second element of the greeting formula, the giver of the greeting, is elaborated in third-person greetings with a descriptive phrase that makes the sender of the greeting more exact and spells out the kind of relationship that exists between this person and Paul: "Gaius, who is host to me and to the whole church, greets you" (Rom. 16:23a); "Erastus, the city treasurer, . . . greets you" (Rom. 16:23b); "Epaphras, my fellow prisoner in Christ, . . . greets you" (Philem. 23).

It is in the third element of the greeting formula, the recipient, however, where the greatest expansion or elaboration takes place. Paul frequently adds the prepositional phrase "in the Lord" or "in Christ (Jesus)."[7] This addition gives a strong element of commendation to the description of the recipient,

---

7. In the twenty greeting formulas that identify the recipient of the greeting, this prepositional phrase occurs eleven times: Rom. 16:3, 5b, 7, 8, 9, 10a, 11b, 12a, 12b, 13; Phil. 4:21a.

for Paul explicitly recognizes the person's relationship to the Lord. Paul often also supplements the greeting with a descriptive phrase about the recipient that expresses a stronger note of endearment or commendation than the descriptive phrase of the giver of the greeting: "my beloved" (Rom. 16:5b, 8, 9, 12b); "approved in Christ" (Rom. 16:10a); "chosen in the Lord" (Rom. 16:13); and so forth. Furthermore, the apostle regularly and sometimes greatly expands these descriptive phrases with a relative clause: "who risked their necks for my life" (Rom. 16:4a); "to whom not only I but also all the churches of the gentiles give thanks" (Rom. 16:4b); "who was the first convert to Christ in Asia" (Rom. 16:5b); and so on. These relative clauses were obviously not intended to help the recipients of the letter identify the person(s) being greeted, for such a person(s) would have been well known to the Christian community. Rather, as their laudatory content makes clear, these lengthy elaborations possess a commendatory function that supports Paul's larger purposes in the letter.[8]

THE GREETING WITH THE "HOLY KISS"

A further distinctive greeting type can be identified in light of four texts where Paul states the manner in which the greeting is to be given: "with a holy kiss" (Rom. 16:16a; 1 Cor. 16:20b; 2 Cor. 13:12a; 1 Thess. 5:26; see also 1 Pet. 5:14). The practice of giving a kiss as part of a greeting was widespread in the Middle East.[9] Jewish examples of greeting others with a kiss, either when arriving or departing, can be found throughout the OT and intertestamental literature.[10] Greeting another person with a kiss continued to be a common practice in Jesus's day (Mark 14:45; Luke 7:45; 15:20; 22:47) and in Paul's (Acts 20:37). Thus the command in the apostle's letters to greet one another with a kiss reflects a widespread custom of that time, which explains why the command can be given in a rather simple and constant formulaic expression, without any accompanying word of explanation.

What is new, however, is that Paul explicitly refers to this kiss greeting as a "holy" kiss. Paul could be referring to the importance of maintaining proper and holy motives while practicing a kiss greeting. But though this concern is surely part of Paul's thought in the exhortation, the reference to a "holy" (*hagios*) kiss suggests that the apostle wants to distinguish the kiss

---

8. For a further discussion of this feature, see the analysis of Rom. 16:3–16 below.

9. On the "holy kiss," as well as the kiss in general in the ancient world, see G. Stählin, *TDNT* 9:119–27; Wünsche 1911; Dix 1945: 105–10; Traede 1968–69; Perella 1969; Benko 1984; Kreider 1987; Klassen 1993.

10. E.g., Gen. 29:11, 13; 31:28, 55; 33:4; Exod. 4:27; 18:7; 2 Sam. 19:39 (19:40 LXX); 20:9; 1 Kings 19:20; Tob. 5:17; 10:12; 3 Macc. 5:49; Add. Esth. 13:13 NRSV (4:17ᵈ LXX); *T. Benj.* 1.2; *T. Reu.* 1.5; *T. Sim.* 1.2; *T. Dan* 7.1; *T. Naph.* 1.7; *Jos. Asen.* 4.1, 7; 18.3; 22.9.

greeting practiced between believers (*hagioi*: "holy" people or "saints") from that practiced between those outside the faith. For others, the kiss greeting "could be simply an expression of friendship and goodwill, but among Christians it assumed a deeper meaning; it symbolized the unity, the belonging together of Christians, in the church of Jesus Christ" (Benko 1984: 98). In other words, the kiss expressed not merely friendship and love, but more specifically reconciliation and peace (see esp. Gen. 33:4; 45:15; 2 Sam. 14:33; Luke 15:20). This idea of the kiss as an outward expression of forgiveness and unity still exists today in the challenge given to a warring couple or two friends arguing that they ought to "kiss and make up." It is this function of the kiss that makes Judas's kiss of Jesus in the garden of Gethsemane so shocking and blasphemous: his action is motivated from an attitude that is completely opposite to its expected expression of unity and concord with the other person. The kiss exchanged between believers soon was referred to by early Christians as the *osculum pacis*, "the kiss of peace" (Tertullian, *On Prayer* 18.14). As a concrete expression of the oneness that exists between followers of Jesus, the exchange of the holy kiss naturally became an introductory step leading up to the celebration of the Eucharist—a further outward act that also powerfully symbolized the unity of believers as the body of Christ (Dix 1945: 106–7).

Paul's command to greet others "with a holy kiss," therefore, expresses more than an exhortation simply to greet one another. It serves instead as an implicit challenge to his readers to remove any hostility that may exist among them and to exhibit the oneness that they share as fellow members of the body of Christ. This function of the kiss greeting explains why this epistolary formula is not found in all of Paul's letter closings but rather is restricted to letters addressed to three churches (Rom. 16:16a; 1 Cor. 16:20b; 2 Cor. 13:12a; 1 Thess. 5:26) where some degree of conflict exists within the congregation and where Paul has addressed the issue of unity earlier in the body of the letter.

Interpretative Significance

ROMANS 16:3–16

The letter closing of Romans (15:33–16:27) is distinctive vis-à-vis Paul's other letter closings in a variety of ways: it has two peace benedictions (15:33; 16:20a), a letter of commendation (16:1–2), and a doxology (16:25–27). Yet its most obvious unique formal feature is the presence of not one but two greetings lists (16:3–16, 21–33), the first of which mentions the names of no less than twenty-six people, together with several unnamed people associated with them. Many scholars have stumbled over the number of people listed in the first greeting list: How can Paul know so many people in Rome when he has neither founded that church nor even been there before? This problem has seemed so great to some that they feel compelled to accept the so-called Ephesian hypothesis: Rom. 16 is a fragment of a genuine Pauline correspondence originally directed to the church at Ephesus and later erroneously attached to the Romans letter. This hypothesis, first proposed already in the early 1800s (Schulz 1829: 609–12), has for many scholars become a certain reality. Günter Klein (1976: 752), for example, states: "The Ephesian destination of 16:1–20 can . . . hardly be disputed."[11]

The boldness of such an assertion, however, cannot hide the fact that this speculative theory lacks any concrete textual evidence: no manuscript of Ephesians has ever been found with the Roman greetings attached; though the location of the doxology varies in some copies of Romans, the rest of Rom. 16, including the greetings of 16:3–16, are found in the oldest and most reliable manuscripts. Even more significantly, all the distinctive aspects of the Romans letter closing, including the first greeting list of twenty-six people, can be readily explained. The key lies in recognizing Paul's preoccupation throughout the epistolary framework of Romans with presenting his apostleship and gospel to unknown readers in Rome in a way that wins their acceptance of both his authoritative status and his gospel message, which is "preached" to them in the body of the letter.[12]

The first greeting list is highlighted by virtue of both its position (it comes in the first and therefore the emphatic position of the two lists) and its size (seventeen greetings in the first list directed to twenty-six people compared to the second list's four greetings for eight people). The strong commendatory manner in which those being greeted are described is a feature not found in any of the other greetings of Paul. This note of commendation is often accomplished by means of a simple term of endearment or praise: "my beloved" (16:5b, 8, 9, 12b), "approved in Christ" (16:10a), "chosen in the Lord" (16:13), "in Christ (Jesus)" (16:3, 7, 9, 10) and "in the Lord (16:8, 11, 12 [2×], 13). Frequently this note of commendation is further stressed by means of a relative clause: "who risked their necks for my life" (16:4a), "to whom not only I but also all the churches of the gentiles give thanks (16:4b), "who was the first convert to Christ in Asia" (16:5b), "who has worked hard among you" (16:6), "who are well known to the apostles" (16:7b), "who also were in Christ before me" (16:7c), and "who has worked hard in the Lord" (16:12b).

11. So also Manson 1948; Kinoshita 1964–65; Suggs 1967; Marxsen 1968: 107–8; Schmithals 1988: 543–65; Fefoule 1990; Whelan 1993: esp. 72–73.

12. See the discussion in chap. 2 of the significantly expanded sender formula in the letter opening of Romans. A fuller exposition of this thesis is found in Weima 1994b.

The reason why Paul includes such commendatory material is obviously not to help the churches in Rome to identify the persons being greeted, for such persons would have been well known to the Christian community there. Instead, these seemingly superfluous additions emphasize the close relations that Paul enjoys with key people in the Roman churches. In colloquial terms, the apostle is name-dropping: he connects himself closely to leading individuals in the Roman churches, enhancing his own status by virtue of these important connections. The situation is similar to a political advertisement in a newspaper where candidates list the names of leading people within the local community who support their candidacy. Paul builds up his own standing in the Roman churches by not merely greeting lots of respected people in Rome but by also associating himself so closely with such persons that he himself shares in the commendations that they receive (so also Gamble 1977: 92).

That Paul uses the greetings to commend himself more fully to the Roman Christians can also be seen in the order in which he greets specific people (Jervis 1991: 151–52). The first persons greeted are Prisca and Aquila. Their stature, both among the Roman believers currently worshiping in their house church (16:5a) and among "all the churches of the gentiles" (16:4), and their previous missionary partnership with Paul (16:3, "my fellow workers") in Corinth and Ephesus (Acts 18:1–2, 18; 1 Cor. 16:19) makes them influential leaders who can testify to the Roman Christians from firsthand experience about Paul's apostleship and the success of his gospel. The second person greeted is Epaenetus, who is "the first convert to Christ in Asia" (16:5b)—literally, the "firstfruit" from that important Roman province. That his conversion happened through the evangelistic activity of Paul seems clear from the parallel with 1 Cor. 16:15: just as the household of Stephanas, the "firstfruits [i.e., first converts] of those in Achaia," were converted by Paul, so also Epaenetus, the "firstfruit" (i.e., first convert) in Asia, was converted by the apostle. This unique status of Epaenetus makes him living proof of the genuineness and effectiveness of Paul's gospel. Similarly, the identification of Andronicus and Junia(s) in the fourth greeting as those who are "well known to the apostles" (16:7) means that they too can function as weighty "character references" for the legitimacy of Paul's apostolic status and his gospel.

The final greeting of the first list is also noteworthy: "All the churches of Christ greet you" (16:16b). Nowhere else does Paul speak so broadly of "all the churches" in conveying the greetings of others. This comprehensive greeting implies that the apostle has the official backing of all the churches in Achaia, Macedonia, Asia, Galatia, Syria, and elsewhere in the eastern part of the empire. As James Dunn (1988b: 899) observes: "The greeting thus has a 'political' overtone: Paul speaks for all these churches, and they are behind him in his mission." The implicit challenge in this greeting is that the churches in Rome ought to join all these worldwide churches in recognizing Paul's apostleship and gospel.

It should now be clear that the first greeting list of 16:3–16, rather than creating a problem for the textual integrity of Romans (as many scholars have claimed), is entirely appropriate to the purpose of Paul that is evident through the rest of the epistolary framework and letter body. The apostle has constructed his closing greetings in such a way that they further establish his apostolic authority over the Roman churches and guarantee their acceptance of his gospel as "preached" to them in the body of the letter.

2 Corinthians 13:12a NRSV

The letter closing of Romans is the longest ending among Paul's extant letters, while the letter closing of 2 Corinthians is among the shortest. Yet despite the brevity of this letter closing (13:11–13 NRSV),[13] every one of its epistolary conventions—including the occurrence of two different types of greetings—has been either chosen and/or adapted by the apostle so that it relates more directly to the specific situation in Corinth and echoes key concerns previously developed in the body of this letter.

The problem of division and disunity—both internally within the Corinthian church, as well as between the majority of the congregation and Paul—is one of the key concerns that manifests itself throughout 1 Corinthians and continues to be addressed in 2 Corinthians, especially in its final chapters (2 Cor. 10–13). Paul fears that among the Corinthian believers there is "quarreling, jealousy, anger, selfishness, slander, gossip, conceit, and disorder" (12:20), and so the body of the letter ends with his expressed prayer for the Corinthians' "restoration" (13:9), that is, for the restoration of unity among all congregational members and with him as their founder.

The apostle then begins his brief letter closing with a hortatory section whose five commands, as has already been highlighted, echo his previous calls for mutual peace and harmony: "Finally, brothers and sisters, rejoice, be restored, be comforted, be of the same mind, live in peace" (13:11a). He then reinforces these closing exhortations with a peace benediction, which, despite being a regular feature of Paul's closing, is especially relevant in the Corinthian context as an implicit challenge for the believers in Corinth to put an end to the division and disorder at work in their church. This particular

---

13. The verse numbering of the NRSV is specified in this discussion because it matches that of the Greek NT, whereas some other modern translations (e.g., NIV) number the final verses of 2 Cor. 13 differently.

peace benediction, however, is made even more relevant by the addition of "love"—a rare instance of Paul expanding the wish of this epistolary convention (elsewhere possibly only Eph. 6:23): "And the God of *love* and peace will be with you" (13:11b). This addition ought not to be regarded as merely a fortuitous expansion. For in light of the broad context of the Corinthian situation and the specific context of the five preceding commands, it can hardly be doubted that "love" has been deliberately added to the peace benediction so that this closing formula better echoes and reinforces the letter's appeal for love and harmony to characterize relations within this fractious church. The same reason accounts for the unique character of the grace benediction that Paul will soon give: "May the grace of the Lord Jesus Christ and the love of God and the fellowship of the Holy Spirit be with you all" (13:13 [NRSV numbering]). This closing formula in 2 Corinthians is distinguished from all other Pauline grace benedictions by virtue of its two additional wishes, "love" and "fellowship," and their two corresponding divine sources, "of God" and "of the Holy Spirit." These supplementary wishes of "love" and "fellowship" fit the thrust of the rest of the letter closing of 2 Corinthians, and they in turn echo the concern of the whole letter: that peace and harmony must exist within the Corinthian church.

Between the expanded peace benediction and the expanded grace benediction occur two types of greetings, each of which are either chosen or adapted by Paul to make them more relevant to the specific historical situation of the Corinthian church. The first type of greeting that the apostle chooses to include in the closing is the kiss greeting: "Greet one another with a holy kiss" (13:12a). We have observed above that the kiss greeting is not merely an exhortation to greet others but rather functions as an implicit challenge for readers to remove any hostility that may exist among them and to exhibit the oneness that they share as fellow members of the body of Christ. Ernest Best's assertion (1987: 136) that "this [the kiss greeting] is not a deliberate attempt to counter disputations," therefore, is surely wrong. Rather, in this context and in light of the epistolary practice of Paul in his other letter closings, the kiss greeting of 2 Cor. 13:12a serves to echo the apostle's concern in the previous verses, as well as that in the whole letter, for unity and peace to prevail in the Corinthian church. As Ralph Martin (1986: 501) correctly comments about this verse: "Paul now turns to the theme of greeting, but in doing so he does not leave behind the theme of peace and harmony discussed in 13.11. To salute one with a holy kiss continues the themes of 13.11."

The second type of greeting that Paul employs and adapts—the third-person type—is also significant: "All the saints greet you" (13:12b). With the exception of Romans 16:16b ("All the churches of Christ greet you"), this is the broadest group of people for whom Paul speaks in his third-person greetings. In this way Paul alludes to his own apostolic authority and so also, indirectly, to the obligation that the Corinthians have to obey his exhortations in the letter. The phrase "all the saints" has the added function of reminding the overly proud and independent-minded Corinthians that they are not a solo group accountable only to themselves, but that they belong to a larger body, the universal church. That this is not reading too much into the text is suggested by the fact that the same corrective—namely, the Corinthians ought to view themselves not as the only Christians in the world but as only a small part of the wider body of Christ—plays an important part in the earlier letter of 1 Corinthians: in the letter opening (see the discussion of 1 Cor. 1:2 in chap. 2), the letter body (4:17; 7:17; 10:32; 11:16, 22; 14:33, 36; 16:1), and the letter closing (16:20). It is further supported by Paul's lengthy exhortation in his later letter (2 Cor. 8–9) that the Corinthians join his other gentile churches in Galatia (1 Cor. 16:1), Macedonia (2 Cor. 8:1–5), and Asia (Acts 20:4) in contributing financially to the collection for needy fellow believers in Judea. All of this justifies D. A. Carson's comment (1984: 185) about the greeting of 2 Cor. 13:12b NRSV: "The sentence 'All the saints send their greetings' . . . is therefore more than courtesy: it is a healthy re-minder to all believers from the Corinthians on to see themselves as part, but only part, of the entire body of Christ" (so also Matera 2003: 314; Seifrid 2014: 496).

The letter closing of 2 Corinthians, therefore, is entirely appropriate to the concerns raised in the letter as a whole, particularly those of chapters 10–13. Every one of the closing conventions of this letter, including the two types of greetings, has been chosen and/or adapted to relate more directly to Paul's preoccupation in the letter: that his Corinthian converts will reject the divisive influence of his opponents and restore peace and harmony within the church and with Paul. Thus 2 Cor. 13:11–13 provides further evidence of Paul's concern to construct letter closings that recapitulate and reinforce the key theme(s) previously raised in their respective letter bodies.

The Autograph

Formal Analysis

Ancient letters frequently ended with an autograph statement. Whereas the opening, body, and first part of the closing was dictated to a secretary (the technical term for such a person is "amanuensis"), the final part of the closing was written by the sender in his own hand. It is not surprising, therefore, that the same phenomenon occurs in Paul's letters. The existence of an autograph is explicitly stated in five of the apostle's letters, always in the closing.

Table 5.4: The Autograph

1 Cor. 16:21	The greeting is written in my own hand, that of Paul.
Gal. 6:11	See with what large letters I am writing to you in my own hand.
Col. 4:18a	The greeting is written in my own hand.
2 Thess. 3:17	The greeting is written in my own hand, that of Paul, which is a sign in every letter; this is the way I write.
Philem. 19	I, Paul, am writing in my own hand.

The phrase "in my own hand (that of Paul)" implies that the apostle had, to this point, been using a secretary to write the letter (note also Rom. 16:22, where the secretary, Tertius, greets the recipients) but now takes up the pen himself to write personally to his readers. In three instances, the autograph statement is part of a greeting formula already examined above: "The greeting is written in my own hand, that of Paul" (1 Cor. 16:21; Col. 4:18a; 2 Thess. 3:17).

Although infrequent, a few parallels to Paul's autograph formula, "in my own hand," can be found in the correspondence of his day. Ferdinandus Ziemann (1912: 365) cites a Greek letter that closes: "I have written these things to you in my own hand." The sender of a papyrus letter (P.Grenf. II 89) states: "I wrote all in my own hand." The letters of Cicero contain a number of references to "in my own hand" (*mea manu*), apparently a preferred formula, signaling the shift from the secretary to his own hand (e.g., *Att.* 8.1; 13.28; see Richards 1991: 173). Despite these examples, Greco-Roman letters rarely speak of a change of hand, since such a shift is visually obvious to the reader. Paul, however, knows that his letters will be read in public worship, where the size of the group prevents everyone from seeing the change in handwriting styles, and so he frequently makes an explicit reference to the closing material that he has written "in my own hand."

But *why* does Paul want his readers to know that he is writing the closing material in his own hand? Does their knowledge of this fact in any way enhance the apostle's persuasive strategy in the letter? In other letters of that day, the autograph was used to accomplish a variety of different tasks, such as to authenticate a letter, to make a letter legally binding, to give a letter a more personal touch, or to ensure confidentiality (Weima 1994a: 48–50). The specific function of any given autograph must be determined by a close examination of the epistolary situation of the particular letter itself. The same is true for determining the function of any autograph found in the closings of Paul's letters.

Interpretative Significance

GALATIANS 6:11–18

The most striking autograph in Paul's letters is Gal. 6:11–18, where not just the final part of the letter closing but also the entire letter closing is explicitly identified by the apostle as being written in his own hand:

> [11]See with what large letters I am writing to you in my own hand! [12]It is those who want to make a good showing in the flesh who are compelling you to be circumcised, only in order that they may not be persecuted for the cross of Christ. [13]Even the circumcised do not themselves obey the law, but they want you to be circumcised so that they may boast about your flesh. [14]But as for me, may I never boast of anything except the cross of our Lord Jesus Christ, by which the world has been crucified to me, and I to the world. [15]For neither circumcision nor uncircumcision is anything; but a new creation is everything! [16]And as many who will follow this rule, peace and mercy be upon them—the Israel of God. [17]From now on, let no one cause trouble for me because I bear on my body the marks of Jesus! [18]May the grace of our Lord Jesus Christ be with your spirit, brothers and sisters. Amen.

This autograph closing is noteworthy for at least seven ways in which it differs formally from the closings of Paul's other letters. First, the autograph formula (v. 11) has been expanded to include a reference to the manner in which Paul writes in his own hand: "with what large letters." This addition functions to underscore to the Galatian readers the importance of Paul's final words in the closing—similar to today's practice of indicating emphasis by placing certain words in bold or italics, or in social media by typing in all capital letters and thereby "shouting." Second, it contains a disproportionately large section of closing statements (vv. 12–15) in which Paul rather angrily contrasts the false gospel and selfish motives of his opponents with the true gospel and selfless motives of himself—a major concern of Paul throughout the letter.[14] Third, the peace benediction (v. 16) is (as has already been noted earlier in our examination of this closing convention) conditional: not all of those in Galatia will receive the divine blessings of peace and mercy but only those who will faithfully follow Paul and his gospel. Fourth, the peace benediction identifies those in Galatia who do faithfully follow Paul and his gospel, using the striking and unparalleled phrase "the Israel of God." Fifth, the hortatory section (v. 17) has a caustic tone that is easily missed in English translation. This closing exhortation is better rendered colloquially as "Don't

---

14. For an exposition of five contrasts in the letter closing that Paul highlights between himself and his opponents, see Weima 1993.

anyone give me a hard time! I bear on my body the marks of Jesus—all kinds of physical scars just because I preach the gospel. What do you have to say against that?!" Paul appeals to his being persecuted on behalf of Christ (in addition to Gal. 5:11, see 1 Cor. 4:11; 2 Cor. 6:4–5; 11:23–27) as proof of the genuineness of his apostleship and gospel in contrast to his "markless" opponents, whose false gospel involving the necessity of circumcision stems only from their selfish desire to avoid persecution (v. 12). Sixth, there is the unusual absence of any personal greetings, either from Paul or from any of "the brothers and sisters" who were with him (1:2). Seventh, the autograph closing lacks any positive note of praise or thanksgiving as would be expressed in a closing doxology or joy expression. The combination of all these unique features of 6:11–18 results in a closing that is truly striking and noteworthy among Paul's letters.

The exceptional character of this autograph closing stems from the letter's specific epistolary situation. A Judaizing theology—"another gospel, which is not at all the same gospel" (1:6–7)—was seriously challenging the spiritual welfare of the Galatians. Because this heretical seed had taken root among believers and was continuing to grow, a serious conflict arose between Paul and his Galatian converts. This conflict manifests itself throughout the letter—in the letter opening (1:1–5), the rebuke section (1:6–10) replacing the expected thanksgiving, and the letter body (1:11–6:10)—and so, not surprisingly, also in the letter closing (6:11–18). Although not unexpected, it is nevertheless impressive how Paul uses this autograph closing to recapitulate the main concerns previously taken up in the body of the Galatians letter. Space constraints do not allow a detailed examination of 6:11–18 at this point (see Weima 1993; 1994a: 157–74); nevertheless, the following observations are sufficient to demonstrate the summarizing function of this autograph.

After the autograph formula (6:11), Paul draws his readers' attention to the false motives of his opponents, who selfishly seek to boast in the circumcision of the Galatians, thereby avoiding persecution for the cross of Christ (vv. 12–13). In the closing autograph, therefore, Paul immediately takes up the problem of his opponents in Galatia, whom he has been attacking throughout the letter (1:7, 8, 9; [2:12]; 3:1; 4:17, 21; 5:7, 10, 12). All the key words in this closing rebuttal are terms that have played a central part in his argument in the letter body:

- The word "flesh" (*sarx*), found twice in the autograph at 6:12 and 13, occurs repeatedly in the letter: both, as is its meaning here in the closing, the physical sense of referring to circumcision (1:16; 2:16, 20; 3:3; 4:13,

14, 23, 29) and the ethical sense of referring to the power of sin (5:13, 16, 17 [2×], 19, 24; 6:8 [2×]).

- The double reference to "the cross of [our Lord Jesus] Christ" at 6:12 and 14 serves as a direct link to Paul's previous statements about the centrality of the cross to the Christian gospel in 2:19–21; 3:1, 13; 5:11, 24. These two closing references to the cross of Christ also look back to Paul's expansion of the greeting formula in 1:3–5 (esp. 1:4a, "who gave himself for our sins in order to rescue us from the present evil age"), where the apostle highlights the centrality of Christ's redemptive work on the cross (see the fuller discussion of this embellished greeting formula in chap. 2).

- The five references to circumcision in the autograph at 6:12, 13 (2×), 15 (2×) echo Paul's earlier discussion concerning this OT rite in 2:3, 7, 8, 9, 12; 5:2, 3, 6, 11, (12), as well as the many references to "flesh" that have the act of circumcision in view (see texts listed above). There is also a striking parallel between 6:15 ("For neither circumcision nor uncircumcision is anything") and the earlier words of 5:6 ("Neither circumcision nor uncircumcision means anything").

- The idea of persecution, important in the closing autograph at 6:12 and 17, also is a subject addressed previously in the letter at 4:29 and 5:11 (see also 1:13, 23).

- The enigmatic phrase "a new creation" in 6:15, probably a well-known maxim of the early church expressing the new order brought about by Christ, serves as an appropriate climax to Paul's argument throughout the letter against those who insist on hanging on to the old order with its legalistic lifestyle in conformity to the Mosaic commandments.

- The striking phrase "the Israel of God" in 6:16 looks back to an important theme developed in the body of the letter, namely the claim of Paul (apparently in reaction to the message of the Judaizers) that gentile Christians are legitimate heirs of Abraham and thus share fully in the blessings of God's covenant with Abraham and his descendants, the people of Israel (3:6–9, 14, 15–16, 26–29; 4:21–31).

- Paul's caustic command to "let no one cause trouble for me" in 6:17 refers to his opponents who have, in fact, been causing the apostle lots of trouble in the Galatian churches and so recalls his rebuke of them throughout the letter (1:7, 8, 9; [2:12]; 3:1; 4:17, 21; 5:7, 10, 12).

Even in such a brief analysis of Gal. 6:11–18, one is struck by the masterful way in which Paul uses his closing autograph to summarize the primary concerns addressed earlier in the letter. This recapitulating or synthesizing function of the Galatian autograph has been recognized by several commentators. More than a century ago Joseph Lightfoot (1890: 220) observed that 6:11–18 functions by way of "summing up the main lessons of the epistle." More recently Richard Longenecker (1990: 298) comments that "6.11–18 must be seen as something of a prism that reflects the major thrusts of what has been said earlier in the letter."

2 Thessalonians 3:17

Another autograph that gives evidence of being altered so that it relates more directly to the specific epistolary situation is 2 Thess. 3:17: "The greeting is written in my own hand, that of Paul, which is a sign in every letter; this is the way I write." Paul draws attention to the fact that he is taking over from his secretary, who has written everything in the letter thus far, and now he, as the letter sender, is writing the closing greeting in his own hand. While the form of the autograph greeting in the first half of this verse follows expected Pauline practice (see table 5.4: The Autograph above), the addition of an explanatory comment in the second half is unique and striking: "which is a sign in every letter; this is the way I write." Two questions need to be answered: To what does the "sign" refer? And what is Paul trying to signal to the Thessalonian readers by this sign?

On the first question, the sign could refer either to the greeting itself or to the fact that the greeting is written in Paul's own hand. The former option must be rejected on grammatical grounds: the relative pronoun "which" (*ho*) introducing this clause is neuter and so refers not to the preceding noun "greeting" (which is masculine) but to the whole preceding clause. Additionally, the greeting formula is *not* found in every letter of the apostle. The "sign," therefore, has in view the handwritten script of Paul, the autograph itself. The phrase that concludes this explanatory comment supports this interpretation, since "this is the way I write" refers to the *manner* in which Paul closes his letters (with an autograph) and not to the *content* of his closing (with a greeting). The phrase "in every letter" suggests, therefore, that Paul always ended his letters with an autograph statement and that this fact should be assumed to be true even in those letters that make no such explicit reference to the apostle's own handwriting. This conclusion receives further support from the secular papyrus letters of that day, the vast majority of which indicate that the sender closed the correspondence in his own hand, yet without expressly saying so (see the examples and discussion in Weima 1994a: 45–50). Recognizing the weight of these parallels, Adolf Deissmann

(1910: 158–59) concluded that it would be wrong to assume that Paul "only finished off with his own hand those letters in which he expressly says that he did."

Thus, for example, it is most probable that in the closing of his previous letter to the Thessalonians, Paul also takes over from the secretary, likely at 1 Thess. 5:27, where in his own hand he pens a command written no longer with the literary plural "we" but with the singular "I" ("I cause you to swear an oath . . ."). Another possible autograph is the hortatory section of Rom. 16:17–20.[15] Not only would this explain the sudden shift in these verses to a harsher tone, but it also parallels Paul's practice elsewhere of giving a closing warning in his own hand (Gal. 6:11–18; 1 Cor. 16:22). Yet another candidate for a closing autograph is Phil. 4:10–20. There are several compelling reasons to conclude that the closing of this letter begins not with the greetings of 4:21 but much earlier, with the hortatory section of 4:8–9a and the peace benediction of 4:9b (see the discussion earlier in this chapter). If so, then Paul may well have taken over from the secretary at 4:10 in order to thank the Philippians in a more personal, handwritten way for their generous financial gift.[16]

On the second question, the vast majority of commentators believe that by sending the Thessalonians his handwritten "sign," Paul intends to signal the authenticity of this letter. The possible existence of a forged correspondence claiming to be from Paul and his fellow workers (2 Thess. 2:2) caused the apostle to write part of the closing in his own hand, thereby establishing the letter's genuineness. This interpretation leads Fred Danker, for example, to render the explanatory clause as "this is the mark *of genuineness* in every letter" (in BDAG 920.1, emphasis added).

A couple of factors, however, suggest a different or at least additional purpose. First, as noted above, a closing autograph in letters of that day functioned not just to authenticate a letter but also to accomplish a variety of different purposes: to make a letter legally binding, to give a letter a more personal touch, to ensure confidentially. Paul's autographs, therefore, should not be limited to only one possible function (such as to establish a letter's authenticity) but rather can serve various purposes, depending on the specific context and concern at work in any given letter. Second, there is strong evidence that Paul suspects the source of the false teaching about the day of the Lord to be not from a letter supposedly from him but from

---

15. So Lietzmann 1906: 121–22; Wiles 1974: 93; Morris 1988: 538; Dunn 1988b: 902, 906.
16. So Bahr 1968: 38; Gamble 1977: 94, 145–46; Hawthorne 1983: 210; O'Brien 1991: 17. For a fuller discussion of these and other potential autographs in the closings of Paul's letters, see Weima 1994a: 123–26.

a prophecy claiming his authority (note the striking absence of the phrase "through a prophetic utterance" in the command of 2 Thess. 2:15, in contrast to its inclusion previously in 2:2b; see Weima 2014: 506, 558). This in turn suggests that in this letter closing the apostle is concerned primarily with establishing the *authority* of the letter, not its authenticity. The autograph makes Paul's presence more powerfully felt by the Thessalonian readers. The mention of his handwritten greeting as a distinguishing sign in all of his letters evokes in the readers' minds a more vivid image of the apostle writing to them and so makes his words harder to ignore. As Maarten Menken (1994: 144) states, the autograph "serves to suggest the personal, authoritative presence of the apostle in the letter." Ben Witherington (2006: 263) similarly observes that "the final words in one's own hand is an indirect means of asserting that what is in this letter has the authority of Paul himself and must be taken seriously" (so also Marshall 1983: 232; Holmes 1998: 277; Wanamaker 1990: 292). The apostle may have in view especially the rebellious idlers, who he anticipates will not all obey his command to be engaged in self-sufficient work.[17]

The Grace Benediction

Formal Analysis

Secular letters of Paul's day typically ended with the "farewell wish," expressed either in the form of "Be strong!" (*errōso* (sing.), *errōsthe* (pl.): Acts 15:29; 23:30, variant readings) or, less commonly, "Prosper!" (*eutychei*). This fixed formula served to signal the definitive end of a letter, somewhat like the expression "sincerely" or "yours truly" is used to close our modern correspondence.[18] Paul, however, indicates the end of his letters by replacing this secular closing formula with a distinctively Christian one: "May the grace of our Lord Jesus Christ be with you."

The grace benediction is the most common epistolary convention of Paul's letter closings: it ends every one of the apostle's letters. But not only is the grace benediction the most frequent of the closing conventions; it is also the most formally consistent. It exhibits a striking uniformity (see table 5.5: The Grace Benediction), consisting of three basic elements: the wish, the divine source, and the recipient.

17. Notice the conditional clause of 2 Thess. 3:14: "But if someone does not obey our command in this letter . . ." In Greek, this is a first-class condition, in which the speaker assumes the truth of what is being considered.

18. For examples and further discussion of the farewell wish, see Weima 1994a: 29–34.

Table 5.5: The Grace Benediction

Letter	Wish	Divine Source	Recipient
Rom. 16:20b	May the grace	of our Lord Jesus	be with you.
1 Cor. 16:23	May the grace	of the Lord Jesus	be with you.
2 Cor. 13:13 NRSV	May the grace	of the Lord Jesus Christ and	
	the love	of God and	
	the fellowship	of the Holy Spirit	be with you all.
Gal. 6:18	May the grace	of our Lord Jesus Christ	be with your spirit, brothers and sisters.
Phil. 4:23	May the grace	of the Lord Jesus Christ	be with your spirit.
1 Thess. 5:28	May the grace	of our Lord Jesus Christ	be with you.
2 Thess. 3:18	May the grace	of our Lord Jesus Christ	be with you all.
Philem. 25	May the grace	of the Lord Jesus Christ	be with your spirit.
Eph. 6:24	May grace		be with all who love our Lord Jesus Christ with love incorruptible.
Col. 4:18b	May grace		be with you.
1 Tim. 6:21b	May grace		be with you.
2 Tim. 4:22b	May grace		be with you.
Titus 3:15b	May grace		be with you all.
Heb. 13:25	May grace		be with you all.
Rev. 22:21	May the grace	of the Lord Jesus	be with all.

THE WISH

The wish or content of this benediction is "grace." Thus, in contrast to secular letters where the farewell wish expresses the desire that the recipients would have physical strength ("Be strong!") or prosperity ("Prosper!"), Paul calls on God to give his readers what he believes to be a more valuable gift and one that is needed more: the gift of grace. As noted earlier, this wish for grace—along with the peace benediction, which typically opens the letter closing—forms a chiasm with the greeting of the letter opening: "Grace to you and peace."

THE DIVINE SOURCE

The divine source for fulfilling this wish is expressed by the phrase "of our Lord Jesus Christ." This phrase expresses the source of grace: it is the grace that Jesus Christ has and gives to his followers. Although Paul normally refs to God as the source of grace, he occasionally speaks of Christ in this fashion.[19] On the whole, however, the depiction of Christ as the source of grace is a characteristic feature of the letter closings.

THE RECIPIENT

The recipient of the wish or benediction normally consists of the prepositional phrase "with you" or the fuller phrase "with your spirit." There is no significant difference between these two: "spirit" is used in an anthropological sense so that it means exactly the same as "you."

The omission of the main verb in the grace benediction calls for some comment. Although the verb "to be" is clearly implied, it is less obvious which mood of this verb Paul intends. If indicative, then the benediction would have the sense of a declarative statement: "The grace of our Lord Jesus Christ *is* with you." Another option is the imperative, in which Paul is commanding Christ to give grace to the readers: "The grace of our Lord Jesus Christ *be* with you." A third possibility is the optative, in which the benediction expresses a holy or pious wish: "*May* the grace of our Lord Jesus Christ be with you." This last option is supported by peace benedictions and other benedictions or prayers in Paul's letters, most—but not all (see Rom. 16:20; 2 Cor. 13:11; Phil. 4:9)—of which use the optative (Rom. 15:5–6, 13; 1 Thess. 3:11, 12–13; 5:23; 2 Thess. 2:16–17; 3:5, 16). By analogy, this practice suggests that the same mood is implied in the grace benedictions. Furthermore, although the opening benedictions or greetings of Paul's letters also omit the verb, the opening benedictions of other NT letters have the optative (1 Pet. 1:2; 2 Pet. 1:2; Jude 2). Thus it seems best to view the grace benediction as a prayer to Christ that he send his grace into the hearts and lives of the letter's recipients.

Interpretative Significance

2 CORINTHIANS 13:13 NRSV

An example of how Paul edits the grace benediction so that it better relates to the key issue(s) raised in the letter body can be seen in 2 Cor. 13:13 (NRSV numbering):[20] "The grace of the Lord Jesus Christ and the love of God and

---

19. See 2 Cor. 8:9; 12:9; Gal. 1:6; 5:4; 2 Thess. 1:12. Note also the opening greetings where Christ is similarly listed as the source of grace, albeit in a secondary role to "God our Father": Rom. 1:7; 1 Cor. 1:3; 2 Cor. 1:2; Gal. 1:3; Eph. 1:2; Phil. 1:2; 2 Thess. 1:2; 1 Tim. 1:2; 2 Tim. 1:2; Titus 1:4; Philem. 3.

20. The verse numbering of the NRSV is specified in this discussion because it matches that of the Greek NT, whereas some other modern translations (e.g., NIV) number the final verses of 2 Cor. 13 differently.

the fellowship of the Holy Spirit be with you all." This closing grace benediction differs from all other Pauline grace benedictions by virtue of its two
additional wishes ("love" and "fellowship") and their corresponding divine
sources ("of God" and "of the Holy Spirit"). In light of the fixed form of the
grace benediction in Paul's other letter closings as well as his demonstrated
practice of adapting other epistolary conventions belonging to the final section of his letters, these additions should not be seen as merely an innocent
and innocuous expansion. Rather, the supplementary wishes of "love" and
"fellowship" fit the thrust of the entire letter closing of 2 Corinthians and, in
turn, echo the concern of the whole letter—namely that peace and harmony
must exist within the Corinthian church. In addition to the grace that they
receive from Christ, believers in Corinth also experience love from God and
the unity of fellowship with other believers from the Holy Spirit. As with
the preceding peace benediction of 13:11b (the only instance of this closing
convention where the extra qualifying phrase "of love" is added), so also here
in the grace benediction, Paul's concern to make the letter closing more relevant to the major theme of the Corinthian letter has resulted in a deliberate
expansion of this closing epistolary convention. In fact, every one of the closing conventions of this letter has been written and/or adapted in such a way
that it relates directly to Paul's preoccupation in the letter for his Corinthian
converts to reject the divisive influence of his opponents and to restore peace
and harmony, both within the church and with Paul (see discussion in chap. 4).

2 Thessalonians 3:18

The grace benediction of 2 Thess. 3:18 provides another example of a
minor yet exegetically significant change. Here the recipient of the wish or
benediction is emphasized through the addition of the adjective "all": "May
the grace of our Lord Jesus Christ be with you *all*." Further evidence that
this addition is not accidental but deliberate and thus significant (contra Best
1977: 348, who states, "Little emphasis should be laid on the addition"; also
Malherbe 2000: 463; Furnish 2007: 183) is shown in the word of encouragement two verses earlier: Paul takes the common Jewish greeting "May the
Lord be with you" and expands it to read "May the Lord be with you *all*"
(3:16b). With this addition the apostle stresses that his prayer for the Lord's
grace to be with them includes *all* the members of the Thessalonian church,
both the majority who are fearful in the face of outside opposition (1:3–12)
and end-time confusion (2:1–17), as well as the minority whose rebelliously
idle behavior requires disciplinary action (3:1–15). As Gordon Fee (2009:
342–43) declares, "This [the addition of "all"] seems to be yet another way

(subtle perhaps, but real nonetheless) of embracing the entire community in the concluding grace. Looked at in this way, it is perhaps his own offering of the right hand of fellowship to some who otherwise need correction in order to be part of the 'all'" (see also Hendriksen 1955: 209; Morris 1959: 262n27; Whiteley 1969: 112).

Conclusion

The detailed analysis of Paul's letter closings undertaken in this chapter has convincingly demonstrated that these final sections are not mere literary conventions with little significance for understanding the rest of their respective letters. Paul's letter closings do reflect several epistolary conventions, all of which exhibit a high degree of formal and structural consistency and thereby testify to the care with which these final sections have been constructed. However, the apostle regularly shapes and adapts his letter closings in order to relate this final section directly to the major concerns of the letter as a whole—sometimes even summarizing and recapitulating those concerns. Consequently, the letter closing can have great interpretative value, providing important clues for understanding the key issues and themes addressed in the body of the letter as well as our understanding of the apostle's readers and their historical situation. The letter closings of Paul, therefore, can no longer be ignored but must instead play an important role in any examination and interpretation of his letters.

6

Epistolary Analysis in Practice:
The Test Case of Philemon

Paul's ability as a letter writer to adapt various epistolary conventions so that they strengthen his persuasive strategy has thus far been demonstrated by a detailed survey of the four main sections of his correspondence (opening, thanksgiving, body, and closing) and the diverse epistolary and other literary forms found in those main sections. Throughout this survey the emphasis has been on the exegetical payoff that comes from interpreting Paul's letters using the method of epistolary analysis. Though necessary for a comprehensive introduction to this method as a right reading of the apostle's correspondence, such a survey deals with texts in an atomized way: diverse passages from among all of Paul's letters were selected and studied. In each case, I have tried to do justice to the larger context of each passage under study. Nevertheless, such an approach can make it difficult for the contemporary reader to fully appreciate the cumulative force of Paul's skill as a letter writer in any given document that he has written. The current chapter, by contrast, presents a sustained epistolary analysis of one whole letter of the apostle: Philemon. The choice of this letter as a test case for the method of epistolary analysis stems from two considerations. First, Philemon is a short letter, which makes a detailed study of the entire letter possible in an introductory book like this. Second, it contains many instances where Paul has deftly adapted and cleverly used various epistolary conventions and literary forms to persuade Philemon to obey God's will in the highly sensitive matter of his slave Onesimus.

The Letter Opening (vv. 1–3)

When the letter opening of Philemon is compared with the rather consistent pattern of epistolary conventions found in the opening sections of Paul's other letters, the distinctive character of Philem. 1–3 becomes readily apparent. Although the greeting formula follows Paul's practice elsewhere, the sender formula and the recipient formula, which we will look at in more detail, both contain unique features:

> [1]Paul, a prisoner of Christ Jesus, and Timothy our brother. To Philemon our beloved brother and fellow worker, [2]and to Apphia our sister, and to Archippus our fellow soldier, and to the church in your house: [3]Grace to you and peace from God our Father and the Lord Jesus Christ.

The Sender Formula (v. 1a)

The sender formula is distinctive in the title that Paul uses to identify himself: instead of the expected designation "apostle," the appellation "prisoner" is found. Nowhere else does Paul open a letter by referring to himself as a "prisoner." The uniqueness of this title was not lost on certain copyists who tried to "correct" the text by changing it to "apostle" or "servant,"[1] thereby bringing it into line with the customary Pauline letter openings. Two questions naturally arise: First, why did Paul drop his usual title "apostle"? Second, why did he substitute it with "prisoner" rather than "servant" (as in Phil. 1:1; Rom. 1:1; Titus 1:1) or some other designation?

In response to the first question, some claim that Paul is asking Philemon for a favor and so is hesitant to assert his apostolic status for fear of being too heavy-handed. Peter O'Brien (1982: 272), for example, states, "The authoritative title 'apostle' is dropped, not because Paul has suddenly ceased to be an apostle, but because he has no intention of appealing to his apostolic authority. He desires to entreat Philemon (vv. 8, 9) rather than command, and substitutes for the term 'apostle' a 'designation which would touch his friend's heart.'"

This explanation, however, is only half correct. It is true that the sensitive nature of the letter's request requires that Paul not approach Philemon in an outwardly heavy-handed manner, and so the title "apostle" is dropped in the letter opening. It is not true, however, that Paul is reluctant to exert his apostolic authority over Philemon. For if, as O'Brien asserts, Paul has "no intention

---

1. Codex Claromontanus has "apostle," while several less-weighty manuscripts (323, 945, and a few others) have "servant."

of appealing to his apostolic authority," why does the apostle a few verses later mention that he has "much boldness in Christ to command you to do what is necessary" (v. 8)? Furthermore, the mention of Timothy as a cosender indirectly points to Paul's authoritative status, since Philemon is reminded that the apostle has others who labor with and under him in the work of the gospel (Lohse 1971: 189). Subtle hints of Paul's authority are also found in later references to the good that Philemon might do "under pressure" (v. 14) and his expected "obedience" (v. 21a). Finally, that Paul identifies himself not merely as a "prisoner" but as a "prisoner *of Christ Jesus*" alludes to his apostolic authority and "obligates" Philemon "to obey the apostolic word" (Lohse 1971: 189; also Wickert 1961) contained in this letter. In this delicate situation, therefore, even though Paul does not want to be heavy-handed in an outward and offensive manner, he clearly and cleverly alludes to his apostolic authority in several ways.

In response to the second question, some commentators have been reluctant to see in the substituted title "prisoner" any deliberate attempt by Paul to use this designation to further his central purpose in the letter. Richard Melick (1991: 349), for example, rejects this idea and claims instead that "the best understanding is that Paul used the words ["prisoner of Christ Jesus"] to speak of his location when writing" (so also O'Brien 1982: 271). But Paul was also a prisoner when he wrote Philippians, Colossians, Ephesians, and 2 Timothy, and yet the title "prisoner" does not occur in the openings of any of these letters. The use of this designation, therefore, must be intended to do more than just convey Paul's location or historical situation.

A better explanation is that the title "prisoner" was chosen because of its "emotive and persuasive power" (Dunn 1996: 311) as well as its direct connection to the implied request of the letter. The theme of Paul's imprisonment serves as an important backdrop to the letter as a whole:

- In verse 1 Paul opens the correspondence by identifying himself as a "prisoner of Christ."
- In verse 9 he begins the letter body with the same designation, "prisoner of Christ Jesus."
- In verse 10 he identifies Onesimus as one to whom he has given birth "in prison."
- In verse 13 he states his desire to keep Onesimus with him so that the runaway slave may continue to serve the apostle during his "imprisonment for the gospel."

- Finally, in verse 23, for the fifth time in this brief letter, he draws attention to his own situation of imprisonment by passing on to Philemon the greeting of Epaphras, who is identified as "my fellow prisoner in Christ Jesus."

Paul's present sufferings in prison for the sake of his Lord "allow him to speak to the community with greater authority" (Lohse 1971: 189; so also Wall 1993: 194). For the degree to which the apostle is willing to suffer for Christ places pressure on Philemon to be similarly willing to suffer for Christ in the matter of Onesimus. William Hendriksen (1964: 209) captures the implied contrast that Paul makes between himself and Philemon with the rhetorical question: "In comparison with the *sacrifice* that I am making, is not the *favor* which I am asking you to grant a rather easy matter?"

The term "prisoner," however, in addition to its emotive and persuasive power, also foreshadows the letter's *implied* request. The existence of an implied request is suggested by the confidence formula found in the letter closing, where Paul states, "Confident of your obedience, I write to you, knowing that you will do even beyond the things that I am saying" (v. 21b). The "things that I am saying" refers to the *explicit* request of the letter, given near the end of the letter body in verse 16, that Philemon welcome Onesimus back "no longer as a slave but more than a slave, a beloved brother." But to what is the apostle referring with the words "even beyond the things that I am saying"? A strong candidate is verse 13, where Paul states his strong desire to have Onesimus remain with him and help him carry on his gospel ministry while under house arrest: "whom I was wanting to keep for myself in order that, on behalf of you, he might serve me in my imprisonment for the gospel." This verse in Greek is intensified by both the addition of the personal pronoun "I" (which is already expressed in the verb and, though redundant, adds emphasis) and the use of the rarer and emphatic past tense "I was wanting" (instead of the more common past tense "I wanted"). F. F. Bruce (1984: 214) does not find Paul's intentions in this verse at all subtle, stating that "Paul now makes it very clear what he is asking Philemon to do." John Barclay (1991: 172) likewise states: "The main point of verses 13–14, the implied request that Philemon send Onesimus back to Paul, is tolerably clear." The letter's implied request, therefore, is that Philemon, after forgiving his runaway slave,[2] will send him immediately back to Paul to assist the apostle in his "prison" ministry. Joseph Fitzmyer (2000: 102) is but one of

---

2. An explicit request to *free* rather than *forgive* Onesimus would make the implicit request much more difficult for Philemon to carry out.

several commentators who understand verse 13 as "indirectly suggesting that Philemon might not only forgive Onesimus but also release him so that he might return to work with Paul in his evangelization" (so also Wiles 1974: 216; Allen 1992: 89; Witherington 2007: 76, 86n18).

The substitution of the designation "prisoner" for the expected title "apostle" can now be seen as more than an accidental or innocent alteration of Paul's epistolary practice. At the very opening of the letter, this change of title highlights Paul's imprisonment—an imprisonment that he repeatedly refers to throughout this brief letter (vv. 1, 9, 10, 13, 23)—in order to foreshadow the implicit request to have the slave owner send Onesimus back to serve as the apostle's helper during the time of Paul's house arrest.

The Recipient Formula (vv. 1b–2)

The recipient formula also appears to be deliberately expanded in three subtle but significant ways so as to induce Philemon's obedience to Paul's explicit and implicit requests in the letter: the description of Philemon as "beloved" and also "our fellow worker," as well as the inclusion of other recipients.

First, there is the description of Philemon as "beloved" (*agapētō*). Although Paul uses the word "beloved" in two other letter openings (Rom. 1:7; 2 Tim. 1:2) and just over twenty times in the body sections of other letters to characterize his recipients,[3] here the term has special significance. This is the first of five references in this brief letter to the concept of mutual love—love extended from one Christian to another:

- In verse 1 Paul's identification of Philemon as "*beloved*" reminds the slave owner, right at the outset, that he belongs to a community of mutual love in which he enjoys the affection extended to him by both Paul and his cosender, Timothy.

- In verse 5, in the thanksgiving section, Paul highlights Philemon's demonstrated practice of extending love to fellow believers, referring to his "*love* for all the saints."

- In verse 7, for a second time in the thanksgiving section, Paul mentions Philemon's loving acts to fellow believers, stating "your *love*" brought the apostle much joy and comfort because "the hearts of the saints have been refreshed through you."

3. Rom. 11:28; 12:19; 16:5, 8, 9, 12; 1 Cor. 4:14, 17; 10:14; 15:58; 2 Cor. 7:1; 12:19; Eph. 5:1; 6:21; Phil. 2:12; 4:1; Col. 1:7; 4:7, 9, 14; 1 Thess. 2:8; 1 Tim. 6:2.

- In verse 9 Paul opens the body of the letter with an appeal formula that calls on Philemon to act according to his demonstrated practice of mutual love—a practice emphasized by the word order: "more because of *love* I appeal to you."
- In verse 16 the stage has been well set for the explicit request that is finally made: that Philemon welcome Onesimus back "no longer as a slave, but more than a slave, a *beloved* brother."

The designation of Philemon as "beloved" in the letter opening, therefore, can hardly be accidental. Instead, it has been carefully chosen to anticipate the key appeal in verse 16: Paul asks that the slave owner accept Onesimus back in the same loving manner that he (Philemon) has been accepted by the apostle and that he (Philemon) has extended to other believers. As James Dunn (1996: 311) notes: "Philemon is called 'the beloved one,' preparing in effect for the appeal in verse 16 that he should be willing to accept Onesimus in like manner" (so also R. Martin 1973: 158).

The second description of Philemon as "our fellow worker" is also significant, since it places Philemon in an elite group: Prisca and Aquila (Rom. 16:3); Urbanus (Rom. 16:9); Timothy (Rom 16:21; 1 Thess. 3:2); Apollos (1 Cor. 3:9); Silas (2 Cor. 1:24); Titus (2 Cor. 8:23); Epaphroditus (Phil. 2:25); Euodia, Syntyche, and Clement (Phil. 4:3); Aristarchus and Mark (Col. 4:10–11; Philem. 24); Jesus Justus (Col. 4:11); and Demas and Luke (Philem. 24). By equating Philemon's status to that of these key figures in the apostle's missionary activity, Paul at minimum elevates the status of the slave owner and so makes him more open to the letter's request. More than that, the title "our fellow worker" highlights the bond that exists between Paul and Philemon: they are involved together in a common ministry where the needs and desires of one partner are shared by the other—an intimate interrelationship that Paul will appeal to later in the body of the letter. Just as the first descriptor of Philemon as "beloved" foreshadows the later appeal that he welcome Onesimus back as "a beloved brother" (v. 16), so also the second descriptor of Philemon as "our fellow worker" looks ahead to the later appeal that "if, therefore, you have fellowship with me, receive him as you would receive me" (v. 17).

The third way that the recipient formula has been expanded to intensify the persuasive force of the letter is through the inclusion of other recipients: in addition to Philemon, the letter is addressed "to Apphia our sister, and to Archippus our fellow soldier, and to the church in your house" (v. 2). Some commentators refuse to recognize any persuasive force at work in the inclusion of these additional recipients, attributing their presence to epistolary courtesy. Peter O'Brien (1982: 273, see also 268), for example, rejects the seemingly obvious fact that Apphia, Archippus, and the house church are even included as letter recipients:

> They are not named along with Philemon as recipients of the letter. The matter Paul is dealing with is a personal affair which concerns Philemon alone and the decision to be arrived at is not a concern of the entire community. The inclusion of other Christians' names in this salutation and the benedictions (vv. 3, 25 where the plural "you" occurs) is due to the apostle's courtesy.

Richard Melick (1991: 349) similarly states: "The text appears to address four readers. The letter makes clear, however, that Paul directed his comments to Philemon alone. . . . Most likely, Paul included the others because they were part of Philemon's family and courtesy demanded it."

But while Apphia may well have been Philemon's wife, there is no conclusive evidence that Archippus was his son, and it can hardly be the case that everyone in the church that met in his house was related to him such that "courtesy demanded" their inclusion among the letter recipients. The more plausible explanation for Paul including all these folks in the recipient formula is that he deliberately makes the letter's request a public matter, thereby giving his correspondence greater persuasive power. As any recruiter or fund-raiser today knows full well, a request made in public is much harder to turn down than one made in private. Norman Petersen (1985: 99) is closer to the truth than O'Brien and Melick in observing: "Social pressure on Philemon is secured most conspicuously by Paul's addressing his letter not only to Philemon but also to Apphia, Archippus, and the entire church that meets in Philemon's house." The same point is recognized by other commentators (Dunn 1996: 313; Witherington 2007: 56), including Barth and Blanke (2000: 263): "All those worshiping together, men and women, the rich and the poor, those more and those less educated, including slaves and children, are charged and enabled to exert some pressure on the slave owner, if ever he would prove reluctant to fulfill Paul's expectations." This strategy of making the letter's request a public matter should not be viewed as a sneaky and questionable tactic of Paul but ought to be viewed in the context of the corporate nature of the early church, in which no matter was purely "private" but rather involved indirectly, if not directly, one's relationship to fellow brothers and sisters within the new family of God (Moo 2008: 383–84).

The Cosender (v. 1a)

The persuasive pressure created by the mention of additional letter recipients suggests that the same purpose may also lie behind the mention of

Timothy as a cosender of the letter. As Fitzmyer (2000: 85) notes: "This also means that Timothy is aware of the issue about which Paul writes in this letter, and he lends supports to Paul's appeal." Paul further draws the attention of Philemon to Timothy's role as cosender and thus cosupporter of the apostle's request in his description of the slave owner not with the singular "*my* coworker" but the plural "*our* coworker."

That this strategy of making the letter's request a public matter so as to exert further pressure is, in fact, a deliberate one is strengthened by Paul's similar practice both later in this letter and in his other correspondence. At the end of this brief letter, the apostle sends greetings from five of his fellow workers: Epaphras, Mark, Aristarchus, Demas, and Luke (vv. 23–24). Thus, in addition to Timothy, there are at least five other Christian leaders who are aware of Paul's request to Philemon and who implicitly support the apostle in his request. This persuasive strategy of Paul in letting his recipients know that others are aware of the request that he is making of them is also found in his correspondence with the Corinthians. Paul cleverly tells the Corinthians that he has been "boasting" (2 Cor. 8:24; 9:2, 3) to the churches of Macedonia about their (the Corinthians') "readiness" and "zeal" (9:2) to support his "offering for the saints," all of which is a means of persuading these reluctant believers in Achaia to contribute to his relief collection.

Summary

Our epistolary analysis of the letter opening of Philemon has demonstrated not only the great care with which Paul has written this seemingly simple letter but also his powerfully persuasive prose. In the space of a few brief verses, he has adapted and expanded the epistolary conventions in a way that foreshadows the explicit and implicit requests of the letter and places pressure on Philemon to obey these requests.

The Thanksgiving (vv. 4–7)

Form of the Passage

A formal analysis of the thanksgiving section of Philemon indicates that it closely follows the typical structure of this epistolary unit, containing four of the expected five elements:[4]

---

4. The thanksgiving does not have the fourth element, the "explanation," which clarifies and/or expands the preceding "cause" of thanksgiving.

Statement of Thanksgiving	[4]I give thanks to my God always,
Manner of Thanksgiving	by making remembrance of you in my prayers,
Cause of Thanksgiving	[5]because I hear of your love and your faith, which you have toward the Lord Jesus and for all the saints.
Prayer Report	[6]I pray that the sharing of your faith may become active in the knowledge of everything good among us for Christ.

This formal analysis reveals a fact overlooked by most commentators: verse 7 does not technically belong to the thanksgiving, which comes to a climactic close with the prayer report of verse 6. Even fewer recognize that verse 7 involves an epistolary convention common in Greco-Roman letters: the "joy expression."[5]

Joy Formula	[7]For I have much joy and encouragement on account of your love, because the hearts of the saints have been refreshed through you, brother.

The Greek papyri contain numerous examples of stereotyped expressions of joy that typically consist of three elements:[6]

1. The main verb, either "I rejoice" (*chairō*) or the synonymous expression "I have joy" (*echō charan*), given with the first-person verb;

2. An adverb of magnitude such as "greatly" (*megalōs*), "exceedingly" (*lian*), or "much" (*polla*); and

3. A causal clause giving the reason for joy, introduced either with the conjunction "because" (*hoti*) or the preposition "on account of" (*epi*).

These three formal elements are found in Philem. 7 and are also consistently found in Paul's use of the joy expression elsewhere (Rom. 16:19a; 1 Cor. 16:17; Phil. 4:10–20; see also 2 John 4; 3 John 3).

Six factors make it clear that the joy expression of verse 7, though formally distinct from the thanksgiving section, nevertheless belongs to this epistolary unit instead of marking the beginning of the letter body.

First, the explanatory "for" (*gar*), which opens the joy formula, connects this verse with the preceding thanksgiving. The joy formula takes the place of the missing fourth element of the thanksgiving, the "explanation," which clarifies the reason why Paul brings thanksgiving to God. The apostle explains that his thanksgiving is based on Philemon's track record of demonstrating

5. For more on this epistolary convention, see Koskenniemi 1956: 75–77; White 1971: 95–96; 1972: 39–40; 1986: 201; Stowers 1986: 186: Weima 1994a: 149–50.

6. See, e.g., *BGU* 332.6–7; 632.9–10; P.Eleph. 13.2–3; P.Giss. 21.3–4; P.Lond. 42.7–9; 43.3–4; P.Mert. 12.3–6; P.Mich. 483.3–5; P.Yale 28.10–11.

love to other believers—a love he hopes Philemon will similarly extend to another new believer, his former slave, Onesimus.

Second, the beginning of the body of the letter is signaled grammatically by the inferential conjunction "for this reason" (*dio*) that opens verse 8.

Third, the start of the letter body is further indicated literarily by the twofold occurrence (vv. 9 and 10) of the appeal formula ("I appeal"). This epistolary convention typically has a transitional function, either from one major topic to another within the letter body, or, as here and elsewhere (1 Cor. 1:10), from the thanksgiving to the letter body.

Fourth, 2 John 4 and 3 John 3 provide two important parallels for the location of a joy formula as part of the introductory thanksgiving and located immediately before the start of the letter body.

Fifth, a Pauline parallel can be found in the thanksgiving of 1 Cor. 1:4–9. Though Paul does not here use the joy expression, he does include—after the thanksgiving proper (1:4–8) and immediately before the beginning of the letter body (which similarly opens with the appeal formula in 1:10)—a concluding benediction (1:9, "Faithful is God, through whom you were called into the fellowship of his son, Jesus Christ, our Lord"). Like the joy expression in Philem. 7, this benediction both foreshadows and transitions to the theme of unity taken up as the first topic in the letter body (1 Cor. 1:10–4:21).

Finally, the joy expression of Philem. 7 does not present the main request of the letter, as might be expected if it were part of the letter body, but rather, like the thanksgiving section to which it belongs, foreshadows in a preparatory way the main request of the letter. As Peter O'Brien (1977: 58) observes: "The paragraph (if v. 7 be included) is designed to prepare the way for the specific matter with which the letter is primarily concerned."

There is overwhelming evidence, therefore, that the joy expression belongs not to the body of the letter but to the thanksgiving and that this second major epistolary unit in Philemon consists of verses 4–7.

Function of the Passage

All three typical functions of the thanksgiving section—a pastoral function, an exhortative function, and a foreshadowing function—can be seen in the specific passage of Philem. 4–7, and each function enhances in various ways the persuasive force of the letter.

PASTORAL FUNCTION

The thanksgiving of Philem. 4–7 serves to reestablish Paul's relationship with Philemon, conveying the genuineness and depth of his feelings for the slave owner. The apostle accomplishes this in the second formal element—the "manner" of thanksgiving, where he states that his thanksgiving to God for Philemon is done "by making remembrance of you in my prayers." In Philemon's mind, Paul evokes the moving image of the apostle on his knees praying to God both about and on behalf of the slave owner. Paul conveys the intensity of his pastoral concern for Philemon by mentioning the frequency of his intercessory prayers: the apostle does not offer merely a single or even occasional prayer, but instead he "always" in his prayers gives thanks to God for Philemon (note not only the plural "prayers" but also the present tense of the participle "making remembrance," which in Greek highlights the ongoing or continuous nature of the action).

Paul's explicit reference to his constant prayers about Philemon's love and faith, however, not only allows the apostle to make known his genuine thanksgiving to God for his divine work in Philemon's life and ministry but also serves to create a context in which the slave owner will more likely agree to the letter's request. Paul writes this letter from a powerless position. He is currently under house arrest in Rome,[7] physically separated from Philemon by over a thousand miles—a great distance given the traveling difficulties of the ancient world. Paul also has no legal authority to compel the slave owner to do anything, let alone compel him to commit a shame-inducing act like forgiving a runaway slave who may also have stolen from him.[8] The situation is not helped by the likelihood that it is now at least three years since Paul has had any face-to-face contact with Philemon. In such a context, it would be inappropriate, offensive, and almost certainly futile for the apostle to move directly from the letter opening to the letter body, where he will make his request. The pastoral function of the thanksgiving, therefore, plays a crucial role in reestablishing Paul's relationship with Philemon and creating a context in which the slave owner will be open to hearing and heeding the difficult entreaty from Pastor Paul that lies at the heart of this letter.

EXHORTATIVE FUNCTION

Second, Paul's thanksgiving to God for Philemon has an exhortative function: even though the apostle's words of gratitude are ostensibly addressed to God ("I give thanks to my God . . ."), whom Paul views as the ultimate

---

7. This is the traditional location of Paul's imprisonment. The problems with locating the apostle's detention in Rome are not as great as they are typically claimed to be, and there is no explicit evidence supporting the alternative location in Ephesus.

8. The conditional clause in verse 18 (a first-class condition in Greek) suggests a real rather than hypothetical situation: "If he has wronged you at all or owes you anything."

cause of Philemon's praiseworthy deeds, by sharing with the slave owner the specific content of his thanksgiving to God Paul places pressure on Philemon to continue living up to these words of thanksgiving. This function involves persuasion through praise: the praise that Paul brings to God for specific deeds done by Philemon has the effect of persuading the slave owner to persist in those specific deeds.

The specific deeds of Philemon that cause Paul to give thanks to God are "your love and your faith, which you have toward the Lord Jesus and for all the saints" (v. 5). The difficulty in this verse is to understand the proper relationship between the two nouns and their two objects: are Philemon's "love and faith" directed to *both* "the Lord Jesus" and "all the saints"? The problem with this view is that elsewhere Paul speaks only about having "faith" in the Lord Jesus and never in saints or fellow believers. A better way to interpret this verse is to recognize Paul's use of a literary device, a chiasm:[9]

Chiasm of Philemon 5

Love (A)   Faith (B)

Toward the   For all the
Lord Jesus (B′)   saints (A′)

Paul, then, is giving thanks to God for Philemon's love for all the saints and his faith toward the Lord Jesus. This interpretation is supported by two additional factors: first, the definite article before both "love" and "faith" suggests that these two nouns should be viewed as being distinct from each other; second, the thanksgiving of Colossians states, "we have heard of your faith in Christ Jesus and of the love you have for all the saints" (1:4; see also Eph. 1:15). When Paul's statement about Philemon's love and his faith is considered in light of the exhortative function of a thanksgiving section, such a statement can be seen to place positive pressure on the slave owner to continue to demonstrate love for fellow believers—including his runaway slave (notice Paul's reference to "*all* the saints," Philem. 5)—and faith in the Lord Jesus.

9. So already the fifth-century bishop Theodore of Mopsuestia. See also, e.g., Lightfoot 1897: 334; Harris 1991: 250; O'Brien 1982: 278–79; Moo 2008: 388–89.

The apostle places additional pressure on Philemon in the thanksgiving's prayer report, where the exhortation is no longer implicit but explicit: "I pray that the sharing of your faith may become active in the knowledge of everything good among us for Christ" (v. 6). The precise meaning of this verse is unfortunately not at all obvious, a fact that has led Harald Riesenfeld (1982: 251) to observe, "Few passages in the New Testament have been interpreted and translated in so many different ways." Nevertheless, a good case can be made that Paul here is praying for Philemon's faith—that is, the outward manifestation of his faith in specific deeds of charity (see Rom. 15:26 and Phil. 1:5 for a similar meaning of *koinōnia*)—to be at work for the good of fellow believers. Joseph Lightfoot (1897: 333) offers the following paraphrase of the prayer report: "Your friendly offices and sympathies, your kindly deeds of charity, which spring from your faith." By letting the slave owner know specifically what he is praying will happen in his (Philemon's) life, Paul not so subtly prompts him to continue to demonstrate his faith in concrete acts of goodness toward other believers—including a new believer such as the about-to-be-mentioned Onesimus.

The exhortative function should also be recognized in the joy formula of verse 7: "For I have much joy and encouragement on account of your love, because the hearts of the saints have been refreshed through you, brother." As with the earlier statement of verse 5, here too exists an implicit challenge for Philemon to accomplish—this time to continue his specific deeds of love by which fellow believers from the Colossian church are refreshed and encouraged.

Foreshadowing Function

Paul's thanksgiving to God for Philemon has a third important function: it foreshadows the major topics or central themes of the letter. Douglas Moo (2008: 385) notes, "In no other letter does Paul 'rehearse' so many of the key points of the letter in the thanksgiving section." The "alert" reader of this little letter will find at least three key terms or ideas in the thanksgiving that are picked up and developed later in the letter body and, in some cases, also in the letter closing.

1. *"Love."* The thanksgiving continues to emphasize a theme introduced and stressed in the letter opening: love for fellow believers (in distinction from love for God and/or the Lord Jesus). But whereas the letter opening highlights the love that Philemon *receives* from Paul and Timothy ("To our *beloved* Philemon," v. 1b) in anticipation of the later request that Philemon extend this same love to Onesimus (vv. 15b–16: "that you have him back . . .

as a *beloved* brother"), the thanksgiving focuses on the love that the slave owner *gives* to other believers.

The apostle stresses Philemon's love for fellow believers in at least three ways. First, he reverses his typical word order: instead of the expected "faith and love" (Col. 1:3–4; 1 Thess. 1:2–3; 2 Thess. 1:3; Eph. 1:15; 1 Tim. 1:14; see also 1 Cor. 13:13; 1 Tim. 6:11), Paul gives thanks to God for Philemon's "love and faith" (v. 5). Eduard Lohse (1971: 193) correctly observes that the noun "love" is placed "in an accentuated position," so that "in this way the reference to 'love' gains special emphasis" and that "'love' is at the front and center of the stage" (so also Moo 2008: 389).

Second, in the thanksgiving Paul refers to Philemon's love for fellow believers: "For I have much joy and encouragement on account of your love" (v. 7a). If one were to think of the situation as a banking transaction, this marks the second time in the letter thus far that Paul has deposited praise for Philemon's love, thereby creating a greater reserve of goodwill from which the apostle may confidently expect to exact a withdrawal in the appeal of the letter body (notice the word order in v. 9 to emphasize this point: "more because of love I appeal").

Third, both references to Philemon's love have in view his love directed not to God and/or the Lord Jesus but to fellow believers: it is a love that is "for all the saints" (v. 5) and through which "the hearts of the saints have been refreshed" (v. 7). As has been highlighted above in the exhortative function, this places pressure on Philemon to live up to the praise that Paul has given him: to extend the same love to a new saint, Onesimus, that he has shown "to all the saints." Even the adjective "all" here may be related to the overall persuasive prose of the letter. For instead of viewing "all" as a Pauline exaggeration or hyperbole, it may well have in view the love that Paul hopes Philemon will have not only for him and his future visit but even more so for the returning Onesimus. As Markus Barth and Helmut Blanke (2000: 280) explain, "In addition, the term 'all the saints' may be used to prepare the way and the reception not only of Paul, if the Lord wills that he comes around (v. 22), but even more of an earlier arrival: Paul's alter ego, Onesimus (v. 12, 16–17). Certainly the fugitive slave is an ugly bird when he attempts to find a nest in Philemon's house and to be included in his love."

2. *"Refresh the hearts."* A second way in which the thanksgiving both foreshadows the explicit request of the letter and also increases the document's persuasive power is found in the unique and unparalleled phrase (so A. Clark 1996: 300) "the hearts of the saints have been refreshed though you" (v. 7). Instead of the much more common Greek word for "heart," *kardia* (fifty-two occurrences in the Pauline letters), the apostle uses the rarer term *splanchna* (only eight occurrences, three of which are in this brief letter). The reason for

this word choice stems from the fact that *splanchna*—which literally refers to human entrails (in colloquial language, "guts"), where it was believed that the deepest feelings were located—is a more emotive term than the common word *kardia*. In today's world it is common to say to one's beloved: "I love you with all my heart!" In Paul's world, one would say instead: "I love you with all my guts!" Dunn (1996: 321) comments about the apostle's word choice: "The emotional bonds between Philemon and 'the saints' were strong. No doubt Paul hoped that this would be a factor in his favor when he came to make his appeal to Philemon in the next paragraph."

That Paul's word choice can hardly be fortuitous is clear from the way he echoes this term in the rest of the letter. In the body of the letter, the apostle describes Onesimus with the clause "this one is my very heart" (v. 12b), again using the rarer term *splanchna*. Then Paul picks up this key term yet again in the letter closing with the command, "Refresh my heart in Christ" (v. 20b). This threefold repetition of the rarer term *splanchna* involves advancing a three-step deductive argument whose implications for Philemon's conduct are quite clear and persuasive:

Step 1:   Paul has joy because of Philemon's actions of "refreshing" the "hearts" of fellow believers (v. 7).

Step 2:   Paul tells Philemon that the slave Onesimus is his very "heart" (v. 12).

Step 3:   Paul commands Philemon to "refresh my heart" (v. 20).

The logic of the apostle's three-step argument is impossible to miss: if Philemon is to obey Paul's closing command to "refresh my heart," this will require that the slave owner deal with the one who is the apostle's heart— Onesimus—in the way that Paul has been carefully hinting at throughout the letter: to forgive the runaway slave (explicit request) and then send him back to Paul to help the apostle in his ministry during his Roman imprisonment (implicit request).

3. *"Sharing/fellowship"* (koinōnia) *and "the good."* Paul's careful selection of the term "love" and the unique expression "refresh the hearts" in the thanksgiving in order to anticipate the main request of the letter suggests that other words or phrases found in this epistolary unit may similarly be preparing the ground for the request that will follow in the letter body. This possibility exists for the terms "sharing/fellowship" (*koinōnia*) and "the good" in the prayer report of verse 6: "I pray that the sharing of your faith may become active in the knowledge of everything good among us for Christ."

We have already seen how Paul, by letting the slave owner know specifically what he is praying, induces Philemon to continue to demonstrate his faith in concrete acts of goodness toward fellow believers—including the new believer who is his runaway slave. The reference to the term "sharing/fellowship" (*koinōnia*) may also have in view more specifically the implicit request of the letter, that Philemon return the forgiven Onesimus to Paul, where the slave can resume helping the apostle to carry on his ministry while under house arrest. In support of this interpretation, Gordon Wiles sees Paul here making an oblique reference similar to that made in the thanksgiving section of Philippians, where the apostle also uses the same word *koinōnia* to refer to that church's gift of both finances and the sending of Epaphroditus to help the apostle during his prison ministry:

> Judging by the careful selection of terms throughout the present thanksgiving as he prepares for the details of his request, we may take *koinōnia* as prefiguring the business language of verse 17, "So if you consider me your partner (*koinōnon*), receive him as you would receive me." Here [in v. 6], then, he is making his first allusion to the actual subject matter of the appeal—generous sharing on the part of Philemon. (Wiles 1974: 223; see also Moo 2008: 391)

If, as I have just argued, the term *koinōnia* in the prayer report of verse 6 looks ahead to the letter's implicit request, this increases the likelihood that the same subject is in view with the verse's reference to "the good." That Paul here is not making a generic reference to things that are "good" but instead has a specific "good" deed in mind is suggested by the clarifying phrase "among us" (Greek, lit., "the good—the among us one," *tou en hēmin*). This phrase locates Philemon's good action as that which is done either in the midst of or for fellow Christians. That Paul is thinking particularly about his implicit request that Philemon send Onesimus back to assist him in his gospel ministry is suggested by his later description in verse 14 (concerning Paul's desire to keep the runaway slave), which uses the identical term "your good thing/deed" (*to agathon sou*). Paul's choice of the term "good" in both the thanksgiving and again in the implicit request of the letter body, therefore, does not appear to be accidental. Rather, as Ben Witherington (2007: 77) notes on verse 14, "The reference to Philemon's 'good deed' picks up on what was said in verse 6."

Summary

Our analysis of the thanksgiving of Philemon has demonstrated that this epistolary unit, like the letter opening, has been constructed with great skill so as to foreshadow the explicit and implicit requests of the letter and also to increase the document's persuasive power. The assertion of John Knox (1935: 21–22) some time ago about the thanksgiving of Philemon, therefore, has been shown to be entirely justified: "The paragraph is clearly designed to prepare the way for the specific matter with which the rest of the letter is to be largely concerned. It [the thanksgiving] is the overture in which each of the themes, to be later heard in a different, perhaps more specific, context, is given an anticipatory hearing."

The Letter Body (vv. 8–18)

The Appeal Formula (vv. 8–10)

The transition from the thanksgiving section to the body of the letter is clearly signaled by the presence of not one but two appeal formulas:

> [8]Therefore, although having much boldness in Christ to command you to do what is necessary, [9]more because of love *I appeal* to you—I, Paul, an old man and now also a prisoner of Christ. [10]*I appeal* to you concerning my child, to whom I gave birth in prison, Onesimus.

The two functions of the appeal formula are well illustrated in these verses. The first and primary function of the appeal formula is transitional: it signals a major shift in the text, either from the end of the thanksgiving section to the beginning of the letter body, as is the case here (see also 1 Cor. 1:10; 1 Tim. 2:1) or, as more typically happens, a transition within the body of the letter (Rom. 15:30–32; 16:17; 1 Cor. 4:16; 16:15–16; 2 Cor. 10:1–2; Phil. 4:2 [2×]; 1 Thess. 4:1; 4:10b–12; 5:12, 14; 2 Thess. 2:1–2). The second function of the appeal formula is to convey a softer, more user-friendly tone to the request of the letter: in situations where Paul's authority is not questioned and he is confident that his exhortation will be obeyed, the apostle chooses not to aggressively "command" his readers and so unnecessarily risk causing offense, but instead he more diplomatically "appeals" to them to do something. Paul is clearly familiar with the softer tone expressed in the appeal formula because here he opens the letter body of Philemon by explicitly contrasting his right to "command" the slave owner with his preferred choice to "appeal" to him.

Thus, on the one hand, the softer, less heavy-handed side of Paul is expressed by the twofold occurrence of the appeal formula. As F. F. Church notes, "By doubling the verb 'I appeal,' Paul pulls Philemon's heart-strings not once, but twice" (1978: 26). What is more, Paul bases his double appeal "more because of love": Paul is now withdrawing or cashing in on the double praise of Philemon's "love" that he deposited in the thanksgiving section (vv. 5 and 7a). Pressure is thus applied to Philemon to act according to the principle of love for which the apostle twice praised him in the preceding epistolary unit.

On the other hand, the harder, more authoritarian side of Paul reveals itself in his not very subtle reminder that he could, if he wanted, instead "command"[10] Philemon to do "what is necessary."[11] Paul could have easily omitted any reference to his authority to issue a command and simply given an appeal, as he does so often in his other letters. Here, however, the apostle chooses to highlight that he has "much boldness in Christ to command you to do what is necessary" (v. 8). While it would be going too far to conclude that Paul's "strategy is little more than blackmail" (A. Wilson 1992: 115), it would be a mistake not to see how Paul's language cleverly compels Philemon to accede to his yet-to-be-mentioned request by reminding the slave owner of Paul's own apostolic authority. John Barclay (1991: 171) is more correct to find "evidence here of Paul's diplomatic skill, exerting authority while appearing to leave the matter entirely in Philemon's hands."

Appeal to Paul's Old Age (v. 9b)

The letter body of Philemon does not contain any additional letter-writing conventions (beyond the appeal formula) that are distinctively epistolary, that is, stereotyped expressions that originate from or are unique to the genre of letters. Nevertheless, Paul in this section of the letter is still very much concerned with influencing Philemon and thus employs a number of persuasive techniques to bring about the slave owner's compliance with the letter's explicit and implicit requests. It is important, therefore, to include in my epistolary analysis of this brief letter a recognition of how these persuasive techniques supplement Paul's skillful adaptation of the opening, thanksgiving, and closing sections so as to enhance the letter's overall persuasive power. Several terms and ideas from the letter body have already been noted and their significance explained in our previous discussion of the letter opening and thanksgiving:

- the phrase "more because of love" in verse 9a
- the three (out of five total) references in this brief letter to Paul's imprisonment in verses 9b, 10b and 13 (see also vv. 1 and 23)
- the implicit request in verses 13–14

---

10. The verb *epitassen* (v. 8) is a strong term describing the authority a higher-ranking person has to command someone of lower position.

11. The participle *anēkon* (v. 8) is another strong term denoting "not merely what is fitting but that which is almost legally obligatory" (H. Schlier, *TDNT* 1:360).

- the reference to "your good deed" in verse 14
- the identification of Onesimus as "beloved" in verse 16
- Paul's appeal to the "sharing/fellowship" he has with Philemon in verse 17

There is no need to repeat those explanations, so in the following paragraphs I will highlight three of the persuasive techniques that have not yet been commented on and are easily missed by the contemporary reader.

The first involves the apostle's appeal to his old age in verse 9b: "I, Paul, an old man."[12] Some commentators see here the use of *pathos*—Paul's attempt to create sympathy for himself (and thus also for his requests) by evoking the image of himself as an old man who is suffering in prison. Witherington (2007: 67), for example, states, "Paul calls himself an old man to provoke sympathy in Philemon and the rest of the audience." Although this interpretation is possible, elsewhere the apostle reminds readers of his difficult circumstances for a variety of reasons but never seemingly to evoke pity; in fact, he seems to eschew sympathy, claiming to have learned how to be content in all circumstances (Phil. 4:11–13).

A more likely explanation is that Paul's appeal to his old age is intended to induce respect and obedience. As James Dunn (1996: 327) puts it: "Since age usually brought with it the wisdom of experience, the appeal is for the respect that a younger member of the same family or circle should pay to the elder" (so also Lohse 1971: 199). It is true that an appeal to age does not carry much weight in our contemporary Western culture, where youthfulness and vitality are often prized more than the wisdom and experience that come with years. But deference toward the elderly was a powerful social convention in the ancient Mediterranean world (Lev. 19:32; Sir. 8:6; see also Prov. 23:22; 1 Tim. 5:1) and continues to be so in many parts of the world today. The

---

12. Many scholars take *presbytēs* (v. 9) not as a reference to an "old man, aged man" (BDAG 863) but "envoy, ambassador" (so, e.g., Lightfoot 1897: 339; Moule 1957: 144; Petersen 1985: 125–28; Barth and Blanke 2000: 321–23). If this reading were correct, then Paul would be appealing to the authority he has as an ambassador of Christ. But there are major weaknesses with this alternative reading. First, it conflicts with Paul's just-stated claim that, though he did have authority to command Philemon, he instead preferred to "appeal" to him and to do so "more because of love." Second, if Paul did intend the meaning of "ambassador," why did he not use the Greek word for this office (*presbeutēs*, which differs in only one letter from the word for "old man"), especially since he is familiar with the verbal form of this word (2 Cor. 5:20; Eph. 6:20)? Third, if Paul intended to use a term that conveyed his authority, why did he not use his more customary title of apostle? Fourth, the common claim that the Greek word for "old man" can *also* mean "ambassador" is not supported by a careful survey of the evidence, which is why the standard Greek lexicon, BDAG, does not list this meaning as even a possibility for the word.

authority that accompanied old age explains how the word for an elderly person[13] evolved from its literal meaning of "old(er) person" and took on (in both the synagogue and church communities) the technical meaning of "leader, elder."[14] The honor-shame aspect of ancient society, therefore, would have made Paul's not-so-innocent aside concerning his old age yet another powerful inducement for Philemon to acquiesce to the apostle's requests in the letter. As Robert Wall (1993: 205) rightly observes: "Paul's appeal is made within a culture where the request of an elderly person would be granted; not to do so would have been considered shameful."

It is also possible that Paul intends the appeal to his old age to strengthen the implicit request of the letter. Ronald Hock (1995) argues that the apostle, by identifying himself as an old man and prisoner and Onesimus as his child, "cast Paul in the role of an old father who is in need of his child's support—an accepted convention of children toward their aged parents" (81). Paul's portrayal of the situation would enhance his implicit request that Philemon send Paul's child, Onesimus, back to his elderly and needy parent in prison to assist his spiritual father in the ministry taking place there.

Appeal to Onesimus's Former Uselessness and Current Usefulness (v. 11)

Another persuasive technique employed by Paul in the letter body involves a pun on Onesimus's name meaning "useful, profitable" (v. 11): "Formerly he was useless [*a-chrēston*] to you, but now he has become useful [*eu-chrēston*] both to you and to me." Paul's clever wordplay, though easy enough to pick up in translation, is even more obvious in the Greek text: the name "Onesimus" is the final word of the previous verse and also the word on which the whole clause of verse 11 is grammatically dependent. It is worth noting—especially if there is any doubt about whether this pun is actually intended by Paul or is instead the creation of overly imaginative biblical scholars—that such word-plays on a person's name still occur today. For example, an advertisement campaign to raise awareness and money to combat Parkinson's disease has a photograph of the actor Michael J. Fox, who suffers from this disease, and the caption "Determined to outfox Parkinson's." In one of the "Got Milk?" advertisements, which feature close-up pictures of big-name stars who are wearing a milk-mustache, the actress Glenn Close appears with the heading "Look Close."

The pun itself has some persuasive force since it either amuses or impresses Philemon and other hearers from the Colossian house church such that they

---

13. Greek *presbytēs* and its synonym *presbyteros*.
14. Dunn 1996: 327, who cites Günther Bornkamm (*TDNT* 6:651–80) and Campbell 1994.

are more positively disposed to Paul and the request that he is making in this letter. Human nature is such that people tend to view in a more positive light those who make them smile or laugh or who impress them with a clever wordplay, and consequently are more likely to agree to what they say or ask. As the famous Roman rhetorician Quintilian, a close contemporary of the apostle Paul, observed centuries ago,

> Rhetorical ornament contributes not a little to the furtherance of our case. For when our audience finds it a pleasure to listen, their attention and their readiness to believe what they hear are both alike increased, while they are generally filled with delight and sometimes even transported by admiration. (*Institutio oratoria* 8.3.5, cited by Lampe 2010: 74)

More important, however, the pun skillfully draws attention to the contrast between Onesimus's former status as "useless" and his current state as "useful." This highlighted contrast in turn strengthens both the explicit and implicit requests of the letter. By reminding Philemon of his slave's former uselessness, Paul minimizes the loss that the slave owner has suffered (v. 18, "If he has wronged you or owes you anything") and so makes it easier for him to forgive his slave and welcome him back as a "beloved brother" (explicit request). By reminding Philemon further of the contrast between his slave's former and current value, Paul also minimizes the cost for the owner to send his slave back to Paul to help the apostle in his prison ministry (implicit request). Philemon would not really be losing anything by sending Onesimus back to Paul, since his slave, while working in his household, was "useless" to him anyway. In fact, Philemon would actually be gaining a greater profit by acceding to the implicit request, since then at least his slave would be living up to his name of "useful" as he serves Paul on his master's behalf (v. 13, "in order that he might serve me on behalf of you").

Appeal to Providence (v. 15)

An additional way that Paul seeks to induce Philemon's obedience involves an appeal to providence in verse 15: "Perhaps this is why he was separated from you for a little while in order that you might have him back forever." Rather than explicitly refer to the illegal escape of Onesimus and so risk raising the rage of the slave owner, the apostle instead alludes to the crime by means of the euphemistic expression "he was separated [*echōristhē*] from you." This verb choice likely involves the use of the divine passive—the use of the passive voice where the unspoken agent of the action is assumed to be God (this interpretation of v. 15 goes back at least to the time of Chrysostom, *Homilies on*

Philemon 2). As Eduard Lohse (1971: 202–3) states, "The passive verb 'he was separated from' plainly intimates that God's hidden purpose may have been behind this incident which has caused Philemon so much annoyance." That this passive verb ("he was separated") is immediately followed by a purpose clause ("in order that you might have him back") strengthens the likelihood that God is the implied agent who has been at work behind the scenes in a way that his divine intention is carried out (Moo 2008: 419).

Paul, therefore, is reframing the action of the runaway slave as something that is part of God's providential plan. Such a view of the situation would be understandable for the apostle, who knew well the words of Joseph to his brothers, "You intended to harm me, but God intended it for good" (Gen. 50:20), and who comforted his readers with the assertion "We know that God works all things for the good of those who love him" (Rom. 8:28). The persuasive force of recasting Onesimus's flight as part of God's providential plan is great, since it suggests that any rejection by Philemon of the apostle's requests would involve a rejection not merely of the human Paul but also of the divine God and his sovereign purpose. It is one thing to disagree with a church leader, even an important one like Paul; it is quite another thing to go against an action that God has sovereignly ordained! The persuasive power of Paul's appeal to providence is recognized by F. F. Church (1978: 28), who views this verse as "the capstone of Paul's proof" and that "by receiving Onesimus back as a beloved brother, he [Philemon] is completing God's designs."

The Letter Closing (vv. 19–25)

There is little agreement among commentators as to where the letter closing in Philemon begins. This is surprising in light of the weighty and compelling evidence that this final section of the letter begins with the autograph formula in verse 19 ("I, Paul, write this in my own hand"):

1. Foremost is the fact that every other autograph formula in Paul's letters belongs not to the body of the letter but to its closing (1 Cor. 16:21; Gal. 6:11; 2 Thess. 3:17; Col. 4:18a).

2. In secular letters of Paul's day, the autograph is always part of the letter closing. So there is the strong presumption that the apostle would follow this epistolary practice in Philemon, especially when there is evidence that he does exactly this in his other letters.

3. There is the close parallel of Gal. 6:11–18: just as Paul in Galatians takes over from his secretary (6:11, "See with what large letters I am writing

to you in my own hand") and personally pens a lengthy closing in which he summarizes in a pointed fashion the key issues of the letter, so also the apostle in Philemon begins writing "in my own hand" in verse 19, not only signing the IOU note to cover any losses that Philemon may have incurred with Onesimus's escape (v. 18) but also cleverly echoing key points raised earlier in the body of the letter (for more on this recapitulating feature in the closing of Philemon, see discussion below).

4. A hortatory section introduced by the vocative "brother(s and sisters)," such as is found in verse 20, is an epistolary convention that regularly appears in Paul's other letter closings (Rom. 16:17; 1 Cor. 16:15; 2 Cor. 13:11a; Phil. 4:8–9a; 1 Thess. 5:25).

5. Additional support for beginning the letter closing of Philemon at verse 19 comes from the fact that the letter body reaches a certain climax in the immediately preceding material of verses 17–18, where Paul moves beyond the thinly disguised request of the previous verses and explicitly challenges Philemon to receive Onesimus as he would receive the apostle himself. As Norman Petersen (1985: 75) writes, "He [Paul] had brought Onesimus' story to a close when he offered to repay Onesimus' debt in verse 18." That Paul in this verse is reaching the end of the body section of the letter is also suggested by the presence of the concluding particle "therefore" (*oun*) in verse 17 and the presence of the first imperatives in verses 17–18, despite his professed reluctance at the beginning of the letter body to command Philemon (v. 8).

Thus, even though there is little scholarly consensus on the extant of this letter's final section, there exists ample epistolary evidence to identify with confidence the letter closing of Philemon as consisting of verses 19–25.[15]

A formal analysis of Philem. 19–25 reveals that this letter closing consists of the following elements:

Autograph Formula (v. 19a)

Parenthetical Comment (v. 19b)

Hortatory Section (v. 20)

Confidence Formula (v. 21)

Apostolic Parousia (v. 22)

Greetings (vv. 23–24)

Grace Benediction (v. 25)

---

15. So Bahr 1966: 467–68; Richards 1991: 173, 178–79; see also Dunn 1996: 324; Moo 2008: 428.

Paul's practice in other letter closings is also evident here: the apostle skillfully shapes and adapts this epistolary unit so that in various ways it recalls the key issue dealt with in the body of the letter, thereby enhancing the document's persuasive power.

Autograph Formula (v. 19a)

After making use of a secretary in the writing of the letter opening, thanksgiving, and body, Paul takes over at the beginning of the letter closing at verse 19a to write a personal promise of payment—an IOU note: "I, Paul, write this in my own hand. I will repay it." The verb "repay it" (*apotinō*), like the verb "charge it" (*ellogeō*) in the immediately preceding verse, is a technical term used in commercial and legal documents of that day (BDAG 124). Paul does not merely issue a weak word about repayment but instead writes a weighty handwritten promissory note. This autographed promise of repayment echoes in an official or legally binding manner Paul's promise made at the end of the letter body (v. 18) to reimburse Philemon for any losses he may have incurred because of Onesimus's actions.

Parenthetical Comment (v. 19b)

The parenthetical comment in verse 19b involves the use of paraleipsis, a rhetorical device in which a speaker or writer declares that they will not say something, thereby saying it after all. A teacher, for example, might say to students: "I know that I don't have to remind you about the test next week and how important it is to review our class material before then." Such a statement cleverly allows the teacher to make a point to the students about the importance of preparing well for the test while outwardly claiming not to need to do so, thereby not insulting the students about their need to do something obvious. In a similar manner, Paul writes to Philemon: "I do not want to mention to you that you, in fact, owe me your very self" (v. 19). Paul is being heavy-handed here.[16] In gambling terms, the apostle is "cashing in his marker," namely reminding Philemon of the huge spiritual debt that he owes Paul for the apostle's key role in his conversion. This reminder places a great sense of obligation on the slave owner to acquiesce to the request extended to him in the body of the letter. As John Barclay (1991: 171–72) observes, this parenthetical comment "is here used to transform Philemon's position from creditor to debtor and so to put him under a limitless moral obligation to comply with Paul's requests."

---

16. Contra Dunn 1996: 340, who finds here "a certain hesitation on Paul's part to lean on Philemon too heavily"; see also Wright 1986: 188.

Hortatory Section (v. 20)

The hortatory section in verse 20 consists of two commands,[17] and both of them recall the main request of the letter. The first command of verse 20a involves a play on Onesimus's name: "Yes, brother, may I have some *benefit* from you in the Lord." The Greek verb used here is the same root for Onesimus's name, which was a common name for slaves, since it was hoped that such a person would live up to his name and be "beneficial" or "useful." Some commentators have questioned this wordplay on Onesimus's name because the verb used in verse 20 was frequently used in other literature of the day.[18] That this expression was well known, however, in no way precludes the possibility that Paul is using it as a deliberate pun. Rather, the additional fact—that (1) this word is used nowhere else in Paul's writings, (2) there are other Greek verbs that Paul could have used to express the same idea, (3) Paul creates a deliberate wordplay on Onesimus's name in verse 11, and (4) the whole letter exhibits a highly skillful argumentation—all suggest that the pun in verse 20a was intended.[19] The wordplay is nicely captured in the translation: "Yes, brother, may I have some 'Onesimus' from you in the Lord."

The first command of verse 20a, therefore, echoes in a general way the primary issue of the letter body and indeed of the letter as a whole, namely Paul's appeal for the runaway slave, Onesimus. This command also looks back in a more specific way to the wordplay of verse 11, which likewise involves a pun on Onesimus's name.

The second command of verse 20b also recalls two key words employed earlier in the letter: the verb "refresh" and the noun "hearts" (the rarer term *splanchna* instead of the common word *kardia*). In the thanksgiving section, Paul commends Philemon for being the kind of person through whom "the *hearts* of the saints have been *refreshed*" (v. 7b). In the body of the letter, Paul not so innocently identifies the slave Onesimus with the expression "this one is my very *heart*" (v. 12b). Therefore, when Paul closes the letter with the command "*Refresh* my *heart* in Christ" (v. 20b), he clearly is intending to echo his previous use of these two key terms. The not-so-subtle fuller meaning of the elliptical command "Refresh my heart" is "Obey my appeal in the body of the letter for the one who is my heart, Onesimus."

17. Technically the mood of the first verb is optative and so expresses not a command but a wish or polite request.

18. So BDF §488.1b; Lohse 1971: 205; R. Martin 1973: 167; O'Brien 1982: 302; Fitzmyer 2000: 119.

19. So most commentators; e.g., Lightfoot 1897: 345; Vincent 1897: 191; Church 1978: 30; Bruce 1984; Wright 1986: 189; Dunn 1996: 341; Barth and Blanke 2000: 486; Nordling 2004: 277; Moo 2008: 432.

Finally, Paul's introduction of the hortatory section with the identification of Philemon in verse 20 with the vocative "brother" may also be significant. Even though this use of the vocative is a regular feature of Paul's closing hortatory sections, it nevertheless recalls both the apostle's identification of Philemon in verse 7 as "brother" and also the letter's key request in verse 16 that this Christian slave owner welcome Onesimus back no longer as a slave but as a beloved "brother."

Confidence Formula (v. 21)

The confidence formula in verse 21 is yet another epistolary convention in the closing section that both recalls earlier material in the letter body and also possesses a persuasive function: "Confident of your obedience, I write to you, knowing that, even beyond the things that I am saying, you will do" (v. 21). As noted in our earlier treatment of this epistolary convention in chapter 4, the confidence formula involves persuasion through praise, since people generally want to live up to the confidence or praise that others have in them. Thus, in a general way, this verse prompts Philemon to prove Paul's confidence in him to be justified by following through on the apostle's request in the letter.

Paul's word choice in verse 21, however, makes this pressure even more pointed: the apostle is confident not simply in Philemon but also in his "obedience." This word raises the stakes of Paul's appeal on behalf of the runaway slave, since it implies that the apostle's request does not really involve an option on Philemon's part that he can either accept or reject but rather is something that requires his "obedience." This undertone of obligation is also found earlier in the letter, in Paul's statement that he could "command" Philemon to do "what is necessary" (v. 8), and even though Paul outwardly states that his preference is that "your good deed might not be by compulsion but by your own free will" (v. 14), such a statement at least hints at the possibility that Paul could instead force Philemon to acquiesce to his request. Commenting on the word "obedience," Douglas Moo (2008: 434) states, "Paul now makes explicit what, in fact, has been implicit in the letter at a number of points: that, while he wants Philemon to respond voluntarily, there is nevertheless a sense in which Philemon is also under obligation to meet Paul's wishes."

Also significant is Paul's additional confidence that Philemon will do "even beyond the things that I am saying" (v. 21b). This comment almost certainly refers back to the implicit request made in verse 13 that Philemon send the forgiven Onesimus back to Paul to assist the apostle in carrying out his apostolic ministry while under house arrest in Rome. The confidence formula in verse 21, therefore, exerts positive pressure on Philemon to agree to Paul's implicit and explicit requests by praising the slave owner in advance for his expected obedience.

Apostolic Parousia (v. 22)

If the confidence formula exerts *positive* pressure on Philemon (positive because Paul confidently expects that Philemon will do what the apostle is asking), then the apostolic parousia places *negative* pressure on him (negative because it involves an indirect threat): "At the same time, prepare a guest room for me, because I hope to be restored to you in answer to your prayers" (v. 22). This statement is hardly a "throwaway remark" given "in the more relaxed mood of the conclusion" (Dunn 1996: 247, 245). Rather, about the places in the letter where Paul tries to make his apostolic *parousia*, or "presence," more powerfully felt by referring to his future visit, the future visit of his emissary, or the act of letter writing, Robert Funk (1967: 249) observes, "All of these [three means] are media by which Paul makes his apostolic authority effective in the churches. The underlying theme is therefore the apostolic *parousia*—the presence of apostolic authority and power." In the context of the letter closing of Philemon, Paul's statement about an upcoming visit functions as an indirect threat: the apostle will be coming to the Lycus valley and the city of Colossae and see firsthand whether Philemon has obeyed his request. Yet, despite the threatening undertone, Paul's apostolic parousia here involves a more "gentle compulsion" (Lightfoot 1897: 345) than some of his other apostolic parousias (compare, e.g., the more threatening tone of 1 Cor. 4:21: "What would you prefer? Shall I come to you with a rod or with love in a spirit of gentleness?").

There is another subtle way in this verse by which Paul increases the pressure on Philemon to obey his request—a subtle way that is hidden in English translation but clear in the original Greek: both the pronoun "you" and the possessive pronoun "your" in "your prayers" are plural. Even though this is a private letter in which Paul couches both the thanksgiving and body sections in the singular, the apostle deliberately makes the situation addressed in the letter a public matter by broadening the audience in both the opening and closing sections, likely under the conviction that a request made in public is harder to turn down than one made in private. The use of the plural also subtly reminds Philemon that he ought to view the situation of his runaway slave not just from his own individual perspective but also from the perspective of how it impacts the larger Colossian church of which he is a part.

Greetings (vv. 23–24)

Paul adds still more weight to his request by bringing this brief letter to a close with a greeting that mentions five people: "Epaphras, my fellow prisoner in Christ Jesus, sends greetings to you, and so do Mark, Aristarchus, Demas, and Luke, my fellow workers." Just as Paul opens the letter by addressing it not merely to the slave owner, Philemon, but also to Apphia, Archippus, and the whole Colossian congregation (v. 2), so he also closes the letter by including the greetings of five people who, in addition to the apostle and Timothy (v. 1), know about the letter's request to Philemon and await his response. A modern analogy would be sending a letter to request a favor from someone and then including at the bottom of the correspondence "cc:," listing the names and perhaps even the official titles of other individuals to whom you have copied the letter. The recipient of such a letter is fully aware of the public nature of this request and would no doubt feel the pressure that this wider knowledge brings.

The issue of Onesimus's return, therefore, is not a private matter limited to Paul and Philemon alone. Instead, it appears that Paul has deliberately made it a public matter so as to exert further pressure on Philemon and those with him to agree to the request of his letter. As Norman Petersen (1985: 100) notes, "With this wider public cognizant of the local problem, the pressure on both Philemon and his church is magnified. The problem is not his or theirs alone. Others know about it and await its resolution."

The order of the names and their accompanying titles may also be significant for increasing the persuasive force of this letter.[20] The name of Epaphras, the pastor of the Colossian church and thus the spiritual leader over Philemon, is mentioned first in the greeting list, in contrast to the closing of Colossians—a letter almost certainly written and delivered at the same time as the letter to Philemon—where Epaphras is mentioned fourth (Col. 4:12). Also, the title given to Epaphras, "fellow prisoner," brings to Philemon's attention yet again the imprisoned state of Paul, which the apostle has been stressing throughout the letter (vv. 1, 9, 10, 13) and which is part of his implicit request. Finally, the use of the title "fellow workers" to describe the remaining four people who send their greetings recalls Paul's opening identification of Philemon as one of his "fellow workers" (v. 1) and so emphasizes the solidarity and common mission that exists between the slave owner and the rest of the apostle's co-missionaries.

---

20. The same phenomenon occurs in the greeting list of Rom. 16:3–16; see discussion in chap. 5.

Grace Benediction (v. 25)

Paul brings his letter to a close with a grace benediction, an epistolary convention found in all of his letter closings and one that is formally most consistent: "May the grace of the Lord Jesus Christ be with your spirit" (v. 25). Even though the apostle here chooses not to make any changes or additions to the grace benediction, there are two ways in which the standard form of this epistolary convention is nevertheless relevant for the specific request of this letter and enhances its persuasive force. First, the wish for God to grant grace can never be for Paul merely a stereotyped prayer but instead is the foundation of the apostle's theology, and thus it is intimately connected with his explicit request to Philemon to forgive Onesimus. The apostle is asking Philemon to do something that is, humanly speaking, impossible to do: his justified anger at Onesimus's flight and possible theft (v. 18), as well as the social pressure in an honor-shame culture for a slave owner to respond to such a situation with harsh punishment, means that forgiveness and receiving Onesimus back as a "beloved brother" (v. 16) is possible only through the divine gift of grace. Second, by using the plural "your" in his grace wish to Philemon ("with your spirit"), Paul again subtly reminds Philemon of the larger community of which he is a part and who will be watching to see whether he will demonstrate grace by acquiescing to Paul's appeal for Onesimus.

Persuasion or Manipulation?

Ralph Martin, in his commentary on Philemon (1973: 165–66), states, "In a letter which is so full of nuances and hidden meanings it may well be believed that Paul's expressions are carefully contrived." This tentative and understated conclusion has been amply proved to be true by the epistolary analysis carried out in this chapter. Paul has skillfully adapted every major unit of this letter—the opening, thanksgiving, body, and closing—so that the persuasive force of his correspondence is greatly enhanced, and he places powerful pressure on Philemon to agree to both the explicit and implicit requests. In fact, Paul's arguments in this brief letter are at times so strong that some might be tempted to accuse the apostle of moving beyond persuasion to manipulation.

This charge, however, is unjustified for at least three reasons. First, Paul does not compromise his integrity by resorting to false praise or feigned emotions: the apostle really does give thanks to God for Philemon's love and his ability to refresh the hearts of the saints; he really is confident that Philemon will not only be obedient but also do even beyond the things that he is explicitly saying in the letter; and he really does believe that this situation falls under the providence of God. Nowhere in the letter does the apostle resort to false statements or outright lies in order to get Philemon to agree to the requests in the letter.

Second, we ought to judge Paul's actions not by our modern, Western standards but by the social norms of his day. As Dunn (1996: 327) points out: "We should hesitate to judge Paul harshly for lowering the tone of the appeal, as if it were emotional blackmail; on the contrary, appeal to the emotions was standard practice in Greek rhetoric." Witherington (2007: 87) makes the same important point: "If this [Paul's techniques of persuasion] makes us uncomfortable because it seems manipulative by modern standards, it is because we do not live in the kind of social and rhetorical environment where Paul did, where this kind of discourse was not only commonplace but actually relished and applauded." That the apostle is indeed employing the kind of persuasive techniques typical of that day can be seen from parallels with the letter of Pliny the Younger in which he skillfully writes on behalf of a freedman, that is, a former slave, who wants to be reconciled to his master:

> C. Pliny to Sabinianus, Greetings. Your freedman, whom you had mentioned as having displeased you, has come to me; he threw himself at my feet and clung to them as he could have to yours. He cried much, begged constantly, even with much silence; in short, he has convinced me that he repents of what he did. I truly believe that he is reformed, because he recognizes that he has been delinquent. You are angry, I know, and rightly so, as I also recognize; but clemency wins the highest praise when the reason for anger is more righteous. You once had affection for (this) human being, and, I hope, you will have it again. Meanwhile it suffices that you let me prevail upon you. Should he again incur your displeasure, you will have so much more reason to be angry, as you give in now. Allow somewhat for his youth, for his tears, and for your own indulgent conduct. Do not antagonize him, lest you antagonize yourself at the same time; for when a man of your mildness is angry, you will be antagonizing yourself. I fear that, in joining my entreaties to his, I may seem rather to compel than to request (you to forgive him). Nevertheless, I shall join them so much more fully and unreservedly, because I have sharply and severely reproved him, positively threatening never to entreat again on his behalf. Although I said this to him, who should become more fearful (of offending), I do not say it to you. I may perhaps have occasion to entreat you again and obtain your forgiveness, but may it be such that it will be proper for me to intercede and you to pardon. Farewell. (*Epistles* 9.21, trans. Fitzmyer 2000: 21–22)

Like Paul in his letter to Philemon, Pliny employs a variety of arguments to make his appeal on behalf of the former slave more persuasive: he cleverly appeals to the genuineness of the slave's repentance, the slave's reformed or changed character, the former affection that the master had for his slave, the young age of the slave, the master's mild temperament, how the master's forgiveness now will make his future punishment for any possible misconduct yet to come that much more justified, and how Pliny himself has already strongly rebuked the slave. Pliny's claim that he does not want to seem "to compel rather than to request you to forgive him" provides an especially strong parallel to Paul's expressed preference to Philemon that "your good deed might be not by compulsion but by your own free will" (v. 14). Paul's argumentation, therefore, should not be judged manipulative but rather in keeping with what was considered acceptable and even expected in his day when dealing with a sensitive matter between a slave and his master.

Third, it must be remembered that Paul writes from a powerless position, being in prison at a great distance away and with no legal authority to compel Philemon to act. How else can the apostle bring about what he believes to be God's will in this difficult situation other than by making use of all the persuasive means available to him? What options did Paul have other than "pulling out all the stops, including combining references to persuasion and command and playing the emotion card repeatedly, to give [his] discourse the necessary weight to achieve its goal" (Witherington 2007: 87)?

Conclusion

Our epistolary analysis of Philemon has clearly demonstrated the great care and impressive skill with which Paul has constructed this letter so as to enhance the document's overall persuasive power. As such, this chapter has illustrated well, in the shortest of Paul's extent letters, what the preceding chapters have established in the apostle's other letters—the exegetical benefits that the method of epistolary analysis has for the proper interpretation of Paul's writings. Modern readers of the apostle's correspondence need to take much more seriously the truth that the rhetoric-loving Corinthians grudgingly admitted about Paul: "His letters are weighty and strong" (2 Cor. 10:10).

Works Cited

Adams, Sean A. 2010. "Paul's Letter Opening and Greek Epistolography: A Matter of Relationship." In *Paul and the Ancient Letter Form*, edited by Stanley E. Porter and Sean A. Adams, 33–55. Pauline Studies 6. Leiden: Brill.

Allen, David L. 1992. "The Discourse Structure of Philemon: A Study in Textlinguistics." In *Scribes and Scripture: New Testament Essays in Honor of J. Harold Greenlee*, edited by D. A. Black, 77–96. Winona Lake, IN: Eisenbrauns.

Arzt, Peter. 1994. "The 'Epistolary Introductory Thanksgiving' in the Papyri and in Paul." *Novum Testamentum* 36 (1): 29–46.

Arzt-Grabner, Peter. 2010. "Paul's Letter Thanksgiving." In *Paul and the Ancient Letter Form*, edited by Stanley E. Porter and Sean A. Adams, 130–58. Pauline Studies 6. Leiden: Brill.

Aune, David E. 1987. *The New Testament in Its Literary Environment*. Library of Early Christianity 8. Philadelphia: Westminster.

———. 1997. *Revelation 1–5*. Word Biblical Commentary 52A. Nashville: Nelson.

Bahr, G. J. 1966. "Paul and Letter Writing in the First Century." *Catholic Biblical Quarterly* 28:465–77.

———. 1968. "The Subscriptions in the Pauline Letters." *Journal of Biblical Literature* 87:27–41.

Bailey, J. A. 1978–79. "Who Wrote II Thessalonians?" *New Testament Studies* 25:131–45.

Balch, David L. 1981. *Let Wives Be Submissive: The Domestic Code in I Peter*. Society of Biblical Literature Monograph Series 26. Chico, CA: Scholars Press.

———. 1988. "Household Codes." In *Greco-Roman Literature and the New Testament*, edited by D. E. Aune, 25–50. Sources for Biblical Study 21. Atlanta: Scholars Press.

Barclay, John M. G. 1991. "Paul, Philemon and the Dilemma of Christian Slave-Ownership." *New Testament Studies* 37:161–86.

Barth, Markus, and Helmut Blanke. 2000. *The Letter to Philemon: A New Translation with Notes and Commentary*. Eerdmans Critical Commentary. Grand Rapids: Eerdmans.

Bauckham, Richard. 1979. "Barnabas in Galatians." *Journal for the Study of the New Testament* 2:61–72.

Belleville, Linda L. 1987. "Continuity or Discontinuity: A Fresh Look at 1 Corinthians in the Light of First-Century Epistolary Forms and Conventions." *Evangelical Quarterly* 59:15–37.

Benko, S. 1984. "The Kiss." In *Pagan Rome and the Early Christians*, 79–102. Bloomington: Indiana University Press.

Best, E. 1977. *A Commentary on the First and Second Epistles to the Thessalonians*. Reprinted with additional bibliography. Black's New Testament Commentaries. London: Black.

———. 1987. *Second Corinthians*. Atlanta: John Knox.

Betz, Hans Dieter. 1979. *Galatians*. Hermeneia. Philadelphia: Fortress.

Bjerkelund, C. J. 1967. *Parakalō: Form, Funktion und Sinn der parakalō-Sätze in den paulinischen Briefen*. Oslo: Universitetsforlaget.

Bligh, J. 1969. *Galatians: A Discussion of St. Paul's Epistle*. London: St. Paul.

Blomberg, Craig. 1989. "The Structure of 2 Corinthians 1–7." *Criswell Theological Review* 4 (1): 3–20.

Boers, Hendrikus. 1975–76. "The Form Critical Study of Paul's Letters: I Thessalonians as a Case Study." *New Testament Studies* 22 (2): 140–58.

Boring, M. Eugene. 2015. *I & II Thessalonians*. New Testament Library. Louisville: Westminster John Knox.

Bradley, D. G. 1953. "The 'Topos' as a Form in the Pauline Paraenesis." *Journal of Biblical Literature* 72:238–46.

Bruce, F. F. 1982. *The Epistle to the Galatians*. New International Greek Testament Commentary. Grand Rapids: Eerdmans.

———. 1984. *The Epistles to the Colossians, to Philemon, and to the Ephesians*. New International Commentary on the New Testament. Grand Rapids: Eerdmans.

Bryant, Robert A. 2001. *The Risen Crucified Christ in Galatians*. Society of Biblical Literature Dissertation Series 185. Atlanta: Society of Biblical Literature.

Byrskog, Samuel. 1996. "Co-senders, Co-authors and Paul's Use of the First Person Plural." *Zeitschrift für die neutestamentliche Wissenschaft* 87:230–50.

Campbell, R. A. 1994. *The Elders: Seniority within Earliest Christianity*. Edinburgh: T&T Clark.

Carson, D. A. 1984. *From Triumphalism to Maturity: An Exposition of 2 Corinthians 10–13*. Grand Rapids: Baker.

Champion, Leonard G. 1934. *Benedictions and Doxologies in the Epistles of Paul*. Oxford: Kemp Hall.

Church, F. F. 1978. "Rhetorical Structure and Design in Paul's Letter to Philemon." *Harvard Theological Review* 71:17–33.

Ciampa, Roy E. 1998. *The Presence and Function of Scripture in Galatians 1 and 2*. Wissenschaftliche Untersuchungen zum Neuen Testament 2/102. Tübingen: Mohr Siebeck.

Ciampa, Roy E., and Brian S. Rosner. 2010. *The First Letter to the Corinthians*. Pillar New Testament Commentary. Grand Rapids: Eerdmans.

Clark, Andrew D. 1996. "'Refresh the Hearts of the Saints': A Unique Pauline Context?" *Tyndale Bulletin* 27 (2): 277–300.

Clark, D. J. 1975. "Criteria for Identifying Chiasm." *Linguistica Biblica* 35:63–72.

Classen, C. J. 2000. *Rhetorical Criticism of the New Testament*. Tübingen: Mohr Siebeck.

Collins, Raymond F. 2010. "A Significant Decade: The Trajectory of the Hellenistic Epistolary Thanksgiving." In *Paul and the Ancient Letter Form*, edited by Stanley E. Porter and Sean A. Adams, 159–84. Pauline Studies 6. Leiden: Brill.

Cook, D. 1992. "The Prescript as Programme in Galatians." *Journal of Theological Studies* 43:511–19.

Craig, C. T. 1953. "The First Epistle to the Corinthians." In *The Interpreter's Bible*, edited by G. A. Buttrick, 10:3–262. Nashville: Abingdon.

Crouch, J. E. 1972. *The Origin and Intention of the Colossian Haustafel*. Göttingen: Vandenhoeck & Ruprecht.

Dahl, N. A. 1950. "Der Name Israel, I: Zur Auslegung von Gal. 6,16." *Judaica* 6:161–70.

Das, A. Andrew. 2014. *Galatians*. Concordia Commentary. St. Louis: Concordia.

Deissmann, Adolf. 1910. *Light from the Ancient East: The New Testament Illustrated by Recently Discovered Texts of the Graeco-Roman World*. Translated by L. R. M. Strachan. London: Hodder & Stoughton.

Dibelius, Martin. 1936. *A Fresh Approach to the New Testament and Early Christian Literature*. London: Nicholson & Watson.

———. 1937. *An die Thessalonicher I, II*. Handbuch zum Neuen Testament 11. Tübingen: Mohr.

Dix, Gregory. 1945. *The Shape of the Liturgy*. Glasgow: Glasgow University Press.

Doty, William G. 1973. *Letters in Primitive Christianity*. Philadelphia: Fortress.

Dunn, James D. G. 1988a. *Romans 1–8*. Word Biblical Commentary. Dallas: Word.

———. 1988b. *Romans 9–16*. Word Biblical Commentary. Dallas: Word.

———. 1993. *The Epistle to the Galatians*. Black's New Testament Commentary. Grand Rapids: Baker Academic.

———. 1996. *The Epistles to the Colossians and to Philemon: A Commentary on the Greek Text*. New International Greek Testament Commentary. Grand Rapids: Eerdmans.

du Toit, André B. 1989. "Persuasion in Romans 1.1–17." *Biblische Zeitschrift* 13:192–209.

Edsall, Benjamin A. 2013. "Paul's Rhetoric of Knowledge: The OΥΚ ΟΙΔΑΤΕ Questions in 1 Corinthians." *Novum Testamentum* 55:252–71.

Elliott, Neil. 1990. *The Rhetoric of Romans: Argumentative Constraint and Strategy and Paul's Dialogue with Judaism*. Sheffield: JSOT Press.

Exler, F. X. J. 1923. *The Form of the Ancient Greek Letter. A Study in Greek Epistolography*. Washington, DC: Catholic University of America.

Fallon, Francis T. 1980. *2 Corinthians*. New Testament Message 11. Wilmington, DE: Michael Glazier.

Faw, Chalmer E. 1952. "On the Writing of First Thessalonians." *Journal of Biblical Literature* 71:217–25.

Fee, Gordon D. 1987. *The First Epistle to the Corinthians*. New International Commentary on the New Testament. Grand Rapids: Eerdmans.

———. 2009. *The First and Second Letters to the Thessalonians*. New International Commentary on the New Testament. Grand Rapids: Eerdmans.

Fefoule, F. 1990. "A contre-courant: Romains 16,3–16." *Revue d'histoire et de philosophie religieuses* 70:409–20.

Findlay, G. G. 1900. "St. Paul's First Epistle to the Corinthians." In *The Expositor's Greek Testament*, edited by W. R. Nicoll, 2:727–953. London: Hodder & Stoughton.

Fitzmyer, Joseph A. 1992. *Romans*. New York: Doubleday.

———. 2000. *The Letter to Philemon*. New York: Doubleday.

Fowl, Stephen E. 2005. *Philippians*. Two Horizons New Testament Commentary. Grand Rapids: Eerdmans.

Frame, J. E. 1912. *A Critical and Exegetical Commentary on the Epistles of St. Paul to the Thessalonians*. International Critical Commentary. Edinburgh: T&T Clark.

Fung, R. Y. K. 1988. *The Epistle to the Galatians*. New International Commentary on the New Testament. Grand Rapids, Eerdmans.

Funk, Robert W. 1967. "The Apostolic *Parousia*: Form and Significance." In *Christian History and Interpretation: Studies Presented to John Knox*, edited by W. R. Farmer, C. F. D. Moule, and R. R. Niebuhr, 249–68. Cambridge: Cambridge University Press.

———. 1970. "The Form and Function of the Pauline Letter." In *SBL Seminar Papers*, 8. Missoula, MT: Scholars Press.

Furnish, Victor Paul. 1984. *II Corinthians. A New Translation with Introduction and Commentary.* Anchor Bible 32a. New York: Doubleday.

———. 2007. *1 Thessalonians, 2 Thessalonians.* Abingdon New Testament Commentaries. Nashville: Abingdon.

Gamble, Harry, Jr. 1977. *The Textual History of the Letter to the Romans.* Grand Rapids: Eerdmans.

Garland, David E. 2003. *1 Corinthians.* Baker Exegetical Commentary on the New Testament. Grand Rapids: Baker Academic.

Gaventa, Beverly R. 1986. "Galatians 1 and 2: Autobiography as Paradigm." *Novum Testamentumn* 28 (4): 309–26.

———. 1998. *First and Second Thessalonians.* Interpretation. Louisville: Westminster John Knox.

George, Timothy. 1994. *Galatians.* New American Commentary. Nashville: B&H.

Green, Gene L. 2002. *The Letters to the Thessalonians.* Pillar New Testament Commentary. Grand Rapids, Eerdmans.

Guthrie, George H. 2015. *2 Corinthians.* Baker Exegetical Commentary on the New Testament. Grand Rapids: Baker Academic.

Hansen, G. Walter. 1994. *Galatians.* IVP New Testament Commentary Series. Downers Grove, IL: InterVarsity.

Harnisch, W. 1973. *Eschatologische Existenz.* Göttingen: Vandenhoeck & Ruprecht.

Harris, Murray J. 1991. *Colossians & Philemon.* Exegetical Guide to the Greek New Testament. Grand Rapids: Eerdmans.

———. 2005. *The Second Epistle to the Corinthians.* New International Greek Testament Commentary. Grand Rapids: Eerdmans.

———. 2008. "2 Corinthians." In *The Expositor's Bible Commentary*, ed. T. Longman and D. E. Garland, 11:415–545. Rev. ed. Grand Rapids: Zondervan.

Harvey, J. D. 1998. *Listening to the Text: Oral Patterning in Paul's Letters.* Evangelical Theological Society Studies 1. Grand Rapids: Baker.

Hawthorne, Gerald F. 1983. *Philippians.* Word Biblical Commentary. Waco: Word.

Hays, Richard B. 1997. *First Corinthians.* Interpretation. Louisville: Westminster John Knox.

———. 2000. "The Letter to the Galatians: Introduction, Commentary, and Reflections." In *The New Interpreter's Bible*, edited by L. E. Keck et al., 11:181–348. Nashville: Abingdon.

Hendriksen, William. 1955. *Exposition of I and II Thessalonians.* New Testament Commentary. Grand Rapids: Baker.

———. 1964. *Exposition of Colossians and Philemon.* New Testament Commentary. Grand Rapids: Baker.

Hock, Ronald F. 1995. "A Support for His Old Age: Paul's Plea on Behalf of Onesimus." In *The Social World of the First Christians: Essays in Honor of Wayne A. Meeks*, edited by L. M. White and O. L. Yarbrough, 67–81. Minneapolis: Fortress.

Holmes, Michael W. 1998. *1 and 2 Thessalonians.* NIV Application Commentary. Grand Rapids: Zondervan.

Holtz, T. 1986. *Der erste Brief an die Thessalonicher.* Evangelisch-Katholischer Kommentar zum Neuen Testament. Zurich: Benziger.

———. 2000. "On the Background of 1 Thessalonians 2:1–12." In *The Thessalonians Debate: Methodological Discord or Methodological Synthesis?*, edited by K. P. Donfried and J. Beutler, 69–80. Grand Rapids: Eerdmans.

Hurd, John C. 1983. *The Origin of 1 Corinthians.* 2nd ed. Macon, GA: Mercer University Press.

Hurtado, Larry W. 1981. "The Doxology at the End of Romans." In *New Testament Textual Criticism: Its Significance for Exegesis;*

Essays in Honour of Bruce M. Metzger, edited by E. J. Epp and G. D. Fee, 185–99. Oxford: Clarendon.

Jervis, L. Ann. 1991. *The Purpose of Romans: A Comparative Letter Structure Investigation.* Journal for the Study of the New Testament Supplement Series 55. Sheffield: JSOT Press.

Jewett, Robert. 1969. "Form and Function of the Homiletic Benediction." *Anglican Theological Review* 51 (1): 18–34.

———. 1972. "Enthusiastic Radicalism and the Thessalonian Correspondence." In *1972 Proceedings of the Society of Biblical Literature,* 1:181–232. Missoula, MT: Scholars Press.

———. 1986. *The Thessalonian Correspondence: Pauline Rhetoric and Millenarian Piety.* Foundations and Facets. Philadelphia: Fortress.

Johnson, Lee A. 2006. "Paul's Epistolary Presence in Corinth: A New Look at Robert W. Funk's Apostolic Parousia." *Catholic Biblical Quarterly* 68 (3): 481–501.

Käsemann, E. 1980. *Commentary on Romans.* Translated and edited by G. W. Bromiley. Grand Rapids: Eerdmans.

Kim, C.-H. 1972. *The Familiar Letter of Recommendation.* Missoula, MT: Scholars Press.

Kim, Seyoon. 2005. "Paul's Entry (εἴσοδος) and the Thessalonians' Faith (1 Thessalonians 1–3)." *New Testament Studies* 51:519–42.

Kinoshita, J. 1964–65. "Romans—Two Writings Combined." *Novum Testamentum* 13:258–77.

Klassen, W. 1993. "The Sacred Kiss in the New Testament." *New Testament Studies* 39:122–35.

Klein, Günter. 1976. "Romans, Letter to the." In *The Interpreter's Dictionary of the Bible: Supplementary Volume,* edited by Keith Crim, 752–54. Nashville: Abingdon.

Kloppenborg, John. 1978. "An Analysis of the Pre-Pauline Formula 1 Cor. 15:3b–5 in

Light of Some Recent Literature." *Catholic Biblical Quarterly* 40:351–67.

Knox, John. 1935. *Philemon among the Letters of Paul: A New View of Its Place and Importance.* Chicago: University of Chicago Press.

———. 1959. *Philemon among the Letters of Paul: A New View of Its Place and Importance.* Rev. ed. New York: Abingdon.

Koskenniemi, Heikki. 1956. *Studien zur Idee und Phraseologie des griechischen Briefes bis 400 n. Chr.* Suomalaisen Tiedeakatemian toimituksia, series B, 102.2. Helsinki: Suomalainen Tiedeakatemia.

Köstenberger, A. 2001. "The Identity of ΙΣΡΑΗΛ ΤΟΥ ΘΕΟΥ (Israel of God) in Galatians 6:16." *Faith and Mission* 19:3–24.

Kreider, E. 1987. "Let the Faithful Greet Each Other: The Kiss of Peace." *Conrad Grebel Review* 5:28–49.

Lake, K. 1911. "The Epistles to the Thessalonians." In *The Earlier Epistles of St. Paul: Their Motive and Origin,* 61–101. London: Rivingtons.

Lampe, Peter. 2010. "Affects and Emotions in the Rhetoric of Paul's Letter to Philemon: A Rhetorical-Psychological Interpretation." In *Philemon in Perspective: Interpreting a Pauline Letter,* edited by D. F. Tolmie, 61–77. Berlin: de Gruyter.

Lassen, Eva M. 1991. "The Use of the Father Image in Imperial Propaganda and 1 Cor. 4:14–21." *Tyndale Bulletin* 42:127–36.

Lietzmann, H. 1906. *An die Römer.* Tübingen: Mohr.

Lightfoot, Joseph B. 1881. *St. Paul's Epistle to the Galatians.* New York: Macmillan.

———. 1897. *St. Paul's Epistles to the Colossians and to Philemon.* London: Macmillan.

———. 1904. *Notes on the Epistles of St. Paul from Unpublished Commentaries.* 2nd ed. London: Macmillan.

Lohse, E. 1971. *Colossians and Philemon: A Commentary on the Epistles to the Colossians and to Philemon.* Hermeneia. Philadelphia: Fortress.

Longenecker, Richard N. 1990. *Galatians.* Word Biblical Commentary. Dallas: Word.

———. 1999. *New Wine into Fresh Wineskins: Contextualizing the Early Christian Confessions.* Peabody, MA: Hendrickson.

Longman, Tremper, III. 2008. "Inclusio." In *The Dictionary of the Old Testament: Wisdom, Poetry and Writings,* edited by T. Longman III and P. Enns, 323–25. Downers Grove, IL: InterVarsity.

Luckensmeyer, David. 2009. *The Eschatology of First Thessalonians.* Novum Testament et Orbis Antiquus: Studien zur Umwelt des Neuen Testaments 71. Göttingen: Vandenhoeck & Ruprecht.

Lund, Nils Wilhelm. 1942. *Chiasmus in the New Testament: A Study in Formgeschichte.* Chapel Hill: University of North Carolina Press.

Lütgert, E. W. 1909. "Die Volkommenen im Philipperbrief und die Enthusiasten in Thessalonich." *Beiträge zur Förderung christlicher Theologie* 13 (6): 547–654.

Lyons, George. 1985. *Pauline Autobiography: Toward a New Understanding.* Society of Biblical Literature Dissertation Series 73. Atlanta: Scholars Press.

MacDonald, M. Y. 2000. *Colossians and Ephesians.* Sacra Pagina 17. Collegeville, MN: Liturgical Press.

Malherbe, Abraham J. 1970. "'Gentle as a Nurse': The Cynic Background to I Thess ii." *Novum Testamentum* 12:203–17.

———. 1986. *Moral Exhortation: A Greco-Roman Sourcebook.* Philadelphia: Westminster.

———. 1988. *Ancient Epistolary Theorists.* Society of Biblical Literature Sources for Biblical Study 12. Atlanta: Scholars Press.

———. 2000. *The Letters to the Thessalonians: A New Translation with Introduction and Commentary.* Anchor Bible 32B. New York: Doubleday.

Manson, T. W. 1948. "St. Paul's Letter to the Romans—and Others." *Bulletin of the John Rylands University Library of Manchester* 31:224–45. Reprinted in *The Romans Debate: Revised and Expanded Edition,* edited by K. P. Donfried, 3–15. Peabody, MA: Hendrickson, 1991.

Marshall, I. Howard. 1983. *1 and 2 Thessalonians: Based on the Revised Standard Version.* New Century Bible. Grand Rapids: Eerdmans.

———. 1999. "Romans 16:25–27—An Apt Conclusion." In *Romans and the People of God: Essays in Honor of Gordon D. Fee on the Occasion of His 65th Birthday,* edited by Sven K. Soderlund and N. T. Wright, 170–84. Grand Rapids: Eerdmans.

Martin, Dale B. 1990. *Slavery as Salvation: The Metaphor of Slavery in Pauline Christianity.* New Haven: Yale University Press.

Martin, Ralph P. 1973. *Colossians and Philemon.* New Century Bible Commentary. Grand Rapids: Eerdmans.

———. 1983. *Carmen Christi: Philippians 2:5–11 in Recent Interpretation and in the Setting of Early Christian Worship.* Grand Rapids: Eerdmans.

———. 1986. *2 Corinthians.* Word Biblical Commentary. Waco: Word Books.

Martyn, J. Louis. 1997. *Galatians: A New Translation with Introduction and Commentary.* Anchor Bible 33A. New York: Doubleday.

Marxsen, Willi. 1968. *Introduction to the New Testament: An Approach to Its Problems.* Translated by G. Buswell. Philadelphia: Fortress.

Masson, C. 1957. *Les deux Épitres de Saint Paul aux Thessaloniciens.* Commentaire du Nouveau Testament. Neuchâtel, Switzerland: Delachaux & Niestle.

Matera, Frank J. 1992. *Galatians.* Sacra Pagina. Collegeville, MN: Liturgical Press.

———. 2003. *II Corinthians.* New Testament Library. Louisville: Westminister John Knox.

McFarlane, D. J. 1966. "The Motif of Thanksgiving in the New Testament." ThM thesis, St. Andrews University.

Meeks, Wayne A. 1983. "Social Functions of Apocalyptic Language in Pauline Christianity." In *Apocalypticism in the Mediterranean World and the Near East: Proceedings of the International Colloquium on Apocalypticism, Uppsala, August 12–17, 1979*, edited by David Hellholm, 687–705. Tübingen: Mohr-Siebeck.

Melick, Richard R., Jr. 1991. *Philippians, Colossians, Philemon*. New American Commentary 32. Nashville: Broadman & Holman.

Menken, Maarten J. J. 1994. *2 Thessalonians*. New Testament Readings. London: Routledge.

Menzies, Allan. 1912. *The Second Epistle of the Apostle Paul to the Corinthians*. London: Macmillan.

Merklein, H. 1984. "Die Einheitlichkeit des ersten Korintherbriefes." *Zeitschrift für die neutestamentliche Wissenschaft* 75:153–83.

Milligan, George. 1908. *St. Paul's Epistle to the Thessalonians: The Greek Text with Introduction and Notes*. London: Macmillan.

Mitchell, Margaret M. 1989. "Concerning ΠΕΡΙ ΔΕ in 1 Corinthians." *Novum Testamentum* 31 (3): 229–56.

———. 1992. "New Testament Envoys in the Context of Greco-Roman Diplomatic and Epistolary Conventions: The Example of Timothy and Titus." *Journal of Biblical Literature* 111:641–62.

Moo, Douglas J. 1996. *The Epistle to the Romans*. Grand Rapids: Eerdmans.

———. 2008. *The Letters to the Colossians and to Philemon*. Pillar New Testament Commentary. Grand Rapids: Eerdmans.

———. 2013. *Galatians*. Baker Exegetical Commentary on the New Testament. Grand Rapids: Baker Academic.

Morland, Kjell A. 1995. *The Rhetoric of Curse in Galatians: Paul Confronts Another Gospel*. Emory Studies in Early Christianity 5. Atlanta: Scholars Press.

Morris, Leon. 1959. *The First and Second Epistles to the Thessalonians*. London: Marshall, Morgan and Scott.

———. 1988. *The Epistle to the Romans*. Grand Rapids: Eerdmans.

———. 1991. *First and Second Epistles to the Thessalonians*. Rev. ed. New International Commentary on the New Testament. Grand Rapids: Eerdmans.

Moule, C. F. D. 1957. *The Epistles of Paul the Apostle to the Colossians and to Philemon: An Introduction and Commentary*. Cambridge: Cambridge University Press.

Moulton, Richard G. 1895. *The Literary Study of the Bible: An Account of the Leading Forms of Literature Represented in the Sacred Writings*. Boston: Heath.

Muddiman, John. 2001. *The Epistle to the Ephesians*. Black's New Testament Commentary. Peabody, MA: Hendrickson.

Mullins, Terence Y. 1962. "Petition as a Literary Form." *Novum Testamentum* 5:46–54.

———. 1964. "Disclosure: A Literary Form in the New Testament." *Novum Testamentum* 7 (1): 44–50.

———. 1968. "Greeting as a New Testament Form." *Journal of Biblical Literature* 88:418–26.

———. 1973. "Visit Talk in New Testament Letters." *Catholic Biblical Quarterly* 35:350–58.

———. 1977. "Benediction as a New Testament Form." *Andrews University Seminary Studies* 15 (1): 59–64.

Murphy-O'Connor, Jerome. 1981. "Tradition and Redaction in 1 Cor 15:3–7." *Catholic Biblical Quarterly* 43:582–89.

———. 1995. *Paul the Letter-Writer: His World, His Options, His Skills*. Good News Studies 41. Collegeville, MN: Liturgical Press.

Mussner, F. 1977. *Der Galaterbrief*. Herders Theologischer Kommentar zum Neuen Testament 9. Freiburg: Herder.

Nauck, Wolfgang. 1958. "Das *oun*-paräneti-cum." *Zeitschrift für die neutestamentliche Wissenschaft* 49:134–35.

Neil, W. 1957. *St. Paul's Epistles to the Thessalonians: Introduction and Commentary*. Torch Bible Commentaries. London: SCM.

Nordling, John G. 2004. *Philemon*. St. Louis: Concordia.

O'Brien, Peter T. 1977. *Introductory Thanksgivings in the Letters of Paul*. Leiden: Brill.

———. 1982. *Colossians, Philemon*. Word Biblical Commentary 44. Waco: Word.

———. 1991. *Commentary on Philippians*. New International Greek Testament Commentary. Grand Rapids: Eerdmans.

———. 1993. "Benediction, Blessing, Doxology, Thanksgiving." In *Dictionary of Paul and His Letters*, edited by G. F. Hawthorne and R. P. Martin, 68–71. Downers Grove, IL: InterVarsity.

———. 1999. *The Letter to the Ephesians*. Pillar New Testament Commentary. Grand Rapids: Eerdmans.

Oepke, Albrecht. 1963. "Die Briefe an die Thessalonicher." In *Die kleineren Briefe des Apostels Paulus*. By H. W. Beyer, P. Althaus, H. Conzelmann, G. Friedrich, A. Oepke, et al., 157–87. Neue Testament Deutsch 8. Göttingen: Vandenhoeck & Ruprecht.

Olson, Stanley N. 1984. "Epistolary Uses of Expressions of Self-Confidence." *Journal of Biblical Literature* 103:585–97.

———. 1985. "Pauline Expressions of Confidence in His Addressees." *Catholic Biblical Quarterly* 47:282–95.

Osiek, C., and M. Y. MacDonald. 2006. *A Woman's Place: House Churches in Earliest Christianity*. Minneapolis: Fortress.

Pao, David W. 2010. "Gospel within the Constraints of an Epistolary Form: Pauline Introductory Thanksgiving and Paul's Theology of Thanksgiving." In *Paul and the Ancient Letter Form*, edited by Stanley E. Porter and Sean A. Adams, 101–27. Leiden: Brill.

Perdue, Leo G. 1981. "Paraenesis and the Epistle of James." *Zeitschrift für die neutestamentliche Wissenschaft* 72:241–56.

Perella, N. J. 1969. *The Kiss: Sacred and Profane*. Berkeley: University of California Press.

Petersen, Norman R. 1985. *Rediscovering Paul: Philemon and the Sociology of Paul's Narrative World*. Philadelphia: Fortress.

Plummer, A. 1918. *A Commentary on St. Paul's First Epistle to the Thessalonians*. London: Robert Scott.

Popkes, W. 1996. *Paränese und Neues Testament*. Stuttgarter Bibelstudien 168. Stuttgart: Verlag Katholisches Bibelwerk.

Porter, Stanley E. 1993. "The Theoretical Justification for Application of Rhetorical Categories to Pauline Epistolary Literature." In *Rhetoric and the New Testament: Essays from the 1992 Heidelberg Conference*, edited by S. E. Porter and T. H. Olbricht, 100–122. Sheffield: JSOT Press.

Porter, Stanley E., and Bryan R. Dyer. 2012. "Oral Texts? A Reassessment of the Oral and Rhetorical Nature of Paul's Letters in Light of Recent Studies." *Journal of the Evangelical Theological Society* 55:323–41.

Porter, Stanley E., and Andrew W. Pitts. 2013. "The Disclosure Formula in the Epistolary Papyri and in the New Testament: Development, Form, Function, and Syntax." In *The Language of the New Testament: Context, History, and Development*, edited by Stanley E. Porter and Andrew W. Pitts, 421–38. Leiden: Brill.

Porter, Stanley E., and Jeffrey T. Reed. 1995. "Philippians as a Macro-Chiasm and Its Exegetical Significance." *New Testament Studies* 44:213–31.

Prior, Michael. 1989. *Paul the Letter-Writer: And the Second Letter to Timothy*. Journal for the Study of the New Testament Supplement Series 23. Sheffield: JSOT Press.

Reed, Jeffrey T. 1996. "Are Paul's Thanksgivings 'Epistolary'?" *Journal for the Study of the New Testament* 61:87–99.

———. 1997. *A Discourse Analysis of Philippians. Method and Rhetoric in the Debate over Literary Integrity.* Journal for the Study of the New Testament Supplement Series 136. Sheffield: Sheffield Academic.

Reinmuth, Eckart. 1998. "Die erste Brief an die Thessalonicher" and "Die zweite Brief an die Thessalonicher." In *Die Briefe an die Philipper, Thessalonicher und an Philemon,* by N. Walter, E. Reinmuth, and P. Lampe, 105–204. Neue Testament Deutsch 8.2. Göttingen: Vandenhoeck & Ruprecht.

Richard, E. J. 1995. *First and Second Thessalonians.* Sacra Pagina. Collegeville, MN: Liturgical Press.

Richards, E. Randolph. 1991. *The Secretary in the Letters of Paul.* Tübingen: Mohr Siebeck.

———. 2004. *Paul and First-Century Letter Writing: Secretaries, Composition and Collection.* Downers Grove, IL: InterVarsity.

Riesenfeld, Harald. 1982. "Faith and Love Promoting Hope: An Interpretation of Philemon v 6." In *Paul and Paulinism: Essays in Honour of C. K. Barrett,* edited by Morna D. Hooker and S. G. Wilson, 251–57. London: SPCK.

Roberts, J. H. 1986. "The Eschatological Transitions to the Pauline Letter Body." *Neotestamentica* 20:29–35.

Roetzel, Calvin J. 1975. *The Letters of Paul: Conversations in Context.* Atlanta: John Knox.

———. 1982. *The Letters of Paul: Conversations in Context.* 2nd ed. Atlanta: John Knox.

Roller, Otto. 1933. *Das Formular der paulinischen Briefe: Ein Beitrag zur Lehre vom antiken Briefe.* Stuttgart: Kohlhammer.

Ryken, Leland. 1993. "The Literature of the New Testament." In *A Complete Literary Guide to the Bible,* edited by Leland Ryken and Tremper Longman III, 361–75. Grand Rapids: Zondervan.

Sanday, William, and Arthur C. Headlam. 1897. *A Critical and Exegetical Commentary on the Epistle to the Romans.* International Critical Commentary. New York: Scribner's Sons.

Sanders, J. T. 1962. "The Transition from Opening Epistolary Thanksgiving to Body in the Letters of the Pauline Corpus." *Journal of Biblical Literature* 81:348–62.

Schmithals, W. 1972. *Paul and the Gnostics.* Translated by J. E. Steely. Nashville: Abingdon.

———. 1988. *Der Römerbrief.* Gütersloh: Mohn.

Schnider, Franz, and Werner Stenger. 1987. *Studien zum neutestamentlichen Briefformular.* New Testament Tools and Studies 11. Leiden: Brill.

Schoon-Janssen, J. 1991. *Umstrittene Apologien in den Paulus-briefen: Studien zur rhetorischen Situation des 1. Thessalonicherbriefes, des Galaterbriefes und Philipperbriefes.* Göttinger theologische Arbeiten 45. Göttingen: Vandenhoeck & Ruprecht.

Schrage, W. 1991. *Der erste Brief an die Korinther (1 Kor 1,1–6, 11).* Evangelisch-Katholischer Kommentar zum Neuen Testament 7/1. Zurich: Benziger; Neukirchen-Vluyn: Neukirchener Verlag.

Schreiner, Thomas R. 1998. *Romans.* Baker Exegetical Commentary on the New Testament. Grand Rapids: Baker.

———. 2010. *Galatians.* Zondervan Exegetical Commentary on the New Testament. Grand Rapids: Zondervan.

Schubert, Paul. 1939. *Form and Function of the Pauline Thanksgivings.* Berlin: Töpelmann.

Schulz, David. 1829. Review of Johann Eichhorn, *Einleitung in das neue Testament,* and Wilhelm de Wette, *Lehrbuch der historisch-kritischen Einleitung in die kanonischen Bücher des Neuen Testaments.* *Theologische Studien und Kritiken* 2:563–636.

Schütz, John H. 1975. *Paul and the Anatomy of Apostolic Authority*. Society for New Testament Studies Monograph Series 26. Cambridge: Cambridge University Press.

Seifrid, Mark A. 2014. *The Second Letter to the Corinthians*. Pillar New Testament Commentary. Grand Rapids: Eerdmans.

Shogren, G. S. 2012. *1 and 2 Thessalonians*. Zondervan Exegetical Commentary on the New Testament. Grand Rapids: Zondervan.

Silva, Moisés. 2005. *Philippians*. 2nd ed. Baker Exegetical Commentary on the New Testament. Grand Rapids: Baker Academic.

Smiles, Vincent M. 1998. *The Gospel and the Law in Galatia: Paul's Response to Jewish-Christian Separatism and the Threat of the Galatian Apostasy*. Collegeville, MN: Liturgical Press.

Stamps, D. L. 1995. "Rhetorical Criticism of the New Testament: Ancient and Modern Evaluation of Argumentation." In *Approaches to New Testament Studies*, edited by S. E. Porter and D. Tombs, 77–128. Sheffield: Sheffield Academic.

Stegemann, W. 1985. "Anlass und Hintergrund der Abfassung von 1 Th 2,1–12." In *Theologische Brosamen für Lothar Steiger*, edited by C. Freund and E. Stegemann, 397–416. Diehlheimer Blätter zum Alten Testament und seiner Rezeption in der Alten Kirche 5. Heidelberg: Esprint.

Still, Todd D. 1999. *Conflict at Thessalonica: A Pauline Church and Its Neighbours*. Journal for the Study of the New Testament Supplement Series 183. Sheffield: Sheffield Academic.

Stirewalt, M. Luther, Jr. 2003. *Paul, the Letter Writer*. Grand Rapids: Eerdmans.

Stowers, Stanley K. 1986. *Letter Writing in Greco-Roman Antiquity*. Philadelphia: Westminster.

Stuhlmacher, Peter. 1994. *Paul's Letter to the Romans: A Commentary*. Translated by Scott J. Hafemann. Louisville: Westminster/John Knox.

Suggs, M. Jack. 1967. "'The Word Is Near You': Romans 10:6–10 within the Purpose of the Letter." In *Christian History and Interpretation: Studies Presented to John Knox*, edited by W. R. Farmer, C. F. D. Moule, and R. R. Niebuhr, 289–312. Cambridge: Cambridge University Press.

Thielman, Frank. 2010. *Ephesians*. Baker Exegetical Commentary on the New Testament. Grand Rapids: Baker Academic.

Thiselton, Anthony C. 1977–78. "Realized Eschatology at Corinth." *New Testament Studies* 24:510–26.

———. 2000. *The First Epistle to the Corinthians*. New International Greek Testament Commentary. Grand Rapids: Eerdmans.

Thompson, Michael B. 1993. "Teaching/Paraenesis." In *Dictionary of Paul and His Letters*, edited by G. F. Hawthorne and R. P. Martin, 922–23. Downers Grove, IL: InterVarsity.

Thomson, Ian H. 1995. *Chiasmus in the Pauline Letters*. Journal for the Study of the New Testament Supplement Series 111. Sheffield: JSOT Press.

Tite, Philip L. 2010. "How to Begin, and Why? Diverse Functions of the Paul Prescript within a Greco-Roman Context." In *Paul and the Ancient Letter Form*, edited by Stanley E. Porter and Sean A. Adams, 57–99. Pauline Studies 6. Leiden: Brill.

Tolmie, D. Francois. 2005. *Persuading the Galatians: A Text-Centred Rhetorical Analysis of a Pauline Letter*. Wissenschaftliche Untersuchungen zum Neuen Testament 2/190. Tübingen: Mohr Siebeck.

Traede, K. 1968–69. "Ursprünge und Formen des 'Heiligen Kusses' im frühen Christentum." *Jahrbuch für Antike und Christentum* 11–12:124–80.

Trebilco, Paul. 1993. "Itineraries, Travel Plans, Journeys, Apostolic Parousia." In *Dictionary of Paul and His Letters*, edited by G. F. Hawthorne and R. P. Martin, 446–56. Downers Grove, IL: InterVarsity.

Trilling, W. 1980. *Der zweite Brief an die Thessalonicher*. Evangelisch-katholischer Kommentar zum Neuen Testament. Neukirchen-Vluyn, Germany: Neukirchener Verlag.

Unger, M. F. 1962. "Historical Research and the Church at Thessalonica." *Bibliotheca Sacra* 119:38–44.

Van Voorst, Robert E. 2010. "Why Is There No Thanksgiving Period in Galatians? An Assessment of an Exegetical Commonplace." *Journal of Biblical Literature* 129:153–72.

Verner, David C. 1983. *The Household of God: The Social World of the Pastoral Epistles*. Society of Biblical Literature Dissertation Series 71. Chico, CA: Scholars Press.

Vincent, M. R. 1897. *A Critical and Exegetical Commentary on the Epistles to the Philippians and to Philemon*. Edinburgh: T&T Clark.

Vouga, François. 1998. *An die Galater*. Handbuch zum Neuen Testament 10. Tübingen: Mohr Siebeck.

Wall, Robert W. 1993. *Colossians and Philemon*. IVP New Testament Commentary Series. Downers Grove, IL: InterVarsity.

Walton, S. 1995. "What Has Aristotle to Do with Paul? Rhetorical Criticism and 1 Thessalonians." *Tyndale Bulletin* 46 (2): 229–50.

Wanamaker, Charles A. 1990. *The Epistles to the Thessalonians: A Commentary on the Greek Text*. New International Greek Testament Commentary. Grand Rapids: Eerdmans.

Weatherly, Jon A. 1996. *1 & 2 Thessalonians*. College Press NIV Commentary. Joplin, MO: College Press.

Weima, Jeffrey A. D. 1993. "Gal. 6:11–18: A Hermeneutical Key to the Galatian Letter." *Calvin Theological Journal* 28:90–107.

———. 1994a. *Neglected Endings: The Significance of the Pauline Letter Closings*. Journal for the Study of the New Testament Supplement Series 101. Sheffield: JSOT Press.

———. 1994b. "Preaching the Gospel in Rome: A Study of the Epistolary Framework of Romans." In *Gospel in Paul: Studies on Corinthians, Galatians and Romans for Richard N. Longenecker*, edited by L. A. Jervis and Peter Richardson, 337–66. Sheffield: JSOT Press.

———. 1997a. "An Apology for the Apologetic Function of 1 Thessalonians 2.1–12." *Journal for the Study of the New Testament* 68:73–99.

———. 1997b. "What Does Aristotle Have to Do with Paul? An Evaluation of Rhetorical Criticism." *Calvin Theological Journal* 32:458–68.

———. 2001. "Literary Criticism." In *Interpreting the New Testament: Essays on Methods and Issues*, edited by David Alan Black and Davis S. Dockery, 150–69. Nashville: Broadman & Holman.

———. 2003. "The Reason for Romans: The Evidence of Its Epistolary Framework (1:1–15; 15:14–16:27)." *Review & Expositor* 100 (1): 17–33.

———. 2014. *1–2 Thessalonians*. Baker Exegetical Commentary on the New Testament. Grand Rapids: Baker Academic.

Whelan, C. F. 1993. "Amica Pauli: The Role of Phoebe in the Early Church." *Journal for the Study of the New Testament* 49:67–85.

White, John L. 1971. "Introductory Formulae in the Body of the Pauline Letter." *Journal of Biblical Literature* 90:91–97.

———. 1972. *The Form and Function of the Body of the Greek Letter: A Study of the Letter-Body in Non-literary Papyri and in Paul the Apostle*. Society of Biblical Literature Dissertation Series 2. Missoula, MT: Scholars Press.

———. 1983. "Saint Paul and the Apostolic Letter Tradition." *Catholic Biblical Quarterly* 45:433–44.

———. 1984. "New Testament Epistolary Literature in the Framework of Ancient Epistolography." In *Aufstieg und Niedergang der römischen Welt*, part 2, *Principat*, edited by Hildegard Temporini and Wolfgang Haase, 25.2:1730–56. Berlin: de Gruyter.

———. 1986. *Light from Ancient Letters.* Foundations and Facets. Philadelphia: Fortress.

———. 1988. "Ancient Greek Letters." In *Greco-Roman Literature and the New Testament*, edited by D. E. Aune, 85–105. Atlanta: Scholars Press.

Whiteley, D. E. H. 1969. *Thessalonians in the Revised Standard Version, with Introduction and Commentary.* Oxford: Oxford University Press.

Wickert, U. 1961. "Der Philemonbrief—Privatbrief order apostolisches Sendschreiben?" *Zeitschrift für die neutestamentliche Wissenschaft* 52:230–38.

Wiles, G. P. 1974. *Paul's Intercessory Prayers: The Significance of the Intercessory Prayer Passages in the Letters of St. Paul.* Cambridge: Cambridge University Press.

Wilson, Andrew. 1992. "The Pragmatics of Politeness and Pauline Epistolography: A Case Study of the Letter to Philemon." *Journal for the Study of the New Testament* 48:107–19.

Wilson, Geoffrey B. 1975. *I & II Thessalonians: A Digest of Reformed Comment.* Edinburgh: Banner of Truth Trust.

Wilson, Todd A. 2004. "Wilderness Apostasy and Paul's Portrayal of the Crisis in Galatians." *New Testament Studies* 50:550–71.

Winter, Bruce W. 1993. "The Entries and Ethics of Orators and Paul (1 Thessalonians 2:1–12)." *Tyndale Bulletin* 44 (1): 55–74.

Witherington, Ben, III. 1995. *Conflict and Community in Corinth: A Socio-Rhetorical Commentary on 1 and 2 Corinthians.* Grand Rapids: Eerdmans.

———. 1998. *Grace in Galatia: A Commentary on Paul's Letter to the Galatians.* Grand Rapids: Eerdmans.

———. 2006. *1 and 2 Thessalonians: A Socio-Rhetorical Commentary.* Grand Rapids: Eerdmans.

———. 2007. *The Letters to Philemon, the Colossians, and the Ephesians: A Socio-Rhetorical Commentary on the Captivity Epistles.* Grand Rapids: Eerdmans.

Wright, N. T. 1986. *Colossians and Philemon.* Tyndale New Testament Commentaries. Grand Rapids: Eerdmans.

Wünsche, August. 1911. *Der Kuss in Bibel, Talmud und Midrasch.* Breslau, Poland: Marcus.

Zaas, Peter S. 1988. "Catalogues and Context: 1 Corinthians 5 and 6." *New Testament Studies* 34:622–29.

Ziemann, Ferdinandus. 1912. *De epistularum Graecarum formulis sollemnibus quaestiones selectae.* Berlin: Haas.

Index of Modern Authors

Index of Scripture
and Other Ancient Sources

The letter *t* following a page number denotes a table. Bold page numbers indicate extended discussion.

Index of Subjects

Bold page numbers indicate extended discussion.